ENCYCLOPAEDIA OF WATER RESOURCE MANAGEMENT PLANNING AND DEVELOPMENT

ENCYCLOPAEDIA OF WATER RESOURCE MANAGEMENT

Planning and Development

PARIKSHIT BALLABH

CYBER TECH PUBLICATIONS
4264/3, Ansari Road, Daryaganj, New Delhi-110002 (India)
Ph.: 011-23244078. Fax: 011-23280028
E-Mail: cyberpublicationsdelhi@yahoo.com

Encyclopaedia of Water Resource Management: Planning and Development

First Edition 2009

Published by G.S. Rawat

For Cyber Tech Publications

4264/3, Ansari Road, Daryaganj, New Delhi - 110 002

E-mail : cyberpublicationsdelhi@yahoo.com

Phone : 011-23244078,

Fax : 011-23280028

Printed at

Asian Offset Printers

PREFACE

India is rich in water resources, being endowed with a network of great rivers and vast alluvial basins to hold groundwater. Conditions, however, vary widely from region to region. Whereas there are some chronically drought affected areas, there are others which are frequently subject to damage by floods.On the whole, under the pressure of rapid population growth, the available resources of water are being developed and depleted at a fast rate & the situation seriously underlines the need for taking up integrated plans for water conservation and utilization for every agro-ecological area to meet the increasing demands of irrigation, water harvesting, human & livestock consumption,expanding industry, hydro-electric power generation, recreation,navigation and other uses.

Water is our lifeline that bathes us and feeds us. In ancient cultures water represented the very essence of life. The Romans were the first to pipe water into their growing cities, especially with their aqueducts. They also realized that sewage water could cause damage to their people, and needed to be removed from large areas of people.

Water has played a role not only in the history of countries, but in religion, mythology, and art. Water in many religions cleanses the soul through holy water

Water has always been perceived as a gift from the gods as it rained from the heavens. The water or hydrologic cycle explains interactions between the atmosphere, hydrosphere, and lithosphere. The water or hydrologic cycle is a major driving force on our planet.

In the present work, an attempt has been made to analyse briefly some of the water acts like the clean water act, federal water pollution act, etc.

The purpose of the work is to enlighten some of the main water resources and the dire need to save it. The work is meant not only for the aspirants of science but also for the general readers. It will be a useful guide to all of them who are really interested to investigate on the water resources.

Editor

CONTENTS

1

WATER MANAGEMENT AND PLANNING

Water is a prime natural resource, a basic human need and a precious national asset. Optimum development and efficient utilization of water resources, therefore, assumes great significance. The Ministry of Water Resources lays down policies and programmes for development and regulation of the county's water resources. It covers sectorial planning, coordination, policy guidelines, technical examination and techno-economic appraisal of projects, providing Central assistance to specific projects, facilitation of external assistance and assistance in the resolution of inter-state water disputes, policy formulation, planning and guidance in respect of minor irrigation, command area development and development of ground water resources, etc. Planning is the process of thinking ahead to achieve desired future outcomes and to avoid undesired future pitfalls. It is something we all do at many levels everyday of our lives. There are benefits to be gained and risks to be avoided by water management planning.

The National Water Policy lays emphasis on integrated water resources development and management for optimal and sustainable utilization of the available surface and groundwater. Creation of well-developed information system, water conservation, and demand management have been recognized in the Policy. Drinking, water has been accorded the first priority in allocation of water for diverse uses. It integrates quantity and quality aspects as well as environmental considerations for water through adequate institutional arrangements. The involvement of beneficiaries and stakeholders in the project planning and participatory approach in water resources management have been focused in the Policy. The Policy also envisages Private Sector Participation for providing facilities in water resources sector. Resettlement and rehabilitation aspects of projected affected persons have been emphasized in the Policy. The policy also recognized adequate training and research in water resources sector.

In recent research scientists believe that earth formed from materials that came from the hot sun. These materials included water (hydrogen) as one of the important elements. When earth cooled and grew solid the water got trapped in rocks in the earth's crust. This water was gradually released by volcanic activity and formed the oceans. Later water vapours also rose in atmosphere which fell back to the surface in the form of precipitation. The earth's water budget never changes. This means that total amount of water remains the same but it may change in its forms of solid, liquid and gaseous. The ocean which cover 70 per cent of earth's surface contain 97 per cent of all water on earth. The oceans are the source of satly. Only 3 per cent of water on earth is fresh. The fresh water includes water locked in glaciers and ice caps which account for 2 per cent of total water. Out of the remaining 1 per cent halt of it is in the form of ground water leaving only just half per cent of total water on earth in gaseous form in atmosphere and as fresh water in rivers and lakes. The water that we use for irrigation, drinking and various other purposes accounts for just one-fiftieth part of earth's total water resources. Can you imagine how precious is this water.

In quantitative terms the total water on earth is 1.4 billion cubic kilometres, the one-fiftieth part found in rivers, fresh water lakes, springs, pools and ponds account for only 280 million cubic kilometres. The unit for measuring water is cubic metre. This means that if water is stored in one metre wide (length and breath each) reservoir to the depth of one metre total volume of water contained will be one cubic metre. One hectare metre (10,000 square metre) area will contain 10,000 cubic metres of water or one square kilometre will contain 1,000,000,000 cubic metres of water.

The land part of the earth receives water only through precipitation. This water does not fall on earth evenly. If it were to fall evenly all parts would receive 86 centimeters of precipitation a year Do you know that Mawsynram in Meghalaya receives about 1200 cms of rainfall a year? It is the most wettest place on earth. Similarly, Jacobabad in Sind in Pakistan receives just 15 cm of rainfall a year. It is the driest place on earth. This means that precipitation is most uneven on earth. This is shown in the map.

It is interesting to note that world's most heavily populated areas also receive enough rain for their needs. It is not without reason. The human settlements first began near water courses and civilizations came up along river valleys. The areas where water is generally found in good measure include countries of Europe, South and South-East Asia, the Eastern USA and much of China. The drier areas include most of Central and West Asia, Central Australia, northern Africa and the Middle East.

Benefits of Good Water Management Planning

Water management planning can benefit both the irrigation district and the irrigator, as well as third parties and the environment. The range of potential benefits includes:

- Better water service to customers
- More effective use of available water supply
- Reduced operating costs
- Improved revenues to the district
- Improved crop yields and quality
- Reduced on-farm costs
- Development of additional water supply capabilities
- Improved water quality and aquatic habitat
- Habitat maintenance for endangered species
- Better documentation of uses and accomplishments
- Education of customers and the public
- Diminished groundwater overdraft
- Improved system and water supply reliability
- Postponed need for new or expanded water supplies
- Reduced drought impacts.

There are a variety of problems and pitfalls that can be avoided by good water management planning. Some of these could affect the district and its customers immediately and others could pose future threats. Some examples of undesirable situations that might be avoided through good planning are:

- Daily and seasonal water shortages
- Excessive losses or spills from water delivery systems
- Over-or under-application of water on farm fields
- Insufficient carryover supplies in reservoirs
- Loss of water rights through waste or abandonment
- Adverse relationships with other water users and publics
- Drainage and erosion control problems
- Ill-timed water deliveries to farm fields
- De-watered streams and wet lands.

The main sources of water, as elsewhere in the world, are Surface water and Ground water.

River water or running water following on the surface of the land is called surface water. The rivers of India can be divided into two broad types-Perennial rivers and Seasonal rivers. Pernnial rivers are snowfed. They generally flow throughout the year. Almost all Himalayan rivers are perennial rivers.They receive water both from snow-melt and rainfall. All the rivrs of South Indian receive water from ranfall only. Most of the southern rivers dry up during summer season. Only a few rivers haver reduced level of water in dry season. In Indian most of the rainfall is received during monsoon months from July to September. Therefore, a large part of the cuntry goes dry for eight months of the year. It is on accunt of this unequal distribution that the problems of floods and drought occur in low lying parts of the country.

Development of a Water Management Plan

The steps involved in the development of the water management plan are not complex, but will require some time and participation from all levels of personnel at the facility. Given a working knowledge of the facility, the facility manager should not have a difficult time in gathering the necessary information. The result of this effort will be a better understanding of where and how much water is used throughout the facility, where best to implement conservation efforts and what benefits can be expected from implementation of the management actions.

Plan Outline

The initial goals set for water use reduction should be as specific and measurable as possible. As more information is gathered and the water management plan develops, these goals may be revised to reflect achievable management actions. Prior to implementing the chosen actions, the goals should be expressed in terms of gallons or percentage saved and include dates for when the goals will be achieved.

Develop a Water Use Inventory

This is where the majority of your effort will be focused. Initially, however, this step can begin with generating a very basic list of water uses at the facility. You might start by listing the most significant water uses at the site or those uses which are believed to be most in need of conservation measures (noticeably inefficient water use). This will be a good starting point for the more detailed facility survey discussed later in this guide.

Identify Water Management Actions

A plan should be developed which outlines and determines the feasibility of each management action by presenting simple cost/benefit analyses and the projected payback periods where applicable. Current or proposed water/wastewater rates should be used when determining the costs and benefits of the actions. The plan should include actions that are no-cost or low-cost, actions which require capital expenditure and actions which require changes in water use procedures by facility personnel. Details of possible water management actions are presented in Section III of this guide.

Implement the Water Management Plan

Implementation of the water management actions selected in the previous step should begin with the prioritisation and scheduling of the actions. Thought should be given to scheduling the actions in a logical manner. For example, it may make more sense to postpone retrofitting of plumbing fixtures if a remodel of the facility is planned for the near future.

This step also includes the communication of water management actions to all levels of personnel. This can help foster a facility-wide awareness that management is dedicated to the concept of water conservation. Communication is especially important if the water management actions include changes in the staff's work procedures or habits.

Implementation of the management actions should be followed by some form of monitoring to determine if the actions achieved the desired effect. Long term dedication to monitoring the water consumption of the facility can also help in identifying future problems with water use such as system leaks.

The Importance of Top Management Support

It is crucial that the top management at the facility support the water conservation plan in a material way. This requires not only dedication to a written policy statement, but also willingness to provide the money, staff, time and other resources necessary to implement the water management plan. Water conservation must be seen as a long term investment rather than a short term budget enhancement.

Large corporations are frequently seen as environmentally wasteful and as if they are not held accountable for their use of natural resources. Many companies, however, have had the forethought to start energy and water conservation programs and have made water conservation one of their decision filters and management policies.

Developing a Policy Statement

For a company plan to have the impact of a directive, a company policy statement is necessary. This statement will reflect the intentions of management and therefore will be different for every company. We offer one example here:

"Water conservation as a way of life is encouraged not only at work, but also at home for our employees. To that end, the company is committed to developing and maintaining a comprehensive water-saving and management program which will help ensure our continued ability to grow as well as to provide and increased dollar-saving potential."

Without support from management, it is much more difficult to implement an effective plan. The genuine desire to conserve water must be present—from the top and on down the line.

Developing a Water Management Plan

The following discussion provides a more detailed examination of the steps involved in the development of the water management plan.

Develop a Water use Inventory

Gather Information

Before starting your survey, collect the information that already exists. This will save time during the facility survey. The people who are familiar with daily operations, especially operating and maintenance personnel, can be very helpful in this step. Some information will be readily available; other data may take some time to collect.

Examples of data collection forms are included in this guide to assist personnel in gathering necessary information. It may be helpful to copy some of these sheets and use them directly for recording information. In some cases, such as consumption history data, it may be more helpful to use the provided form as a template for recording the data in a computer spreadsheet. By using a computer, statistics such as total annual water consumption or average gallons per day may be easier to compile and maintain.

Specifically, gather the following:

* Building floorplan and list of water meters serving the building. When multiple water meters serve multiple buildings at the facility, it is recommended to group meters serving each building. Worksheet II-1 provides a table for recording the meter account information. It is recommended that the local water utility be contacted to get a complete list of all meters serving the facility. The utility may also be able to provide information regarding the type of use that each meter serves (landscape, fireline etc.). By recording both the billing account number and the meter number (usually stamped on the dial cover for the meter), you may be able to determine which meter(s) serve a particular building or area of the facility.

* Water and sewer bills for the last two years. Worksheet II-2 presents an example of data collection table for this purpose. However, for multiple meters at a facility, it may be easier to record the years of billing data on a computer spreadsheet.

* List of outdoor water uses and two years of consumption data, if available. Outdoor water use may include make-up water for pools and spas, supply water for evaporative misting systems, as well as landscape irrigation. As noted previously, the local water utility may know which meters are solely for landscape use. If possible, the landscape water use data should be separated from the indoor or process water use data on the Water Consumption History sheet (Worksheet II-2). However, many older facilities will have meters with combined landscape and indoor service. In these cases, it may not be possible to separate the water uses. Installing separate meters for irrigation can sometimes save on sewer use fees.

* Submeter consumption data for two years. Your facility may submeter process water use or make-up water for cooling towers. If possible, the submeter data should be collected to separate these consumptions from the other water uses recorded on the city meters. The results of any water submeter calibration tests should be reviewed so that meter reading can be adjusted to reflect actual water use. Any submeters used should be American Water Works Association (AWWA) approved.

* Typical facility operating schedules, number of employees and visitors maintenance and janitorial work schedules. This information can be recorded on the Building Water Survey Form presented as Worksheet II-3.

* Lists of all water using equipment with manufacturers' recommended or specified flow rates, where available.

* A complete inventory of plumbing fixtures.

* Any prior water and energy surveys.

Conduct a Comprehensive Facility Survey

After you have collected the available existing information, you are ready to begin the survey. The exact extent of a water survey will depend upon the size of the building, the complexity of its systems and the survey budget (if any). The more comprehensive the survey, the greater the value of the resulting water management options and cost savings. An inventory form for Existing Plumbing Equipment is provided in Worksheet II-4. Details associated with the assignment of responsibilities for the survey are discussed in Section IV—Participation.

A Water Use Inventory table is provided in Worksheet II-5. Copy this form and use it to record information while performing the detailed facility survey. The following steps should be performed while recording information on the Inventory forms.

* Walk through your facility and through direct observation and measurements, identify and list any equipment that uses water: faucets, toilets, showerheads, drinking fountains, kitchen equipment, water-using process equipment, cooling towers, boilers, ice machines etc.

* Determine the amount of water used by each type of plumbing fixture or device within the facility. Log or record the consumption data for each device. When field-testing the flow of water through fixtures, it is usually sufficient to take sample readings at a few representative fixtures, located throughout the facility. When measuring the flow rate of fixtures, such as faucets, adjust the fixture to an average or typical flow rate. Keep in mind that measured flows may vary on different floors because of pressure losses at higher elevations.

* Where possible, install temporary water meters to gauge water use by large water-using equipment. Compare the equipment water use measurements with the manufacturers' rated flow amounts; some equipment may be operating at higher water consumption rates than necessary. If there is a significant difference, consider having qualified personnel review equipment operation and make adjustments to lower water consumption.

* Record hours of operation for plumbing fixtures, devices and all water-using processes or pieces of equipment. Not any particular fixture, device or piece of equipment that uses water for more than one operation. Ice makers, for example, can use water for both making ice and for cooling. When possible, determine actual schedules of plumbing fixture use by talking to operating personnel familiar with the fixture use.

* Verify operating schedules and the number of building occupants during different times of the day.

* Determine daily facility consumption rates from water meter and submeter readings and other sources. This step will also help to prepare for monitoring water use reductions after beginning the water management program. After the survey is completed, continue to take meter readings on a monthly basis.

* As you list the water using equipment and fixtures during the survey, note any issue which have an impact on water consumption. Leaking faucets and valves, single-pass cooling flows and outdated fixtures are examples of some of the observations that should be recorded. These issues should be addressed when developing the Water Management Actions.

Prepare the Estimated Water Balance

After completing the inventory of water uses around the facility, you should take the time to group the uses by category. Categories which might apply to your facility could include:

- Domestic Plumbing (restroom consumption such as toilets, urinals, showers and faucets)
- Heating and Cooling (evaporative cooler and/or cooling tower make-up, boiler blow-down, etc.)
- Kitchen Plumbing (ice machines, food preparation, dishwashers etc.)
- Process Water (process cooling, rinsing operations, chemical dilution etc.)
- Water Features (pools, spas, fountains etc.)
- Landscape Irrigation.

As you group the various water consumptions of your facility, you will be able to generate an estimated water balance. This water balance will provide you with an estimate of the total amount of water that your facility consumes on a daily and annual basis. It provides an Estimated Water Balance table which you may use to summarise and total the consumptions of your applicable categories. At the bottom of the table, you can compare the estimated total water consumption with the total metered water consumption. This is an excellent way to check the accuracy of your water use inventory. It will probably be easiest to compare these consumption numbers based on a gallons per day (gpd) basis. If the difference of the estimated and metered consumptions is greater than 15 percent, you may have forgotten to include some water uses in the inventory or your water use assumptions for some items may not be accurate. You may need to revise your water use inventory and the associated water use assumptions.

Note that in the Estimated Water Balance table (Worksheet II-6), there are columns for listing average gpd for three separate time periods; may to October, November to April and Annual (January through December). This allows you to recognise that some water uses will be seasonal. For example, the occupancy of your facility may vary from winter to summer (like a hotel or resort); this will have an effect on the average daily domestic plumbing water consumption. Alternatively, water use items such as cooling towers, evaporative coolers, and landscaping irrigation will have significantly greater average daily consumption in the summer compared to the winter season. The seasonal uses should also be compared to the corresponding seasonal metered consumption. If your water provider charges seasonal rates, it may be helpful to group your months to correspond to those seasons.

Identify Water Management Actions

Examine Possible Management Actions

By grouping the various uses in the water balance into categories, you will be able to verify which categories use the largest amounts of water. This information should guide your efforts in determining the most effective water management actions. For example, if the cooling system accounts for half of your facility's total water consumption, this could be a good area on which to focus conservation efforts.

Your approach to evaluating the water management options for each water use category should be comprehensive. Complete replacement is typically not an option for most facilities and may not necessarily be the best solution. Often, simple procedural changes in maintenance or operation can produce substantial water savings. A constantly running toilet, for example, can waste 4,000 gallons of water per day. Checking and replacing valves and ballcocks regularly can save this otherwise wasted water.

A checklist of conservation measures is provided in Worksheet II-7 at the end of this section. This checklist will provide you with an excellent starting point for determining possible water management actions at your facility. The checklist will allow you to note which conservation actions you have already implemented, which actions you can implement without further evaluation (such as actions which require little or no cost to implement), and which actions need to be investigated to determine cost effectiveness. Some of the actions listed may not apply to your facility.

As you weigh, your fixture and equipment options, consider federal legislation and state water conservation and plumbing regulations. Some states and municipalities that have experienced water shortages in the past and those concerned about water use and conservation in general have passed stringent legislation.

While reviewing and selecting the possible water management options, you will want to determine how much water will be conserved by implementing this action (gallons per day) and how much it will cost to implement this action. This information will be critical to performing the economic analysis.

Section III provides detailed discussions of a variety of Water Management Options that you may consider for your facility.

Perform an Economic Analysis of Actions

After you have examined and selected a number of Water Management Actions, you must then determine which actions will be economically feasible.

Since some water efficiency options can be expensive and budgets are usually limited, it is critical that you choose those options most appropriate and cost-effective to your facility. At the same time, initial cost should not be the only reason for deciding which option is best. For example, replacing an existing frequently used or older toilet with a low-flow model will require a larger initial investment than simply installing a retrofit device. However, the device will require regular observation and maintenance and eventual replacement. The labour costs may quickly offset the initial low cost of the device. Replacing the toilets that get the greatest mount of use will have a quicker pay-back than less frequently used toilets.

At this point you will have information pertaining to the amount of water each action will conserve. However, this conservation information needs to be translated into a cost (dollar) savings. The savings that a particular action will provide can then be compared to the initial cost of implementing the action.

Total Cost of Water

The basic cost of water can be determined from your utility bills or by calling your local water utility. Water utility bills usually contain two components: fixed charges and charges based on the amount of water used (unit costs). The fixed charges should not be included as a part of the total unit cost, since these amounts do not change relative to the amount of water used. Unit costs on your utility bill may include:

- Basic water unit cost (and associated consumption charges)
- Environmental costs
- Seasonal costs
- Waste water fees
- Additional discharge fees.

The units used for billing these costs may vary from city to city. You should determine whether the billing units are in gallons, thousands of gallons or ccf (100 cubic feet = 748 gallons).

The total unit cost of water at your facility may include more than just the water and wastewater billing rates provided by your local utilities. A number of expenses may be added together to form the total water/wastewater unit cost. These might include:

- Energy cost of pumping water from wells.
- Cost of pre-treating and on-site pumping.

- Cost of water heating and cooling.
- Chemical and/or other treatment costs, including treating cooling tower or boiler feed and reuse water.
- Sewer costs, which can be based on the amount of water, biochemical oxygen demand, dissolved solids and suspended solids.

When combining these costs, you can use current prices. However, if possible, use prices that you expect will be in effect at the time any water efficiency and conservation changes are actually made. In that way, you can assess more accurately the savings realised by reducing water use. You may already have some of these expenses in the form of unit costs (such as dollars per gallon). However, your energy related expenses, such as pumping and heating, may need to be converted into unit costs. This can be done by estimating the costs associated with these expenses over a given time period and dividing these by the estimated volume of water used over this time period. Knowing the total cost per unit of water used is important because it will be used to determine savings realised by conservation actions.

Economic Analysis

The "simple payback" economic analysis compares the total initial cost of a water management action with the annual dollar savings that the action will provide to determine the length of time required before the action will pay for itself. Economic analyses that include the "time value of money" are available. These more detailed approaches may be necessary in situations where long term operating costs of an action will be significant. However, the simple payback method is easy to calculate and generally sufficient for most cases.

Simple payback is calculated by dividing the capital costs of the water management action by the net annual savings that the action will provide:

$$\text{Simple Payback Period} = \frac{\text{Capital cost (\$)}}{\text{Net annual savings (\$/year)}}$$

The following page illustrates an economic analysis for a cooling tower conservation action. For the details involved in the consumption calculations, refer to Section III: Water Management Actions. The provided example calculations indicate that the $5,000 initial cost of implementing the water management action will be paid back in approximately 11 months. Actions with payback periods of three years or less should be considered.

Worksheet II-8 presents a table which can be used in the economic evaluation of the proposed water management actions. The table below summarises the sample calculations for the cooling tower.

Period Action	Annual Water Savings Gal/yr	$/yr	Other $/yr	Total Savings ($/yr)	Annual Savings ($/yr)	Net Costs ($/yr)	Capital Savings ($)	Payback Costs (yr)
Cooling Tower Acid Addition	1,350,000	4,050	1,350	5,400	0	5,400	5,000	0.9

Samples Economic Calculation Cooling Tower Water Consumption

Note: See the Cooling Tower discussion in Section III: Water Management Actions for details of the consumption calculations.

- **Assumptions:**
  - Capacity: 300 tons of refrigeration
  - Operation Time: 250 days per year
  - Efficiency: 2.5 cycles of concentration before conservation
  - Water/Waste-Water Rate: $3.00 per 1,000 gallons

- **Conservation Actions**: Conductivity controller, pH contro-ller, treat with sulphuric acid to increase cycles to 5.0.

- **Consumption Before Actions:**

  Evaporation:(300 tons) x (3 gpm/100 tons) x 1,440 min/day)=12,960 gpd

  Bleed: (12,960 gpd) ÷ (2.5 CR – 1) =8,640 gpd

  Total Make-up:(12,960 gpd) + (8,640 gpd) =21,600 gpd

  21,600 gpd for 250 days/yr = **5,400,000 gal/yr**

- **Consumption After Actions:**

  Evaporation:(300 tons) x (3 gpm/100 tons) x 1,440 min/day) = 12,960 gpd

  Bleed: (12,960 gpd ÷ (5.0 CR —1) = 3,240 gpd

  Total Make-up(12,960 gpd) + (3,240 gpd) =16,200 gpd

  16,200 gpd for 250 days/yr = **4,050,000 gal/yr**

- **Annual Water Savings: 1,350,000 gal/yr**
- **Cost Savings:**

Water & Sewer: (1,350,000 gal/yr)
x ($3.00)/1,000 gallons)=$4,050/yr

Chemical: (1,350,000 gal/yr)
x ($0.10/100 gallons) = $1,350/yr

$4,050/yr + $1, 350/yr= $5,400/yr

- **Capital Cost:** $5,000
- **Payback Period:** $5,000 ÷ $5,400/yr = 0.9 years = 11 months.

Implement the Water Management Plan

Develop a Water Management Plan and Schedule.

Once you have decided to take action to conserve water, choose the specific actions based on the previous examination of current water use, occupant needs and the results of the economic analysis. Prioritising the selected water management options in this way will maximise water, energy and financial savings while maintaining or improving occupant comfort and increasing facility efficiency. Because individual facilities vary, no one plan is right for all facilities. After choosing water efficiency options, you should then develop a comprehensive water management plan work schedule. Determine what funding is available for what improvements, when the funding is available, and the time required to complete the entire water management project. Examine large retrofit or replacement options or high-priority jobs to determine the time necessary to complete each. While many can be implemented in a few hours or days, others may require upto several months and the services of a professional contractor.

When preparing the schedule, do not plan so closely that a delay in implementing one option throws the entire schedule off balance. If a water management programme is expected to take 18 months, the first six months should be planned in detail and progress and savings should be closely monitored. As you develop a sense of your progress in the first six months, you will be better able to plan the next phase (the next six months) with equal detail. In this way, remaining options are continually reviewed, helping to ensure that the plan is as realistic as possible and reflects the realities of actual progress compared to the initial plan.

Note: If you have an energy efficiency plan in place, a "piggy-backed" water conservation plan maximises the effectiveness.

Communicate the Water Management Plan

Before implementing you water management plan, be sure that your employees know what is going on and why. Most water efficiency measures will only yield the savings you expect when *users* are part of the solution. Begin by sending all employees, a letter from management expressing support for the water efficiency programme and urging employees to participate on all levels. The letter should explain why changes are being made, what difference they will make and finally, why water management is necessary. Signs should be posted near equipment, particularly in rest rooms, so visitors are aware that water-savings initiatives are in place.

Since many water efficiency measures produce savings only when used properly, you must teach employees how to operate them. Additional signage may be necessary concerning low-flow toilets and urinals and automatic faucets.

Bulletin boards, newsletters and staff meetings should regularly discuss the progress of the water management programms and might also attempt to change occupant water use overall. As part of your programme, you may wish to incorporate some of the following suggestions:

- Set-up a "hotline' to report leaks or other wastes of water to facility managers or maintenance personnel.
- Start a suggestion and incentives system to recognise water-saving ideas.
- Distribute flyers or pamphlets to promote the facility's water management plan or to educate occupants about good water use habits.
- Organise a slogan or poster competition.
- Start a water column in your regular employee newsletter featuring how much water has been saved through the water management programme.
- Prepare a water conservation display covering different aspects of water use affected by the water management programme (landscaping, low-flow plumbing products, water use habits, process changes etc.) and place it in an appropriate location such as the facility lobby or employee cafeteria. Include ideas for home water conservation so your employees can lower their personal expenses. Contact your water supplier to see if it can contribute literature and/or other items for this display.

Implement the Water Management Plan

Now you are ready to start installing retrofits or replacements and to introduce maintenance or operational changes. Once work begins, closely monitor your programme to ensure that it runs smoothly. This part of your plan should include at least the following items:

- Call contractors to verify that their work is progressing as promised.
- Follow up regularly with operating and maintenance personnel to make sure that their equipment is regularly checked and serviced.
- Listen to your facility's water users and keep communication lines open. Those who regularly use the equipment and fixtures will be able to provide the best feedback, if something is not working as planned. Let them know that their input is important, so repairs or modifications can be made quickly.
- Check your water and sewer bills for decreases in your consumption and billing.

Monitor the Water Management Plan

Once implementation of your water management programme has begun, you will want to carefully monitor water use to see what types of savings you are actually realising. In addition to checking equipment, facility managers should maintain regular contact with operating and maintenance staff to verify that their work continues to produce water savings. After verifying that your conservation efforts have produced positive results, share this information with others. Not only should you let your employees and management know bout how much water they are saving, you may also want to share the news with your customers and community. This may encourage other groups and facilities to develop a similar water management programme. Consider graphing or visually displaying water savings to emphasise successes.

Other water management measures include preventing water being wasted which takes place in hundreds of ways, to prevent breaches in canals and tanks as well as to prevent pollution.

2

CATEGORIES OF WATER RESOURCE

India is rich in water resources, being endowed with a network of great rivers & vast alluvial basins to hold groundwater. Conditions, however, vary widely from region to region. Whereas there are some chronically drought affected areas, there are others which are frequently subject to damage by floods.On the whole, under the pressure of rapid population growth, the available resources of water are being developed & depleted at a fast rate & the situation seriously underlines the need for taking up integrated plans for water conservation & utilization for every agro-ecological area to meet the increasing demands of irrigation, water harvesting, human & livestock consumption,expanding industry, hydro-electric power generation, recreation,navigation & other uses.

Water resources are divisible into two distinct categories : the surface-water resources & the ground-water resources. Each of these categories is a part of the earth's water circulatory system,called the hydrologic cycle, & is ultimately derived from precipitation,which is rainfall plus snow. They are interdependent & frequently the loss of one is the gain of the other. The brief description of the run-off cycle,which is a part of the hydrologic cycle,will help us to understand the origin & the inter-dependence of these two categories of water resources.The precipitation that falls upon land & is the ultimate source for both the categories of water resources is dispersed in several ways. A sizeable portion is intercepted by the vegetal cover or temporarily detained in surface depressions.Most of it is later lost through evaporation. When the available interception or the depression storage are completely exhausted & when the rainfall intensity at the soil surface exceeds the infiltration capacity of the soils, the overland flow begins.Once the overland flow reaches a stream channel, it is called surface run-off, which together with other components of flow, forms the total run-off.Part of the water that infiltrates into the surface soil may continue to move laterally at shallow depth as interflow owing to the presence of relatively impervious lenses just below the soil surface & may eventually reach the stream channel when it is called the sub-surface runoff. A part of the sub-surface run-off may enter the stream promptly, whereas the remaining part may take`a long time before joining the stream flow.A second part of the precipitation which infiltrates is lost through evapo-transpiration via plant roots & thermal gradients just below the soil surface. A third part may remain above the water table in the zone of unsaturated flow.A fourth remaining part percolates deeply into the ground-water.Part of this ground-water may eventually reach the stream channel & become the base flow of the stream. This portion is termed ground-water run-off or ground-water flow.Apart from infiltrated rain-water, the seepage from canals, ponds, tanks, lakes, irrigated fields,etc.is also dispersed & accounted for in the same manner.The total run-off in the stream channel includes the snow-melt, the surface run-off the sub-surface run-off, the ground-water run-off & the channel precipitation, i.e. the precipitation falling directly on the water surface of streams, lakes, etc. It constitutes what is known as the surface-water resources. The portion of the precipitation which, after infiltration,reaches the ground-water-table, together with the contribution made to ground water from a neighbouring basin, influent rivers,natural lakes, ponds, artificial storage reservoirs, canals, irrigation & constitutes the ground-water resources. That quantity of water in the ground-water reservoir, which is not annually replenishable, is not taken into account, as it is a sort of dead storage which cannot be used on a continuing basis from year to year. The above phase of the run-off cycle pinpoints the inflow components for the surface-as well as for the ground-water resources. It has to be appreciated that there is always a balance between the inflow factors making up water resources of a region, whether surface or ground, & the outflow components.The surface water resource of a given basin in excess of the withdrawal use is accounted for on the outflow side by one or more of the following factors:

(i) stream outflow from the basin;

(ii) loss through evaporation;and

(iii) the influent recharge to the ground water.

Similarly, the unutilised ground-water resource of a basin is accounted for by the following outflow factors:

(i) Evapo-transpiration from the ground-water-table;

(ii) outflow to the neighbouring ground-water basin;

(iii) the effluent discharge to the streams;and

(iv) the addition to the ground-water storage.

The interrelationship between the surface-water & the ground-water resources is evident from the above analysis.The surface-water resources contribute to the ground-water recharge in various ways:

(i) by influent recharge from the streams;

(ii) by seepage from natural lakes, ponds, etc;

(iii) seepage from artificial storage reservoirs, canal systems, etc, and

(iv) return flow from irrigation.

These factors presently contribute to about 25 percent of the country's total ground-water resources.On the other hand, the bulk of the base-flow in the rivers, which represents the sustained fair-weather run-off is contributed by the ground-water resources. This contribution,presently, is roughly assessed at about 25 percent of the total surface-water resources of the country.

Factors Affecting Water Resources

The water resources of a region,conceived as a dynamic phase of the hydrologic cycle, are influenced by the following three major groups of factors:

1. Climatic Factors

(a) Rainfall : its intensity, duration & distribution.

(b) Snow

(b) Evapo-transpiration

2. Physiographic Factors

(a) Basic characteristics.

1. Geometric factors : drainage area, shape, slope & stream density.

2. Physical factors : land use, surface infiltration conditions, soil types, etc.

(b) Channel characteristics : carrying capacity & storage capacity.

3. Geological Factors

(a) Lithologic including composition, texture, sequenceof rock types & the thickness of rock formations.

(b) Structural, including chief faults & folds that interrupt the uniformity of occurence of rock types or sequence of rock types also beds, joints, fissures, cracks, etc.

(c) Hydrologic characteristics of the aquifers permeability, porosity, transmissivity, storability, etc.

The physiographic features (including geological factors) not only influence the occurence & distribution of water resources within a region but these, particularly the orography, play a significant role in influencing rainfall & other climatic factors, such as temperature, humidity & wind. However, within a geographical location & physiographic framework, it is primarily the rainfall (its intensity, duration & distribution) & the climatic factors affecting evapo-transpiration that determine the totality of water resources in the region.

Rainfall pattern and distribution.

Rainfall pattern & distribution in a region is a good index of its water resources.A considerable portion of the Indian subcontinent belongs to the subtropical zone. However, the region as a whole shares the characteristics of a tropical climate. Literally, the word 'monsoon' means a wind system which undergoes a seasonal 180 degree reversal of direction. Many regions of the world experience the monsoon. In India, however, two factors make it unique. One is the continuous & high mountain mass in the north which forms an effective barrier to the air movement across them. The second is the peninsular shape of the subcontinent with its land in close proximity to the ocean, thereby providing a rich source of moisture.The rainfall in the country is primarily orographic, associated with tropical depressions originating in the Bay of Bengal & the Arabian sea. The moisture-laden summer monsoon, accounting for the bulk of rainfall in the country, originates from the vast expanse of the Indian Ocean & enters the Indian subcontinent from the south-west as south-westerly current. The physiographic features of the Indian peninsula & the Western Ghats divert the monsoon into two branches, namely, the Arabian Sea branch & the Bay of Bengal branch. The Arabian Sea branch strikes the Western Ghat & precipitates heavily along the Western Ghat from Kerala to Gujarat between the last week of May & the first week of June. After surmounting the Ghats the southern part of the current blows across the Peninsula as a westerly or in places, as a north-westerly wind.The northern portion of the current which crosses the Saurashtra coast blows across Rajasthan as a south-westerly wind & gives rain mostly in the coastal districts near the Aravalli hills & the Punjab Kumaon Hills, but very little in the plains of Rajasthan.The Bay of Bengal branch turns north & enters Bangladesh, Assam & West Bengal in May as a southerly current. With the progress of summer, this current moves northwards & by about June it strikes the Himalayas & precipitates heavily. On being deflected by the Himalayas, it turns westwards & enters northern India as an easterly current. This occurs in the whole country, except in the western parts of Rajasthan, coming under the influence of the monsoon by about the first week of July. However, the advance of monsoon is not regular every year & is governed by the movement of depressions & low-pressure waves travelling from the Bay of Bengal across the country. Whereas Assam, the western coastal plains & the Western Ghats receive heavy rainfall almost every year, rainfall in other parts of the country is dependent on the number of depressions in the Bay of Bengal. Therefore, the annual monsoon variation in the central, northern & the north-western parts of the country is much more pronounced than in the regions of abundant rainfall.The monsoon starts withdrawing from Punjab downwards upto Saurashtra & Gujarat in the first week of September & disappears by the middle of November, except in the extreme south & south-east, where the receding monsoon gives rain as the north east monsoon from the Bay of Bengal.During winter, the northern part of the country gets some rainfall from western disturbances, but these are irregular & not reliable compared with the south-west monsoon. Also, severe cyclonic storms experienced during the transition months of April to June & October to December cause some precipitation. Some parts of the country receive hot-weather rainfall between March & May mainly owing to large-scale thunderstorms called Norwesters. These rains are of substantial importance in West Bengal & Assam.The annual average rainfall in India is about 120 cm, i.e. slightly more than the global mean of 99 cm. The more important fact to reckon with , however, is its extreme spatial & temporal variation. The regional variation is so large that whereas the Khasi Hills in the north-east get as average annual rainfall of more than 1,000 cm, the average annual rainfall received in parts of the Rajasthan desert is even less than 15 cm. Moreover, nearly 75 percent of the total rainfall is received in the four month period from June-September. Even in this season, the rainfall in most parts of the country is subject to uncertainty of occurence, marked by prolonged dry spells & aberration in the time of commencement & withdrawal, & also the total amount received. This explains the dependence of agriculture in most parts of the country on artificial irrigation & gives an insight into the nature of the country's water resources.

Evaporation and evapo-transpiration.

Evaporation is the process by which water vapour escapes from a free water-surface or moist soil. On land, in addition to water lost from the soil, there is also loss of water from plants; the combined loss is termed 'evapo-transpiration'. Evapo-transpiration is an important parameter in determining the water resources of a region. Loss through evapo-transpiration is controlled mainly by two factors, namely, the ability of the atmosphere to supply energy to vaporize water & transport the vapour & enhance the availability of moisture on the earth's surface. The former is determined by such parameters as the short wave & the long-wave radiation, humidity, air temperature, wind movement, albedo & temperature of the evaporating surfaces. The availability of moisture at the earth's surface is influenced by precipitation & the artificial application of water. Evapo-transpiration is also influenced to some extent by such factors as vegetal cover, type of foliage, stage of plant growth, & soil fertility. Because of all these variable complex factors, the estimation of evapo-transpiration becomes very difficult.A number of theoretical & empirical methods, however, have been used for computing the evapo-transpiration. These include methods based on the energy-budget theory, mass-transfer theory, water-budget approach & empirical methods using various equations, the prominent among which are:

(1) Lowry-Johnson;

(2) Thornthwaite;

(3) Blaney-Criddle;

(4) Blaney-Morin;

(5) Penman;

(6) Hargreaves; and

(7) Christiansen.

Whereas some of these equations compute the evapo-transpiration directly, others either determine the potential evapo-transpiration directly, others either determine the potential evapo-transpiration (i.e. the rate of evapo-transpiration, if the supply of water is unlimited), or evaporation equivalent to Class A Pan evaporation, & then use empirical relationships between these factors & the evapo-transpiration. The method commonly adopted is to compute evapo-transpiration from Class A Pan evaporation either actually observed on evapori-meters or empirically determined from equations.In India, the regional values of actual evapo-transpiration have yet not been computed. However, evaporation data based on a network of about 80 stations equipped with wire-mesh covered standard Class A Pan evapori-meters is now available for about 10-15 years. It has been observed that evaporation is lowest in Assam & the adjoining Himalayas & Bengal (the annual value being 150 cm) & the highest value is 387 cm at Jalgaon & Ahmedabad. Evaporation is lowest (from 2mm to 8mm/day) during January & maximum during May (when it ranges from 4 mm to 20 mm/day). The monthly & annual potential evapo-transpiration values have also been computed by applying the Penman formula for about 300 stations in India. The annual variation ranges from 140 cm to 180 cm over a large portion of the country. Values exceeding 200 cm, occur over Western Rajasthan & parts of Saurashtra & Tamil Nadu. This is generally the highest during May (when it ranges from about 10 cm to 30 cm) over most parts of the country. In Rajasthan, it continues to be high in June also. The minimum is usually in December & January, when it ranges from about 3-15 cm per month.

Assessment of Water Resources

Surface-water resources. The most reliable method to assess the surface-water resources is through an accurate & continual study of water flows through rivers & streams over a period of years. The run-off records of the various river systems in India are incomplete & therefore, the assessment of the water resources from actual gauged discharge records is not possible for the whole country. However, the rainfall records are available for a long period & attempts have, therefore, been made to roughly assess the water resources on the concept that the natural run-off (assuming that there is neither any upstream development from the surface or ground-water resources nor any increment or decrement in the ground-water storage) is equal to the total volume of precipitation minus the volume of water lost into the atmosphere through evapo-transpiration.

Dr A. N. Khosla, an eminent engineer, evolved the following relationships in the run-off as the function of rainfall & temperature, assuming that the temperature is the main determinant of evapo-transpiration :

$$R_m = Pm - L_m \quad ....(1)$$

$$L_m = 0.481\ T_m \quad ....(2)$$

in which

R_m= monthly run-off. cm

P_m= monthly rainfall,cm

L_m= monthly evaporation losses,cm

T_m= mean monthly temperature, degree centigrade.

On the basis of this relationship, he estimated the mean annual natural run-off (normally referred to as the surface-water resources) of the six water-resources regions of the country as 167.23 mham. The region-wise distribution is given in Table 1. Later, based on the specific analysis of the stream-flow data from 80 sources, carried out by the Central Water & Power Commision, the Irrigation Commission (1972) has worked out the water resources of the country at 178 mham. This figure includes, besides surface run-off, ground-water run-off (effluent discharge) which is contributed by the ground-water storage as the base flow of the rivers(as shown later the present figure of ground water run-off is roughly assessed at about 45 mham) as well as the sub-surface run-off contributed by rainfall & seepage from surface-water resources, but excludes whatever influent recharge(tank storage) that may have taken place from the flood flows.The above estimate represents the average annual river flow. All this flow cannot be utilised owing to the highly variable character of the flow & other limitations imposed by the physiographic factors. The concentration of flow in a four month period necessitates the construction of storage works, if the flood flows passing to the sea are to be utilised. However, suitable sites for the construction of storage dams are limited.

TABLE 1

Name of Basin	*Catchment area (m ha) precipation (cm)*	*Average annual precipitation (cm)*	*Total Precipitation (degreerun- centigrade)*	*Mean (m temperture off (m ha m)*	*Average annual*
Indus Basin	35.40	56	19.82	12.6	7.94
Ganga Basin	97.60	111	108.34	16.8	48.96
Brahmaputra Basin	50.62	122	61.76	8.2	38.08
West-flowing Rivers	49.16	122	59.98	25.5	31.06
East-flowing Rivers	121.03	100	131.92	26.1	41.19
Loni & Ghaggar Basin	16.80	39	4.87	26.2	..
Total	370.61	549	386.69	..	167.23

The utilisable quantum also depends on the availability of suitable sites for the diversion of water, the quality of water being suitable, the proximity of water to the land fit for cultivation & the dependability of flow. In India, the irrigation projects are usually designed for 75 percent dependability, so that the designed quantity of water is available for at least 75 percent of the year. In view of the limitations imposed by these considerations, the total utilisable flow has been estimated at 66.6 mham, by the Irrigation Commission(1972).Region-wise details of the total available & the utilisable surface-water resources are given in Table 2. With further growth of irrigation, it is likely that sub-surface flow contributing to the total annual run-off may appreciably increase, thus augmenting the present availability of surface-water resources.This increase, however, maybe compensated for by the anticipated reduction in the ground-water run-off owing to the continued development of the ground-water resources. It is therefore, visualised that the total surface-water resources may remain, more or less, steady at the same level as at present.

TABLE 2

S.No	*Name of Basin*	*Average annual run-off (in mham)*	*Utilisable flow Utilisable flow*
1.	Indus Basin	7.70	4.93
2.	Ganga Basin	51.001	8.50
3.	Brahmaputra Basin	54.00	1.23
4.	West-flowing rivers	28.80	6.92
5.	East-flowing rivers	34.80	33.80
6.	Luni & Ghaggar Basin	1.70	1.22
	Total	178.00	66.60

Ground-water resources

The assessment of ground-water resources is much more difficult, as it involves the evaluation of the various hydrologic components within the framework of a complex geological environment. There are as yet numerous gaps in the available information & the stage has not reached when any precise basin-wise assessment of the resource can be made except in highly generalised terms.An attempt was made by the Central Working Group (constituted for working out the Fourth Five-Year Plan proposals for Minor Irrigation in 1968) to work out the rainfall contribution of ground-water recharge by classifying the geological formations in India into 7 categories & assuming, on the basis of the best-informed judgement, different percentage factors for the ground-water recharge for these various categories. The categories & the percentage factors assumed are indicated in Table 3.

On the above basis, the average contribution to ground-water recharge in the country as a whole works out at 10 percent of the total rainfall. Since then, some more reliable regional estimates (though still based on short-cut generalised methods) have been made by the state ground-water organisations, & it is felt that the figure of 10 percent contribution, on the average, maybe somewhat conservative. A figure of 12.5 percent is considered to be more realistic.Reckoning that the total annual volume of rainfall is about 400 mham, on the basis of a mean rainfall of 120 cm over the geographical area of 328 mham, the mean rainfall contribution to the ground-water recharge comes to 50 mham.

S.No.	*Rock type formation*	*Assumed percentage rainfall contributing to ground-water recharge*
1.	Hard-rock formations & the Deccan traps	10
2.	Consolidated rocks(sandstone)	5-10
3.	River alluvia	15-20
4.	Indo-Gangetic alluviam	20
5.	Coastal alluvia	10-15
6.	Western Rajasthan sand dune	2
7.	Intermontane valleys	15-20

As mentioned before, the under-ground aquifers are supplemented from sources other than rainfall, seepage from canals, water-courses, field channels, ponds, tanks, return flow from irrigation in the fields & the influent recharge from rivers. As assessed later, the total volume of surface water presently utilised for irrigation is about 23.5 mham. It is visualised that about 35 percent of this total volume diverted for irrigation would pass as deep percolation to ground-water storage. Hence, the addition to the ground-water recharge on this account maybe taken as about 8.2 mham. The total volume of ground-water presently used for irrigation is estimated at about 10.5 mham. Since in the case of ground-water used for irrigation, the loss in the long conveyance systems is not involved & the efficiency of irrigation is somewhat better, it may be more realistic to assume a figure of 25 percent as the deep percolation contributing to ground-water recharge. The addition to ground-water recharge on this account will thus be 2.75 mham. The total contribution to ground-water recharge from these sources may thus be taken as 10.95(say 11) mham.Assuming that about 4 mham, maybe the influent recharge from the flood flows, the total mean availability of ground-water resources at present maybe reckoned as about 65 mham. It is roughly visualised to be accounted for as below:

1. Withdrawal use:
   - (i) Irrigation 10.5 mham
   - (ii) Other uses 1.5 mham
   - (iii) Total 12.00 mham
2. Loss due to evapo-transpiration from the water table 8.00 mham

3.	Ground-water rainfall (effluent recharge to rivers & streams)	45.00 mham
	Total	65.00

According to the assessment of the National Commission on Agriculture, the contribution from surface-water resources to the ground-water recharge is likely to increase to about 35 mham on the full development of irrigation-25 mham from seepage from canals, tanks etc. & 10 mham as influent recharge (to be increased as a result of special measures for induced recharge). Adding the contribution of rainfall, the total ultimate ground-water resources may be of the order of 85 mham. Reckoning that about 50 mham will be lost as ground-water run-off & evapo-transpiration, the ultimate usable ground water resources may be assessed at 35 mham. The above assessment does not include the additional supplies that may temporarily be obtained by the mining of water in certain regions.

Present utilization of Water Resources

Water resources are utilised mainly for three purposes : irrigation, industrial use & domestic water supply, urban as well as rural. Irrigation is by far the major consumer of water resources.

Irrigation

The development of irrigation has received attention in the country since the beginning of the Indian civilisation. Reference to wells & tanks has been made in the *Vedas*. Some of the existing tanks & canals were constructed centuries back. The British Government remodelled & constructed several major canals in the country during the nineteenth & twentieth centuries. Since the inception of the first Five-Year Plan, concerted efforts have been made to develop irrigation through major, medium & minor irrigation schemes (schemes costing more than Rs 5 crores are classified as major.Those between Rs 25 lakhs & 5 crores as medium & those costing less than Rs 25 lakhs as minor).Table 4 gives the progressive development of irrigation since the beginning of the first Five-Year Plan.It would appear that under minor irrigation, there has been a significant step-up in the development of ground-water, particularly since the end of the Third Plan. The factors responsible for this acceleration were : the realization of the value of ground-water as a source of assured irrigation, the rapid extension of electric power to villages ; the increased production & availability of diesel engines & diesel oil ; the fast development in the extension of cooperative credit for minor irrigation ; & the indigenous production of drilling & other equipment required for the programme. Table 5 gives the progressive increase in the number of wells & pumping sets :

TABLE 4

Period	*Major-medium irrigation (surface)*	*Surface*	*Ground*	*Total*	*Grand total*
Pre-Plan	9.7	6.4	6.5	12.9	22.6
End of the First Plan	11.0	6.5	7.6	14.1	25.1
End of the Second Plan	13.1	6.6	8.2	14.8	27.9
End of the Third Plan	15.2	6.8	10.2	17.0	32.2
End of the three year period-1966-169	17.0	7.0	12.0	19.0	36.0
End of the Fourth Plan	19.4	7.5	16.0	23.5	42.9

TABLE 5

Item	*1950-51*	*1960-61*	*1968-69*	*1973-74*
1. Dug wells	3,500	4,500	5,900	6,920
2. Shallow tube-wells (private)	3	20	250	810
3. Deep tube-wells (public)	3	8	15	20
4. Electrical pumping-sets	18	192	1,089	2,440
5. Diesel pumping-sets	65	230	722	1,753

With more & more area coming under irrigation, there has been a steady increase in the intensity of cropping as well as in the intensity of irrigated cropping. This increase is shown in Table 6.

TABLE 6

Period	*Intensity of cropping*	*Intensity of irrigated cropping*
1950-51	111.12	108.13
1955-56	114.01	112.28
1960-61	114.63	113.36
1965-66	114.10	117.11
1968-69	116.07	122.07
1970-71	118.55	123.32

The total area irrigated from the surface-water sources in 1973-74 is estimated at 26.9 million ha. This area includes about 3 million ha in which the supplemental irrigation is provided by ground-water schemes. Reckoning an average total irrigation depth of 0.9 metre measured at the head of the source, for 23.9 million ha, irrigated exclusively from the surface-water schemes, the total volume of surface-water presently used (in 1973-74) comes to 21.51 mham. Assuming that an irrigation depth of about 0.3 metre on the average will be provided by the ground-water schemes in the area under supplemental irrigation, the average depth provided by the surface-water schemes may be taken as 0.6 metre. The total volume utilised on this account will come to 1.8 mham. The present total utilisation of surface-water for irrigation may then be taken as 23.31, say 23.50 mham.For ground-water irrigation, as in this case conveyance is not involved & also the efficiency of irrigation is somewhat better, a reduced yard stick of 0.6 mham of irrigated area is considered to be realistic. On this basis, the total volume of ground-water utilised in 1973-74 for irrigating 16 million ha would work out at 96 mham.In addition, it is roughly estimated that 9 mham metres of ground-water was used for providing supplemental irrigation to an area of about 3 million ha. under the command of existing surface-water irrigation projects. The total ground-water pumpage for irrigation in 1973-74 is thus assessed at 10.5 mham.

Other uses. No scientific estimate is available of the present utilisation of water resources for industrial & domestic purposes. It is, however, roughly reckoned that the total utilisation for these purposes may be about 2.5 mham, about from surface-water & about 1.5 mham from ground-water.

Total utilisation. The following data give the picture that emerges in respect of the present status of utilisation of the water resources :

PRESENT UTILISATION

S.No.	*Total utilisable resources*	*Irrigation*	*Other uses*	*Total*
1. Surface-water	66.6	23.5	1.0	24.5
2. Ground-Water	35.0	10.5	1.5	12.0

FUTURE PERSPECTIVE AND PORTENTS

Table 7 gives the future perspective for irrigation development in the country based on the present state of knowledge about the usable water resources & the possibility of utilising them :

TABLE 7

	Ultimate gross irrigated area (mham)	*Average total depth of irrigation*	*Ultimate utilisation of water resources for irrigation (mham)*	*Total usable water resources (mham*	*Balance water resources for other uses (mham)*
(a) *Surface Irrigation:*					
(i) Exclusive of surface water	62	0.8	49.6	NA	NA
(ii) Supplemental irrigation*	100.47	4.7	NA	NA	
Total	72**	..	54.3	66.6	12.3
(b) *Ground water*					
(i) Exclusive of ground water	35	0.66	23.1	NA	NA
(ii) Supplemental irrigation	10***	0.33	3.3	NA	NA
Total	35	..	26.4	35	8.6*

This figure includes area partly irrigated from surface waterworks & partly from ground-water schemes.

** It includes 57 m ha from major-medium works & 10 m ha from minor works.

*** Included under surface irrigation.

In the above projections it has been assumed that with more emphasis on the lining of canals, distributaries & water-courses & improving the efficiency of irrigation, the average depth of irrigation in the case of surface irrigation will decrease from the present 0.9 m to 0.8 m in course of years. For ground-water irrigation, on the other hand, it is visualised that the present figure of 0.6m may have a tendency to increase owing to the gradual extension of ground-water irrigation to higher-water-consuming crops, like paddy & sugarcane. Hence a figure of 0.66 m has been asumed in the context of the ultimate development from ground-water. For the area under supplemental irrigation, it is assumed that an average irrigation depth of about 0.47 m will be provided from surface-water & 0.33 m from ground-water.As regards the net area sown, the present figure which is about 142 m ha, the outer limit is considered to be 150 million ha. in view of the paucity of additional land available for bringing under cultivation. The question is : What will be the realistic corresponding figure in the gross cropped area?The data for the years 1955-56 to 1970-71 show the near-linear relationship between the area sown more than once & the gross irrigated area.Further, if the past trend is assumed to continue, the ultimate figure of the areas taken more than once, when the gross irrigated area reaches the ultimate level of 107 m ha, will be 60 m ha. This would mean that the ultimate total cropped area may be reckoned to be of the order of 210 m ha.The past figure shows that the intensity of cropping has a tendency to be somewhat less than the intensity of irrigated cropping, although both of them increase with the growth of irrigation. The ultimate intensity of cropping on the basis of the gross cropped area of 210 m ha & the net area sown covering 150 m ha will be 140. Assuming a somewhat higher intensity of about 150 percent for irrigated cropping, the net irrigated area against the gross irrigated area of 107 m ha may be taken as about 70 million ha.Table 8 gives the overall perspective for the ultimate increases visualised in the areas under cultivation & irrigation.

TABLE 8

S.No	*Item*	*1973-74*	*Ultimate (million ha)*
1.	Gross cropped area	169	210
2.	Net area sown	142	150
3.	Gross irrigated area	42.9	107
4.	Net irigated area	34.8	70
5.	Intensity of cropping	119%	140%
6.	Itensity of irrigated cropping	123%	150%

The above figures give the basis on which the ultimate projections for agricultural production in the country may be made. The present trend shows that about 90-95 percent of the ultimate potential for irrigation from ground-water may be reached by the year 2000. The full exploitation of the potential for irrigation from surface-water sources may extend to about the year 2025.The water resources to be ultimately available for non-irrigation uses amount to 12.3 m ham from surface-water & 8.6 m ham from ground-water. Although the percentage of utilisation of water resources for purposes other than irrigation is low at present, this is expected to rise appreciably in the future with increasing industrialisation & power generation through thermal & nuclear plants. According to the National Commission on Agriculture, by the year 2025 the requirements under these sectors may amount to over 25 percent of the available < normal the from 2025 year by requirements these meeting in constraints be will there that obvious is It period. this beyond further increase may & resources> The above perspective underlines the fact that in the face of anticipated population growth & technological advancement, the country's utilisable water resources are limited & there is no ground for complacency in the matter. There is utmost need for laying maximum emphasis on conservation & efficient utilisation of the available water resources. To achieve this objective, the *laissez-faire* approach in water development should give way to integrated development based on carefully drawn-up plans for every agro-ecological region. Technological & management capabilities will have to be updated for this purpose. The degradation of the environment through pollution, which has so far been neglected, will need to be given serious consideration while making decisions relating to the future development. Above all, there is need that while the available water resources are utilised in the best manner possible, the development of technology for augmenting the water resources through new methods, as artificial recharge, recycling of water, desalinization of sea-water & weather modification should also be given constant attention.

3

PROCESS OF WATER MANAGEMENT AND CONSERVATION PROGRAMMES

In view of the limited water available and, that too, unevenly and polluted, there is a need to adopt some conservation measures for balanced and adequate supply of water to various users. Water is a resource that belongs to the community. Measures for conservation of water resources have to be taken at different levels. Some common measures to increase water resources are creation of more water storage reservaoirs, inter-basin transfer of water and measures to raise underground water level. Water is a national resource. The government has to take a decision to solve the problem of scarcity of water.

Planning is just a logical sequence of decision-making phases or activities that include:

1. Gathering Information and Defining Problems
2. Setting Goals and Priorities
3. Evaluating Options
4. Defining a Plan of Action
5. Implementing and Monitoring

There is nothing magical or complicated about this sequence of activities. If you think about it a little bit, you will realise that you use this thought process for almost every decision you make. In the context of water management, it is simply used as a framework to ensure a systematic and thorough decision-making process.

The five planning phases described above are shown in sequential, step-by-step order. However, the planning process often requires going back and forth between steps. For example, it is very common to determine, in the course of evaluating options, that further information gathering is needed.

It is this back-and-forth approach that makes planning a process. Figure 1, rather than a product. The product (in this case a water management plan) should be viewed as a "snapshot" of an ongoing process, taken at a specific point in time for the purpose of implementing particular management measures.

Water management planning should be viewed as an ongoing activity and not as a one-time effort. Situations change, new technologies arise and problems and opportunities may be seen in a new light. As a result, plans become outdated. Water management planning must become a routine part of district management to be effective in the long run.

GATHER INFORMATION
&
IDENTIFY PROBLEMS

↓

SET GOALS
&
PRIORITIES

↓

EVALUATE
OPTIONS

↓

DEFINE A
PLAN OF ACTION

↓

IMPLEMENT
&
MONITOR

Figure 3.1: The Planning Process

Each of the five planning phases shown on Figure 3.1 are discussed in detail in this section. Hopefully, by the time you have read through the section, you will have a good understanding of the planning process and how it could be applied to your situation.

The Importance of Public Involvement

A basic principle of planning is that it cannot effectively be done in a vacuum. It would be foolhardy to design a new set of policies, procedures or requirements and attempt to implement them without involving the people affected by them. In many cases, district or ditch company by laws would prohibit such actions.

For plans to be credible and effective, it is important to obtain consensus and support from district boards of directors and from potentially affected parties. The parties that are most obviously affected by the water management measures described in this guide book are water users themselves. Involving water users in all phases of the planning process is more likely to produce management plans that address real problems in practical ways. If they feel that the plan is responsive to their needs and to their input, they will be far more likely to support it.

But there are other important "publics" that can also make significant contributions to plan development. Involving local community leaders, state and federal agency staff and representatives of various interest groups in the planning process is more than the application of the "two heads are better than one" principle; it also provides a mechanism for obtaining broader perspectives on the issues and can help head off later obstacles to plan implementation.

For these reasons, it is very important to consider public involvement as an integral part of the water management planning process. The goals of public involvement are:

* To build credibility by establishing an open and accessible planning and decision-making process.
* To identify and understand the diverse concerns and values of the parties potentially affected by your decisions.
* To develop a consensus among these divergent interests in support of your water management plan.

Some methods to provide public involvement opportunities include mail questionnaires and information sheets, public meetings and workshops, focus groups and advisory committees and the use of local media. Reclamation has a substantial amount of experience in developing public involvement programmes and has produced a *Public Involvement Manual* to assist water resource planners in this area (USDI, 1980).

Additional assistance in developing a public involvement programme can be obtained from the Water Conservation Coordinator at Reclamation's Area or Regional Office nearest you.

Information Gathering and Problem definition

The first phase of the planning process includes problem definition and information gathering activities. These activities go hand-in-hand. You probably already have some ideas about water management problems in your district, but having more or better information will help you define those problems more clearly and possibly uncover others. You also probably already have quite a bit of information about water use in your district, but it may be incomplete or not organised in a way that is helpful in problem-solving.

This first phase of the planning process is meant to "flesh out" information gaps and uncertainties about problems and to develop a solid foundation for subsequent planning activities. Before you can effectively set goals and evaluate options, you must have a clear definition of the problem, you are trying to solve.

Input from irrigators and others affected by your district's water use will help you identify important issues. When examined carefully, these issues may turn out to be symptoms of more basic problems. Therefore, you will want to involve a wide range of people at the onset of Phase 1, perhaps through an annual shareholder meeting or public meeting.

Needs for Information of Checklist

Part of the first phase of the planning process is gathering the information you need to identify and analyse water management problems. You will also need some other descriptive information about the district to include in your water management plan document so that people who read it have a good understanding about the district. The checklist below is provided to help you get started assembling the information you will need.

Understanding the local hydrology and climate will help you identify the factors which affect district water supplies and irrigation demands. Data that might be useful include:

* Hydrology of source streams, district reservoirs, area wetlands and ground water.
* Water quality of sources and return flows.
* Climate information such as precipitation and temperature.

Sources of hydrologic, climate and water quality data include extension offices, local universities, the National Climate Data Centre, the U.S. Geological Survey, the EPA, the NRCS, Reclamation and private data publishers.

Water Rights, Permits and Contracts

The legal and institutional constraints under which your district operates will be a factor in your water management plan. Therefore, it would be useful to understand:

* Rights or permits held by the district
* Contracts with Reclamation or others
* Instream flow requirements
* Restrictions on water use
* Endangered Species Act compliance needs.

Sources of information include district by laws, articles of incorporation, decrees, contracts and state water legislation. Pay particular attention to restrictions on the use of conserved or salvaged water, transfers within your district or between districts and any requirements to preserve return flow patterns.

Lands and Crops

Understanding the agricultural details of your district is key to developing a sound management plan. Data that should be collected include:

* Acreage under each crop
* Irrigation methods
* Soils, topography and drainage

The Crop Production and Water Utilisation Data Sheets that districts submit to Reclamation are comprehensive with respect to areas irrigated and crops grown. You should find descriptions of terrain, soil types and soil parameters important to irrigation operations in Reclamation's Land Classification Maps. Your district may have copies of these maps or may wish to obtain them from Reclamation's area office manager. Other sources of soils information may be found in Natural Resources Conservation Service (NRCS) soil surveys.

Operating Policies and District Operations

Your water management plan may involve modifying existing operating policies. Sources of this information include district bylaws, written policies, district rules and regulations, and standard practices. You will first need to understand:

* General operations
* Water ordering and delivery procedures

* Water shortage allocation policy
* Inter-district agreements and operations
* Staffing and training of operators.

Examples include reservoir operations main canal operations, timing of use of different sources, groundwater pumping policies, flood control policies, facilities maintenance and hydropower operations. Many operating policies may not be written down describing your operations in writing will help you and others better understand how the district works.

Water Pricing and Accounting

To understand relationships between water use and revenues, you will want to compile descriptions of:

* Water accounting procedures
* Water user billing procedures

These procedures may be gleaned from standard practices or they may be codified in bylaws and contracts. If some of your district revenue comes from billing water users, you will want to understand the basis for billing.

Water Resources Inventory

The infrastructure and water supplies currently in place in your district twill be the most important factors in determining where water use efficiencies can be improved. Records of flow amounts will be key to estimating losses and potential savings. They types of data you will need include:

* Diversion capacities and diversion records
* Groundwater pumping capacities and pumping data
* Storage capacities, storage and release records and evaporation data
* Delivery records and data, including peak period deliveries
* Drainage and return flow records.

Some districts will have detailed, daily records for diversions, storage and deliveries for multiple points in the system. Others will have diversion and delivery records only for main canals and laterals. Reclamation's Monthly Water Distribution sheets will contain monthly data for your district, though the accuracy and reliability of these data should be verified. You may also have additional records in the form of ditch rider notebooks, water ordering cards etc. Information from drought years will be particularly useful.

Other Water Uses

There may be opportunities and constraints presented to your district by non-agricultural water uses. Your district may provide water supplies for municipal, domestic or industrial uses; you will want to quantify those water uses as much as possible. Some other water uses include:

* Recreational and environmental uses
* Special needs or operations (*e.g.*, sediment flushing)

Existing Water Management and Conservation Programmes

You will want to understand what management measures or programmes have already been implemented in your district. These could range from sprinkler installation to education programmes to variable rate pricing. Understanding the cost and impacts of each measure will help you make informed decisions about future measures. Lessons from programmes that have not succeeded are as valuable as those from programmes that have succeeded.

Identifying Problem Areas

There are a variety of ways to learn about water management problems in your district. Probably the most common way is day-to-day observation and experience. District management and staff members often observe operational problems directly. Water users may complain of difficulties with deliveries. Other persons in the community may bring drainage problems to your attention. Holding informal "brainstorming sessions" with district staff, water users, partners and stakeholders might help to increase information exchange.

Another important way to learn about water management problems is to analyse data. For example, by comparing records of gross diversions with records of farm deliveries you can estimate the amount of water lost in main canals and laterals. This type of quantitative analysis can provide quite specific information about problem areas, provided it is based on accurate data. One very useful method of analysis is the water budget, which is described in more detail below. You also might be able to obtain additional useful data from other agencies (for example, a county extension agent) or by installing new measuring devices.

The Water Budget Concept

The water budget is a convenient tool for analysing water management problems and opportunities, provided that you have adequate and reliable data. It is also a useful way to organise quantitative information you have collected.

The water budget concept, simply stated, is that the sum of system inflows has to equal the sum of system outflows. Inflows consist of all the sources of water supply to the district. Outflows consist of all the ways that water is removed from the district. The various components of inflow and outflow that are usually present in a district water budget.

By comparing inflows and outflows in a water budget, it is possible to identify unaccounted-for losses. For example, if the diversion into a canal and farm turnouts from the canal are all measured, the difference between the diversion and the sum of the turnouts would be the gross loss from the canal. This gross loss is the net result of seepage, evaporation, precipitation and the interception of surface runoff and ground-water flow. If any of these latter quantities (such as precipation evaporation and interception) can be accurately measured or estimated, then the remaining difference provides an estimate of the other quantities.

However, all this is possible only if the records or estimates for all the accounted-for inflows and outflows are accurate and reliable. If any of those records or estimates are unreliable or inaccurate, the losses calculated from the water budget will also be unreliable or inaccurate. Thus it is very important that the data used in water budget analysis be verified. For example, it can encompass the entire district or focus on a specific lateral. By focusing on smaller areas, it is sometimes possible to identify the specific locations of problems such as ditch seepage.

The water budget can also be prepared on an annual basis or a daily basis. A shorter time step sometimes helps identify scheduling problems. Table 3.1 depicts a water budget set up to look at an entire district on a monthly basis for an average year. It might be helpful to prepare such a water budget for a wet year and for a dry year to see how losses change with hydrologic conditions. By analysing several years, your confidence in the results of the analysis will be increased.

The primary limitation on what scales can be used in the water budget is the availability of accurate flow measurements. You should not be tempted to stretch the application of the water budget methodology beyond what you have the data to support. If you are unable to construct a good water budget for the district, you should probably consider the improvement of water measurement systems to be a top priority for your water management plan.

The Crop ET value in Table 3.1 can be calculated from crop acreages and crop consumptive use estimates. Consumptive use estimates are often available from Reclamation or other state or local agricultural agencies. Most districts don't collect seepage and evaporation data. These values may be derived from the water budget if the other data in the table are available.

TABLE 3.1:
Example Monthly Water Budget

Month	*Inflows*					*Outflows*				
	Direct Diversion	*Storag Release*	*Ground Water Pumping*	*Precipi-tation*	*Total Inflows*	*Operational Spills*	*Drainage*	*Evap. and Seepage*	*Grop ET*	*Total Outflows*
January	*0*	*0*	*0*	*1200*	*1200*	*0*	*720*	*480*	*0*	*1200*
February	*0*	*0*	*0*	*1500*	*1500*	*0*	*900*	*600*	*0*	*1500*
March	*0*	*0*	*0*	*2250*	*2250*	*0*	*1350*	*900*	*0*	*2250*
April	*3581*	*0*	*0*	*2700*	*6281*	*1053*	*527*	*1053*	*3648*	*6281*
May	*8723*	*0*	*0*	*2550*	*11273*	*1491*	*1491*	*1988*	*6302*	*11273*
June	9318	0	0	750	10068	705	1411	1411	6541	10068
July	9629	4395	550	450	15024	1053	2107	2107	9757	15024
August	5777	7770	400	300	14247	1208	2416	2416	8207	14247
September	2889	4101	0	600	7589	611	1221	1221	4536	7589
October	654	978	0	750	2382	195	389	389	1409	2382
November	0	0	0	750	750	0	450	300	0	750
December	0	0	0	1050	1050	0	630	420	0	1050
Total	40571	17244	950	14850	73614	6316	13612	13285	40400	73614

One of the most valuable aspects of the water budget is that it provides a means to calculate efficiencies. Estimating efficiencies at different levels will help you identify where improvements are needed the most:

District-wide Efficiency = Crop ET ÷ Total Inflows

Delivery Efficiency = Total Farm Deliveries ÷ Total Inflows

On-Farm Efficiency = Crop ET ÷ Total Farm Deliveries

Monthly calculations of efficiencies will help you determine how well district diversions and deliveries match crop requirements.

Checklist of Typical Problem Areas

A "checklist" is provided below to help you start thinking about where there might be opportunities to improve water management in your district. This checklist is organised into problem areas that are common in irrigation organisations. It may be that your district or ditch company has unique water management problems and opportunities that could be added to this list.

Adequacy of Data

Good information is fundamental to making good decisions. Informed decisions about water management are based on good water measurement and accounting. Without accurate and reliable information about when, where and how much water is used, it is difficult to correctly assess the locations and magnitudes of problems. These assessments, in turn, are key to deciding how to allocate scarce district resources.

1. Do you make regular measurements of flows into all laterals? To your turnouts?
2. Are all measuring devices in good operating condition? Checked regularly?
3. Are you able to base billing to customers on measurements of water they actually use?
4. Do you think you could use more or improved water measurement?
5. Do you have specific ideas about where and how such measurements should be taken?

Adequacy of Supply

The adequacy of the district water supply should be considered at several levels. Income situations it will be clear that water demand chronically exceeds available supply. However, it is more common that supply is adequate on the average, but there are shortages in dry years, in the late season or in certain locations.

1. Do you regularly have difficulties meeting overall district water demands?
2. Are there certain areas of the district that are always a problem?
3. Do you regularly have late season shortages?
4. Have you ever compared actual diversions and deliveries to estimated crop requirements?
5. Have you estimated your overall system efficiency?

Scheduling of Deliveries

Ideally, water is delivered only when it is needed. We are all accustomed to this concept and apply it regularly when we turn on the tap at the kitchen sink. Irrigation water supply systems are usually no pressurised like domestic systems, so matching deliveries and needs is a much more complicated proposition. When deliveries don't match needs, there is the potential for wasted water or unmet demand.

1. Do you run water continuously in canals and laterals.?

2. Do irrigators in your district have access to monitoring and scheduling services telling them when they need to irrigate?

3. Do you use a rigid-schedule (rotation) or advance ordering (arranged) system for water deliveries?

4. How far in advance do users need to place their orders? Can you fill orders on shorter notice?

5. Do you have the ability to quickly check or shut down canals and laterals to avoid spills?

Efficiency of Application

Irrigation water delivered to the farm must ultimately be delivered to the crop root zone. The challenge in water application is to deliver water to the root zone efficiently and uniformly over the entire field, without putting too much in some places and not enough in others. Application efficiency and uniformity are affected by many things, but most prominently by field characteristics, water application methods, and water management skill of the irrigator. Evidence of poor application efficiency includes dry patches or ponding on fields, excessive tailwater runoff and irregular crop stress.

1. Are the farm fields in you district relatively flat or is the land sloping or hilly? Are sprinklers common in the hilly areas?

2. Do soil types differ greatly from field to field? Within fields?

3. Is there a lot of variability in the effectiveness of on-farm water use?

4. Does the district provide demonstration projects or training workshops for irrigators?

5. Does the district have programmes to make improved water application equipment or technologies more accessible to irrigators?

Control of Drainage and Tailwater

Tailwater is produced when irrigation water is applied to fields at rates and in amounts greater than can be infiltrated into the soil profile. Drainage may include both tailwater and seepage water from deep percolation through farm fields. This deep percolation occurs when more water is infiltrated than can be retained in the crop root zone. Sometimes excess water must be applied to leach salts from the soil, but the presence of significant amounts of drainage and tailwaters is often viewed as evidence of over-application of irrigation water.

1. Has your district constructed drains to convey tailwater and seepage away

from irrigated fields?

2. Do you monitor flows in these drains or at other points on local streams to assess the quantities of tailwater and drainage return flow being produced?
3. Do you collect tailwater and drainage flows in ponds?
4. Do you monitor the water quality in drains and ponds?
5. Are there ponds in locations where it is feasible to pump tailwater back into your district's distribution system?

Water Transfer Needs and Opportunities

Water transfer arrangements can take many forms. They may be formal or informal, temporary or permanent, within the district or with outside users. The basic idea behind all of them, however, is to move water from users having more than they need to users having less than they need.

1. Is there a method within your district for irrigators to transfer their water shares or allocations to other irrigators?
2. Can such transfers be made to non-irrigation uses within the district?
3. Have non-irrigation or non-district water users inquired about the district's ability to supply them with water?
4. Are there local water needs that could be met by the district if transfers were allowed?
5. Is the transfer within the district, within or out of the basin?
6. Are there state laws or policies that affect this transfer?

Environmental Considerations

The development of western irrigated agriculture has impacts on the environment and ecosystems of the region. Construction and operation of water storage and diversion projects and their management to varying degrees, have generally modified and depleted natural flow regimes, created wetlands in areas where they did not exist naturally and degraded water quality by adding sediments, salts and chemical residues from fertilizers and pesticides.

1. Are there wetlands or critical habitats affected by water use in you district?
2. Are there endangered species in source or receiving streams?
3. Are drainage waters from your district highly saline?

4. What constraints do these issues impose on your operations?
5. How do your operations affect these environmental values?
6. Are there ways district operations could be modified to improve conditions?

Public Concerns

Irrigated agriculture is undergoing more and more scrutiny by municipalities, industry, environmental groups and the general public. This interest may pose both constraints and opportunities for irrigation districts.

1. Has you district been approached as a potential source of water?
2. Is your district facing new environmental regulations?
3. Is your water storage facility also a recreational facility?
4. Is your water storage facility subject to relicensing?
5. Are there downstream water users who depend on your district's return flows?
6. Are there upstream water users whose activities affect the amount and quality of your water source?

Setting Goals and Priorities

The objective of this second phase of the planning process is to define the goals of your water management planning effort. These goals will help you decide which water management measures make the most sense to implement. They will become the "yardsticks" by which you measure the success of your efforts. They need to state where you are going and why.

Goal-Setting

In addition to addressing specific problems within the district, some other areas where you should consider developing specific planning goals include the following:

- Providing leadership in solving regional water problems
- Improving coordination with neighbouring water supply entities
- Enhancing the value of the water resource within and outside the district

There are some basic principles to follow when it comes to defining the goal statements that will drive your water management planning effort. These principles are derived from strategies for businesses but they are applicable to any directed activity. The principles are that goals should be;

Relevant

Goal statements need to address actual problems and opportunities faced by the district. The objective of the planning process is to identify and take appropriate actions to address potential water management problems and opportunities. Hopefully, the information-gathering and problem-definition activity of Phase 1 will have illustrated for you where some water management problems and opportunities exist. Your goals should build on these findings.

Consistent with Values

District goals will be more readily achieved if they are consistent with the values of district directors, staff and irrigators. Their values are the basis of their motivation to support your management efforts.

Specific and Clearly Stated

Goals need to be expressed in clear terms and directed at specific activities. This principle is necessary in order to choose between management options and to gauge your progress. Vaguely stated goals will leave people uncertain about what they should do. If possible, goals should be stated in quantitative terms.

Written Down

It is essential to write down goal statements in order to communicate them consistently to others. It also makes a commitment that is not present when you just think about them. Use simple, concise, common language when writing goal statements.

Minimal in Number

Having too many goals will diffuse the resources your district can direct toward achieving any one of them. You don't need to include all the possible goal statements that you think of—some probably aren't really important.

Challenging but Realistic

Motivated people generally respond well to challenges, but unrealistic goals will cause everyone involved to become frustrated and disillusioned. Goal statements should reflect the practical ability of your district to direct money and staff resources at the problem to be solved.

Visualised

Painting mental pictures of your goals is a very powerful technique. It helps you see them as more realistic and achievable. To the degree possible, you should **try** to share your vision with others on whom you will rely for help.

Long-term

Many water management improvements take time to develop and will not be realised immediately. Attitudes change slowly and voluntary adoption of new practices occurs incrementally. The district must maintain a leadership role over the long-haul to allow its efforts to bear fruit.

Achievement-oriented

If people don't see results from their efforts, they eventually lose interest. When developing goal statements, try to think of ways in which progress toward those goals might be recognised and publicised. This is specially important for goals that will take a long time to achieve.

Example: Goal Statements

Here are few examples of goal statements that reflect the principles stated above.:

> "Implement a water measurement improvement programme by the end of 1998 to support future studies of district water use and management."
>
> "Reduce seepage losses from system laterals to less than 5% of gross diversions by the year 2000."
>
> "Develop, through improved water management, sufficient surplus supply capacity to provide 2,000 acre-feet of water annually for local industrial needs."
>
> "Implement water pricing structures that will increase district revenues by $1,00,000 per year to support a revolving loan fund for on-farm water management improvements."
>
> "Develop facilities and operating policies to support a 2-day advance water ordering system by the year 2010."

Setting Priorities

Chances are that you will identify several, perhaps many, goals for water management improvement. There may be more things you want to do than you have the resources to accomplish. If this is the case, you will have to decide which goals are the most important.

There are a variety of ways to set priorities among competing goals. Priorities might emphasise goals that are perceived to be important to the greatest number of people. Priorities might emphasise goals that have the least cost or the greatest financial return. Priorities might emphasise goals that enhance the physical performance of your supply system. Priorities might emphasise goals that are most in harmony with existing rules and regulations and with neighbouring water management agencies. Priorities might emphasise goals that contribute more to improved water quality or habitat.

One way to assess the relative importance of problems and goals is to hold workshops or discussion groups with staff and with water users. After describing the water management problems you have identified and the possible goals you have defined, you can ask for a "straw vote." You might list all the possible goals or problems on large sheets of paper, hang them on the wall and ask participants to "vote" on the five most important ones.

Your Board of Directors will obviously also be an important source of input for assigning priorities to the goals of your water management plan.

Given the importance of good information to good decision-making, it is probably safe to say that having good water measurement and accounting should be a top priority in every district. Without good water measurement it is difficult to quantify and evaluate water management problems and opportunities. It is also impossible to base accounting or pricing on actual water delivery unless those deliveries are measured. Accordingly, every district should consider adopting planning goals that include improved water measurement and accounting.

Evaluating Water Management Options

This phase of planning activity involves identifying candidate measures for water management improvement and investigating how well each option might contribute to achieving the goals you defined in Phase 2. Usually this means that you will need to make rough assessments of costs, water savings, political acceptability, etc., of each of the measures being considered.

The evaluation process involves going back and forth between evaluation steps. You may decide, for example, that certain effects of a candidate measure are unacceptable but that the measure could be re-defined to avoid those effects. You would then go through the evaluation process for the modified measure. Hopefully, each time you go through this exercise your are getting more precise and confident in your evaluation.

Later in the planning process you will select from the most promising options to define an action plan. The basic objective of Phase 3 is to develop enough information about potential water management improvements to support these later decisions.

Water Management Measures

District management and staff are probably the people best qualified to identify potential water management improvements for the district. You may already have some ideas about water management improvements you would like to make. However, it is important to take a little time, think about the "big picture" and involve some other people to make sure there aren't other measures that would solve the important problems a little bit better.

The main focus in defining potential water management measures for consideration should be the goals you defined. If your goal statements are specific enough, they will almost "suggest" certain types of measures. Brainstorming in workshops and focus groups of staff members or irrigators is also a good way to generate ideas about potential water management improvements. Thinking of the possibilities is a very creative process. But you should always come back to your goal statements as the guiding principles.

The general areas covered for discussions in thee descriptions include:

- Improvements to water measurement and accounting;
- Changes in water pricing and billing methods;
- Education and training programmes;
- Operational and facility improvements to reduce water losses;
- Improvements to water delivery scheduling;
- Incentives for improving on-farm water management;
- Development of contingency plans for shortage periods;
- Ways to facilitate water transfers.

Once you have identified some specific measures, you think could help achieve your water management goals, the next step is to describe the effects of those measures. A wide variety of effects should be considered. Some of the more important ones include: cost to the district and to irrigators, changes in water flow and use patterns and environmental effects. The discussions of specific measures in Section Three provide you with some ideas about how to estimate the effects of various types of water management measures.

Most water management improvements will have costs of some type. There may be material costs for equipment or construction. There may be labour costs for operation and maintenance. There may be financing costs if money is borrowed to pay for the improvements. There may be costs for more detailed studies or contract negotiations.

It is also important to consider who pays these costs. Some costs may be borne by the district, while some may be passed through to irrigators. The perspectives of both the district and irrigators should be considered when evaluating the costs of water management improvements.

Another important matter to be resolved is how the costs of improvements will be financed. Financing might be available from existing capital or maintenance funds. Some improvements might logically be paid for through user fees. Borrowing and levying taxes are other methods of financing available to some districts.

Each of the measures you are considering should be evaluated in terms of costs and financing requirements. Detailed cost estimates and financing strategies are probably not needed for the early stages of planning, but will likely be required later for some types of improvements.

Water Flow and Use Patterns

Improvements in water management will change water flow patterns in the district. These changes may take many forms, including reduced diversions from streams, reduced seepage from canals, more variable flows in laterals, less runoff from farm fields, increased deliveries to farm turnouts, etc. Changing some of these patterns may be the objective of the improvements, while changing others will be a side-effect of the improvements.

It is important to describe how flow patterns will change in the district as a result of water management improvements. You should attempt to make this description as detailed and quantitative as possible. Developing alternative district water budgets reflecting different potential improvements is a good way to estimate the amounts of water involved in these changes.

It will be particularly important to estimate changes in water use patterns that are related to district revenues. For example, if the district charges irrigators for the amounts of water delivered to them, your evaluation of management measures should estimate how farm deliveries would be changed.

Environment

Altering water flow and use patterns may have environmental effects. These effects are likely to be related to changes in overall diversions and changes in seepage and return flows. In general, water management improvements will result in more efficient water use and will reduce spills and return flows. The effects of this may vary from district to district. Since it is common for return flows to support wetlands and other habitats, these environmental features might be affected by changes in flow patterns.

There also may be changes in water quality. For example, if runoff from farm fields is reduced, there may be less sediment and nutrients in district return flows. Changes in flow patterns, wetlands or water quality may also affect particular fish and wildlife species. Your Reclamation water conservation coordinator can provide additional assistance in this area.

Legal and Institutional Considerations

The implementation of water management and conservation measures must be done within the context of state water law and for some districts, Reclamation law and contracts. Furthermore, some conservation measures may have environmental implications that require local, state or federal permitting or mitigation activities. Water management measures that have been identified as having potential application in your district should be reviewed in light of these legal and institutional considerations before final decisions are made regarding their implemen-tation. The advice of district counsel may be helpful in this regard.

Displaying and Comparing Your Evaluations

You will need to obtain input from management, staff, irrigators, your Board of Directors, and others about the alternative water management measures you are considering. It will be important to do this before you decide to go ahead with specific measures in your action plan.

There may be quite a bit of information available about the alternatives you have evaluated. This can make it difficult to display the effects of the alternatives in a concise way. One approach that may be helpful is to use an evaluation matrix. A simple evaluation matrix format is shown in Figure 3.4.

To use this simple and familiar display method, first list the alternatives down the side and the effect categories across the top. You can make these lists and categories as simple or as complex as you want in order to get your points across. Then, in each "cell" of the matrix, put an indicator of the effect of each alternative. These indicators might be numerical estimates of costs or amounts of water, but they can also be simple terms like "good, neutral or bad" or "high, medium or low."

If more detail is needed to display the information create one matrix for cost information, another for water savings, another for environmental effects etc. This general approach is very flexible and can be easily adapted to suit your needs.

Define A plan of Action

In this phase of the planning process, you will decide which of the measures evaluated in Phase 3 you want to implement. While you may feel that you already know what you want to do, it is a good idea to take a little time to systematically review the information developed and be sure you are starting out with the most useful and effective management improvements.

You may ultimately want to combine various management improvement measures into programmes. A programme is simply a logically-related set of activities. You might, for example, define a water measurement improvement programme that includes three measures: installation of meters or flumes on farm turnouts, more systematic observation of canal and lateral flows by ditch riders and obtaining a database programme for your personal computer to help store and analyse the data.

Your action plan will consist of one or more water management improvement programmes. A schedule and budget to support the activities in each programme should be defined.

Selecting Measures for Implementation

The most important indicator of whether a measure should be selected and incorporated into your action plan is how well that measure contributes to achieving the goals defined. Measures that do a better job of achieving your goals obviously are preferable to those that do a poorer job of achieving your goals.

If some of the goals are expressed in quantitative terms, you should be able to make a very precise comparison of measures relative to those goals. For example, if your goal is to reduce the amount of water lost to seepage from laterals by a certain percent, you can compare canal lining approaches on the basis of what percent seepage reduction each is expected to have.

Comparing Measures by Relative Cost

Another approach to deciding which measures to implement is to rank them on the basis of implementation cost. These costs should be expressed in comparable terms, such as annual or capitalised costs and they should address both initial costs and ongoing maintenance costs. The timing of costs may be important if the district has other special financial requirements or situations.

Comparing Measures by Ease of Implementation

Clearly, some water management measures are easier to implement, politically, institutionally and technically, than others. Another approach to deciding which measures to implement is to rank them according to "ease of implementation" criteria. However, it is difficult to adopt this approach on anything other than a subjective basis. It may be more desirable to use subjective factors as "fatal flaw" screening criteria for elimination of alternatives that pose insurmountable political, institutional or technical problems.

Comparing Measures on Benefit-Cost Basis

In this approach to evaluating alternative water management measures, the district would consider programmes that have the highest benefits relative to costs. The ranking of programmes by benefits and costs ensures that the district pursues those programmes that are economically beneficial. The benefit-cost evaluation may be based on a variety of values. An evaluation based on saved water would involve two components.

- *Evaluating the benefit of saved water:* You should carefully analyse the value of water that your district saves through improved management and how that water can best be used. For example, your district might be able to resell the water to a municipality. The benefit of the saved water in this case would be the price that could be obtained per unit of water sold.
- *Evaluating the cost of saved water:* You should describe the cost of management improvements on a dollars-per-acre-foot basis. This is done by estimating the annual cost of the measure divided by the estimated amount of water saved annually. Measures can be ranked from lowest cost per acre-foot to highest cost per acre-foot.

Comparing Measures by Environmental Effects

Environmental effects are often the hidden costs and benefits of improved water management. Some measures will have more environmental consequences than others. A measure may have positive effects on drainage, erosion and water quality of return flows but may have detrimental effects on wetlands. A preliminary comparison of measures on the basis of environmental effects will help you anticipate what permits will be required which government agencies will be involved and what kind of support you will receive from the community.

Other General Considerations

Another thing to consider is the possibility that some water management measures may be complementary or conflicting. Conflicting measures that, when implemented together, would enhance the effectiveness of each other. Conflicting measures are those for which the successful implementation of one measure diminishes the potential effectiveness of another measure; such measures should *not* be considered for implementation together.

Water measurement and incentive-pricing are examples of complementary measures. Clearly, without good measurement of farm deliveries it would be impossible to know how much water an individual irrigator used during a given billing period. Accordingly, incentive pricing should not be considered unless development of adequate water measurement and accounting systems is considered alongwith it.

An example of conflicting measures would be encouraging installation of sprinklers and construction of on-farm reuse ponds. It is typical for the production of surface runoff (*i.e.,* tailwater) to decline when sprinklers are substituted for surface application methods. Reuse ponds generally are designed to capture tailwater. Accordingly, if these two measures were being considered, it would be advisable to defer constructing the reuse ponds until the effects of sprinklers on tailwater production are well understood.

Conservation Investments by Others

The de-regulation of the electrical utilities industry in the United States holds some potentially interesting lessons for the water industry. One of these is the concept of "privatising" investments in conservation. This concept might be applied to water conservation measures you think may be beyond your financial capabilities to adopt.

Under this concept, the district could define water management and conservation measures which require significant investment (canal lining, installation of sprinkler systems etc.) and which are consistent with the district's overall internal goals, but which are beyond the financial reach of the district and its irrigators. Other entities within or outside the district would then be allowed to invest in one or more of these district-defined water conservation measures and would be entitled to some or all of the water saved, based on a satisfactory demonstration of actual savings achieved.

Projecting Results of Selected Measures

Once you have decided which measures and programmes will be part of your water management action plan, you will develop estimates of programme water savings and other benefits, cost and environmental consequences. You should be able to make these estimates from the information you developed in evaluating alternative measures.

Water Savings

The projected water savings of your plan might be derived by simply adding the projected savings of the measures that make up the plan, unless there are significant interactions between these measures. The water savings associated with some measures may be predicted fairly accurately. For example, concrete lining of distribution canals will predictably reduce losses to a few percent. The water savings associated with some other measures will be more difficult to predict, particularly if the measures rely on voluntary adoption of methods by individual irrigators. Some measures may not have water saving effects.

The timing of water savings should also be considered. For some measures, savings will be immediate once the measure is implemented, while for others, the savings will only be realised over a period of time.

Cost

The cost of programme implementation should be estimated in terms of initial costs and ongoing costs. The projected useful life of facilities or equipment should be considered here, since maintenance and replacement will be required over the long run.

By mapping these costs out over time you can create a cash-flow requirements table. A comparable cash-flow table should be developed for any revenues the district contemplates receiving in connection with the measures (*e.g.*, from the sale or lease of water). These cost and revenue schedules will then facilitate development of net-annual-cost or net-capitalised-cost equivalents for budgeting purposes.

Environmental Consequences

You made some preliminary assessments of the environmental consequences of various plan elements in Phase 3 and made some relative comparisons of possible measures in Phase 4 of the planning process. Once you have decided on the elements that are to be part of your overall plan, you should prepare a written summary description of the probable environmental consequences of the overall plan.

It is not expected that this description be a formal environmental assessment or impact statement or a substitute for such documents. It should simply alert readers to the generally anticipated effects of the selected programme of conservation measures. Specific benefits or impacts of consequence, as well as areas of uncertainty, should be highlighted. You may also wish to contact your local Reclamation Water Conservation Coordinator for further assistance.

Implementation and Monitoring

In order to make your water management plan a reality, you need to define the sequence of activities and then allocate the necessary funds to support those activities.

Schedule

The implementation schedule for your plan should reflect the time required to develop the various measures included in the plan. Certain changes may need to be presented to users as proposals first, allowing for some educational time before implementing actual changes. There also may be time required to develop necessary information and control systems and for district staff training.

Measures involving equipment acquisition or construction will almost certainly require more detailed feasibility study than they have been given in this management plan. This study would then be followed by preliminary and final design and preparation of construction plans. Permitting and environmental compliance may also be required before actual construction can begin.

The district budget for implementing the management plan will be based on the cash-flow requirements of the plan and the net-capitalised or net-annual cost of the plan. Depending on the contents of the plan, it may be possible to allocate funds from existing revenue streams for plan implementation. If additional revenues are needed, the budgeting process will be dependent on the potential sources of that revenue. Some possibilities are increases in water service charges or water rates, increases in mill levies and issuance of revenue or general-obligation bonds.

It is possible that revenues from some of these sources will not develop immediately; if so, the plan implementation schedule will need to reflect the time required for this revenue development. Some aspects of the management plan may require additional effort by district staff. The plan should describe how duties would be assigned or how additional staff would be recruited and supported. An important part of your water management plan is identifying and quantifying the water savings and other effects it achieves. This should take the form of an ongoing monitoring programme because the effects of some measures will not be immediately evident. It will typically not be possible to measure these effects directly. Water savings may be evident in reductions in diversions, farm deliveries, spills, drain flows etc. These quantities have substantial natural variation from year to year and you may need to accumulate several years of data in order to determine whether there has been a significant change.

4

IRRIGATION POTENTIAL OF WATER RESOURCE

The average run-off in the river system of the country has been assessed as 1,869 cubic kilometers. Of this, total utilizable water resource is estimated to be about 1122 cubic kilometers, surface water 690 cubic kilometers and ground water as 432 cubic kilometers. Water is India there are about 1869 cubic kilometres of water Approximately 434 billion cubic metres. Only 1800 cubic metres (down from 5177 cubic metres in 1951). Ground water is being utilised about 37.24 per cent. Water does a person use on an average about 26 litres of water a day at home. It is neither human population nor agriculture but industry (worldwide) but agriculture is major user in India.

It is believed that life first originated in water before it invaded land. Water is in fact a pre-condition of life. It is a very important and critical resource of India. The monsoonal rainfall throughout the coutnry has frther added to its critical nature. The list of its uses has been ambitious because it is required for drinkinn and domestic consumption. It is being put to use for various industrial purposes. Agriculture has been claiming a greater and greater share for irrigation keeping in view the rapid growth of population.

Expansion of Irrigation facilities, along with consolidation of the existing systems, has been the main part of the strategy for increasing production of food grains. With sustained and systematic development of irrigation, the irrigation potential through major, medium and minor irrigation projects has increased from 22.6 million hectares in 1951, when the process of planning began in India, to about 93.95 mha at the end of Ninth Plan. Plan-wise irrigation potential created and utilized through major, medium and minor irrigation projects in the country is given in the table 4.1.

TABLE 4.1.

Development of Irrigation Potential through Plan Periods

Plan Period	*Potential created (Mha)*	*Potential utilized (Mha)*
Pre-Plan period	22.60	22.60
First Plan (1951-61)	26.26	25.04
Second Plan (1956-60)	29.08	27.80
Third Plan (1961-66)	33.57	32.17
Annual Plan (1966-69)	37.10	35.75
Fourth Plan (1969-74)	44.20	42.19
Fifth Plan (1974-78)	44.20	42.19
Fifth Plan (1974-78)	44.20	42.19
Fifth Plan (1974-78)	52.02	48.46
Annual Plans (1978-80)	56.61	52.64
Sixth Plan (1980-85)	65.22	58.82
Seventh Plan (1985-90)	76.53	68.59
Annual Plans (1990-920	81.09	72.86
Eighth Plan (1992-98)	86.26	77.24
Ninth Plan (1997-20020	93.95*	80.06*
Targets for Tenth Plan (2002-07)	109.11*	90.42*

* Provisional and are subject to change

Major and Medium Irrigation Projects

Irrigation projects with a Culturable Command Area (CCA) between 2,000 and 10,000 hectares are classified as medium projects and those with CCA of more than 10,000 hectares as major projects. The expenditure incurred on major and medium projects and the irrigation potential created during the various plan periods are given in table hereunder. At the beginning of the Tenth Plan, there were 162 major projects with a spillover cost of Rs. 140968.79 crore, 221 medium projects with a spillover cost of Rs. 12786.77 crore, and 85 extension, Renovation and Modernisation projects, with a spillover cost of Rs. 21256.50 crore.

TABLE 4.2:

Major and Medium Irrigation projects (Expenditure incurred and potential created)

Period	*Outlay/ expenditure (Rs. Crore)*	*Potential created*	*Cumulative (mha)*
Pre-Plan period	--	9.70	9.70
First Plan (1951-56)	376	2.50	12.20
Second Plan (1956-61)	380	2.13	14.33
Third Plan (1961-66)	576	2.24	16.57
Annual, Plans (1966-69)	430	1.53	18.10
Fourth Plan 91969-74)	1,242	2.60	20.70
Fifth Plan (1974-78)	2,516	4.02	24.72
Annual Plans (1978-80)	2,079	1.89	26.61
Sixth Plan (1980-85)	7,369	1.09	27.70
Seventh Plan (1985-90)	11,107	2.22	29.92
Annual Plans (1990-92)	5,459	0.82	30,74
Eighth Plan (1992-97)	21,669	2.21	32.95
Ninth plan (1997-2002)	42,968	4.10*	37.05*
Tenth Plan outlay (2002-2007)	71,213	9.94*	46.99*

* Provisional and are subject to change

Accelerated Irrigation benefits Programme

The Accelerated irrigation Benefits Programme (AIBP) was launched during 1996-97 give loan assistance to the states to help them complete some of the incomplete major/medium irrigation projects, which were in an advanced stage of completion. The Surface Minor Irrigation Schemes of North-Eastern States, Hilly States of Sikkim, Uttaranchal, Jammu and Kashmir, Himachal Pradesh and KBK districts of Orissa have also been provided Central Loan Assistance (CLA) under this programme since 1999-2000. grant component has been introduced in the programme from April 2004 like other Central sector schemes. The criteria for AIBP have been further relaxed from April 2005 to include minor irrigation schemes of non-special category States with potential more than 100 ha. With preference to Tibal areas and drought prone areas which wholly benefit dalits and adivasis. Extension, renovation and modernization schemes have also been included on a selective basis. The Assistance will be on the pattern of normal central assistance i.e., 70 per cent loan and 30 per cent grant in the case of non-special category states and 10 per cent loan and 90 per cent grant in the case of special category States and KBK districts of Orissa. The drought-prone areas, tribal areas and flood-prone areas in the country, to be identified in consultation with the Planning Commission shall be treated at par with special category states for funding i.e., 90 per cent grant and 10 per cent loan. The state governments have been provided an amount of Rs. 17537 crore as CLA/grant under AIBP since inception of this programme upto March 2005 for 184 major/medium and 4169 surface minor irrigation schemes. After commencement of this programme 37 major/ medium and 2856 surface minor irrigation schemes have been completed. A Statement giving state-wise details of CLA/grant released under AIBP during 1996-97 to 2004 is given in table.

Hydrology Project

The Hydrology Project was implemented with International Development Association assistance of SDR 75.1 million under a credit agreement with Government of India. The credit effectiveness of the project began on 20 December 1995 and the extended closing date was 31 December 2003. The Government of Netherlands provided a grant-in-aid of Euro 14.64 million in the form of technical assistance under a bilateral Indo Dutch agreement.

The Project was implemented by nine states, viz., Andhra Pradesh, Chhattisgarh, Gujarat, Karnataka, Kerala, Madhya Pradesh, Maharashtra, Orissa and Tamil Nadu and six Central agencies. The project enabled establishment of functional Hydrological information system (HIS) and an improved institutional capacity of implementing agencies to build, operate and utilize the HIS to the benefit of different user groups. The development of databases would support major aspects of National Water Policy, particularly with regard to water allocation and planning and management of water resources development at a national, state, basin and project level. To realize the objective, the hydrology project supports: upgrading and expanding physical infrastructure for all aspects of data, viz., collection, collation, processing, storage and dissemination; provision of equipment and material; Institutional strengthening including technical assistance and training and new buildings, laboratories computer hardware and incremental operating and maintenance costs.

TABLE 4.3:

Central Loan Assistance Released Under AIBP

(Rs. In crore)

State	*up to IX Plan*	*2002-03*	*2003-04*	*2004-05*		
				Loan	*Grant*	*Total*
Andhra Pradesh	630.615	33.186	205.530	61.2829	26.2641	87.5470
Arunachal Pradesh	30.000	1.500	20.000	1.0000	9.0000	10.0000
Assam	84.718	16.2738	19.2015	1.6930	15.2370	16.9300
Bihar	339.725	14.481	74.644	26.0505	11.1645	37.2150
Chhattisgarh	86.650	104.0000	74.630	2.0475	0.8775	2.9250
Goa	128.400	-	2.000	0.4550	0.1950	0.6500
Gujarat	1971.733	1000.330	650.359	484.7500	45.7500	530.5000
Haryana	44.500	18.000	7.735	7.7945	3.3405	11.1350
Himachal Pradesh	43.806	8.150	14.492	0.3690	3.3210	3.6900
Jammu & Kashmir	27.510	34.999	21.545	1.274	11.470	12.745
Jharkhand	51.410	9.670	1833	14.8995	6.3855	21.2850
Karnataka	1066.890	620.850	266.478	314.7921	81,5031	396.2952
Kerala	52.425	5.665	31.000	34.6080	14.8320	49.4400
Madhya Pradesh	716.563	220.C00	568.440	361.6907	155.0103	516.7010
Maharashtra	305.855	133.134	164.395	370.5002	158.7858	529.2860
Manipur	73.750	19.500	15.500	1.3000	11.7000	13.0000
Meghalaya	12.676	1.500	1.088	0.1744	1.5694	1.7438
Mizoram	4.866	0.750	9.300	0.5000	4.5000	5.0000
Nagaland	12.730	2.659	8.00	0.4000	3.6000	4.0000
Orissa	563.995	179.570	154.685	16.9561	7.2669	24.2230
Punjab	358.810	36.660	-	-	-	-
Rajastha	466.172	174.385	499.837	247.0328	105.8712	352.9040
Tripura	82.447	13.395	13.377	1.100	9.9011	11.0000
Tamil Nadu	20.000	-	-	-	-	-

Uttar Pradesh	1154.590	359.000	274.1440	52.7760	175.9200	
Uttaranchal	-	25.163	25.5525	3.8992	35.0925	38.9917
West Bengal	125.433	28.133	3.144	9.4227	4.0383	13.4610
Sikkim	3.760	0.750	0.0750	0.6750	0.7500	

Note: 1. The CLA released during 2003 -04 Madhya Pradesh consists of excess release of Rs. 0.204 core which has been deducted in respect of Banjar Project.

2. Out of 11.238 crore CLA released during 2002-03 to Sbernarekha in West Bengal Rs. 10.25 crore transferred to Teesta Barrage in 2003-04.

The total expenditure was Rs. 605.28 crore at the closing of the project on 31 December 2003.

A follow-on Hydrology Project Phase-II is proposed to be taken up. The project objective for this is to extend and promote the sustained and effective use of Hydrological Information System (HIS) by all potential users concerned with water resource planning and management, public and private, thereby contributing to improved productivity and cost-effectiveness of water related investments in the 13 states, viz., Andhra Pradesh, Chhattisgarh Gujrat, Karnataka, Madhya Pradesh, Kerala, Maharashtra, Orissa, Tamil Nadu Goa, Punjab, Pondicherry and Himachal Pradesh and 8 central agencies, viz., Central Water Commission, Central Ground Water Board, Indian Meteorological Department, National Institute on of Hydrology, Central Water and Power Research Station, Ministry of water Resources, Central Pollution Central Board and Bhakhra-Beas management Board.

Water Quality Assessment Authority

In view of the multiplicity of agencies involved in water management in the country, with no virtual co-ordination among them, the problem of pollution of national water resources has become a matter of serious concern. To circumvent the situation, the Ministry of Environment and Forests, issued an Extraordinary Notification on 22 June 2001 constituting the "Water quality Assessment Authority" with effect from 29 May 2001.

The Ministry of Water Resources is assisting the WQAA in carrying out and coordinating its functions The Water Quality Review Committees have been constituted by 34 out of 35 states/UTs with an objective to improve coordination amongst the Central and state agencies in the respective States/USs, review/assess schemes launched/ to be launched to improve quality of water resources, review Water quality data Analysis and interpretation in order to identify problem areas and developing Action Plans for improving quality on a sustainable basis, identify hot spots for surveillance monitoring, and to look into other specific miscellaneous issues related to Water Quality arising from time to time.

Expert Group constituted by WQAA with a view to unifying and streamlining the widely varying Water Quality Monitoring Systems being followed by various central and State agencies had submitted its report. A Task Force was also constituted by WQAA to recommend measures for optimum water quality observation network and coordinate data collection and dissemination system to assist WQAA. The Task Force has now submitted its report.

Command Area Development and Water Management Programme

The Generally-Sponsored Command Area Development (CAD) Programme was launched in 1974-75, with the main objectives of improving the utilization of created irrigation potential and optimizing agriculture production and productivity from irrigated lands on a sustainable basis, by integrating all functions related with irrigated agriculture through a multi-disciplinary team under an area Development Authority.

The CAD programme was initiated with 60 major and medium irrigation projects So far 310 irrigation projects with a Culturable Command Area (CCA) of about 28.45 Mha have been included under the programme, out of which 133 projects are ongoing.

Based on suggestions received from beneficiaries and implementing agencies and recommendation of the Working Groups of the Planning Commission on 'Command area Development programme' and 'Private/ beneficiary participationin the irrigation management' for Tenth plan, the CAD Programme has been restructed and renamed as "Command Area Development and Water Management (CADWM) Programme w.e.f 1 April 2004.

The Programme involves execution of On-Farm Development (OFD) works like construction of field channels and field drains, reclaimation of water logged areas, renovation and rehabilitation of M1 tanks, correction of system deficiency above outlets upto distributaries of 4.25 cumec (150 cusec) capacity. The Programme also involves software activities like adaptive trials, demonstrations, training of farmers, evaluation studies, etc. Central assistance of 50 per cent (limited to the prescribed cost norms) is provided to the State Governments for construction activities and of 75 per cent for the software activities. Warabandi or a rotation system of distribution of irrigation water in order to ensure equitable and timely supply of water to the farmers' fields is also a component of the programme. Central assistance was provided for this item till 31 March 2004 but this item is now continuing under the restricted CADWM Programme without any Central assistance.

The National Water Policy 2002 stresses participatory approach in water resources management. It has been recognized that participation of beneficiaries will help greatly for the optimal upkeep of irrigation system and utilisation of irrigation water. The participation of farmers in the management of irrigation would give responsibility for operation and maintenance and collection of water charges from the areas under the jurisdiction of the Water Users' Association. To encourage the formation and functioning of farmer's Associations, a one time functional grant of Rs. 600 per ha. To be shared by Centre, State and farmers at the rate of Rs. 270:270:60 respectively is being provided, under the restructured programme. Moreover, minimum contribution of 10 per cent of beneficiaries has been made mandatory in the cost of construction of field channels, full package OFD works, reclaimation of water logged areas and renovation of MI tanks.

The evaluation made in the past has revealed that the CAD Programme made a positive impact on various important indicators, like increase in the irrigation area, productivity and production, irrigation efficiency, etc. Despite best efforts for efficient irrigation water management, the problem of water logging has surfaced in many irrigated commands. Under the component on reclaimation of water logged areas, 445 schemes of nine states namely, Bihar, Gujarat, Madhya Pradesh, ammu and Kashmir, Karnataka, Kerala, Maharashtra, Orissa and Uttar Pradesh have been approved till now at an estimated cost of Rs. 45.18 crores for reclamation of 57700 ha. Of water logged area. Out of this, an area of about 44135 ha. Has been reported to be reclaimed by these states up to March 2004.

Minor Irrigation

All Ground Water and Surface Water Schemes having a Culturable Command Areas (CCA) up to 2,000 ha. Individually are classified as Minor Irrigation schemes. The development of Ground water is mostly done through individual and cooperative efforts of the farmers, with the help of institutional finance and through own savings. Surface Minor Irrigation Schemes. The development of Ground Water is mostly done through individual and cooperative efforts of the farmers, with the help of institutional finance and through own savings. Surface Minor Irrigation schemes are generally funded from the Public sector outlay. Irrigation Potential created and utilized under Minor Irrigation up to various plan periods as per Minor Irrigation Development Report from State Governments compiled by Ministry of Water Resources is given in table 4.4.

The Ministry of Water Resources has been implementing the Centrally sponsored Plan Scheme "Rationalisation of Minor Irrigation Statistics (RMIS)" since the Seventh Five Year Plan. Under the RMIS scheme the first Census of Minor Irrigation Projects with reference year 1986-87 was conducted in all the States/UTs except Rajasthan and the Census Report was published in November 1993. The second Census of Minor Irrigation Projects was conducted with reference year 1993-94 and the Census Report was published in March 2001. The second Census Report provides detailed information giving District wise information on construction of Minor Irrigation Schemes of each type over the years, their distribution according to ownership, holding size, social status, distribution of schemes by its types, and status, distribution of schemes according to finance source, schemes according to water distribution system adopted, water lifting device, schemes according to horse power, schemes in the command of major/medium projects, average pumping hours, average length of water conveyance channel, culturable command areas, potential created, potential utilized, Irrigation through supplementary sources and schemes. The data contained in the Second MI census report has been put on Internet and the same is also available in Compact Disk (CD).

TABLE 4.4:

Irrigation Potential Created and Utilised under Minor Irrigation

Period	*Potential Created (mha)*	*Potential utilized (mha)*
Pre-Plan Period	12.90	12.90
First Plan	14.06	14.06
Second Plan	14.75	14.75
Third Pland	17.00	17.00
Annual Plans (1966-69)	19.00	19.00
Fourth Plan	23.50	23.50
Fifth Plan	27.30	27.30
Annual Plan(1978-80)	30.00	30.00
Sixth Plan	37.52	35.25
Seventh Plan	46.61	43.12
Annual Plans (1990-92)	50.35	46.54
Eight Plan	53.31	48.77
Ninth Plan	56.90	49.05
Tenth Plan	63.71	54.49

The third Census of Minor Irrigation Projects with reference year 2000-01 has been conducted in all the States/UTs except the UTs of Daman and Diu and Lakshadweep. Thirty-two States/UTs have completed the fieldwork relating to census and computerized the Census data. Scrutiny of data in respect of rest of the States have been completed and for the remaining States is in the final stage of completion.

Preparatory work for conducting fourth Minor irrigation census in the country with reference year 2005-06 is in progress.

Since 1999-2000, Central Loan Assistance of Rs. 416.75 crores has been released to these states for completion of 4169 Minor Irrigation Projects. As reported by the concerned States about 2850 schemes have been completed creating an additional irrigation potential of 1.08 lakh hectatres by the end of March 2005.

Pilot Scheme National project for repair, renovation and restoration of water Bodies directly linked to Agriculture : The Pilot Scheme was approved at an estimated cost of Rs. 300 crore to be implemented during the remaining period of the Tenth five-Year Plan with a funding pattern Centre: State: 75; 25. Under the scheme, pilot projects are to be taken up in one or two districts each in the states for taking up restoration of water bodies having original irrigation culturable command area of 40 ha up to 2000 ha to revive, augment and utilize their storage and irrigation potential. The districts are to be selected by the states. Detailed project Reports are to be prepared by the states as per the guidelines for approval and consideration for funding. The scheme also provides for involvement of the community and stakeholders in implementation and related matters. During 2004-05, Ministry of Water Resources approved 16 district projects of 9 States namely, Andhra Pradesh, Chhattisgarh, Jharkhand, Karnataka, Madhya Pradesh, Orissa, Rajasthan, Tamil Nadu and wet Bengal at an estimated cost of Rs. 168.29 crore.

Once the pilot scheme is completed and validated this will form the basis for launching of the National water Resources Development Project to include all water bodies.

Flood Management

Of the country's total geographical areas of 329 m.ha. 40 m.ha I prone to floods, out of which 32 million ha. Can be provided with reasonable degree of protection. Till March 2004 an area of 16.46 m.ha has been provided with a reasonable degree of protection against flood by construction of embankments, drainage channels town protection works and by raising villages.

Although Flood Management comes within the purview o the State Governments the Union Government provides Central assistance to the flood prone States to take up critical works. The central Government also provides special assistance to the border States and North Eastern States for taking up some special priority works.

In order to mitigate the damages from floods, a nationwide Flood Forecasting and Warning System has been established by the Central Water Commission on interstate river basins. Flood Forecasts are issued through 173 Stations out of which 145 are river level forecasting Stations and 28 are inflow forecasting stations on major dams/ barrages, throughout the country. Forecasts about water level in rivers likely to be attained as a result of floods and volume of inflow into reservoirs are formulated and disseminated to various administrative authorities of Central Government State Government ad District Administration, media and other users. With reliable advance information/ Warning about impending floods, loss of human lives and immovable properties and human miseries can be reduced to a considerable extent the above measures provide immense benefits to the authorities of concerned dams and barrages for systematic operation of he reservoirs for optimum utilisation of water resources and for the control of floods.

5

WATER RESOURCES IN INDIA

India is one of the few countries of the world with adequate water resources. Because of its highly uneven relief feature this water is not evenly distributed over the entire land. The average runoff of water in rivers has been assessed at L869 cubic kilometers. Of this only 690 cubic kilometers is being utilized through storage and diversion in various forms. On account of rapid population growth per capita availability of water has reduced from abut 5177 cubic metres in 1951 to 1800 cubic metres in 2000. At world level the largest single use of water is not for personal use but by industry. The industry uses more than double of what all the people together use.

The main sources of water, as elsewhere in the world, are

(a) Surface water

(b) Ground water.

(a) Surface water

Surface Water: River water or running water flowing on the surface of the land is called surface water. The rivers of India can be divided into two broad types- Perennial rivers and Seasonal rivers. Perennial rivers are snowfed. They generally flow throughout the year. Almost all Himalayan rivers are perennial rivers. They receive water both from snow-melt and rainfall. All the rivers of South India receive water from rainfall only. Most of the southern rivers dry up during summer season. Only a few rivers have reduced level of water in dry season. In India most of the rainfall (abut 90%) is received during monsoon months from July to September. Therefore, a large part of the country goes dry for eight months of the year. It is on account of this unequal distribution that the problems of floods and drought occur in low lying parts of the country.

Ground Water: The water obtained from beneath the ground is called underground water or ground water. It is used for drinking, irrigation and industrial use by digging wells and tubewells. Ninety per cent of India's ground water resources are found in unconsolidated rock formations of North India specially in the plain regions. The Penninsular Plateau holds very little ground water resources. It is due to hard lava rock which is impervious, found in plateau region. Only in coastal plains have rich reservoir of ground water. The result of unconsolidated rock formation in North India is that ground water can be obtained at deep depths of more than 15 metres. It is estimated that India has abut 44,000 million cubic metres of groundwater. Major part of it is found in states of Uttar Pradesh, Maharashtra, Andhra Pradesh, Madhya Pradesh Tamil Nadu, Orissa, Gujarat, Bihar and Assam in that order. Level of ground water development (or its biggest users) is highest in Punjab, Rajasthan and Haryana followed by Tamil Nadu, Uttar Pradesh and Gujarat in that order. The Union Territory of Delhi has already almost exhausted its ground water replenishment resources and its drawing on original ground resources. This means that its ground water use is more than what is replenished in natural course. It is now popularizing water harvesting.

National water budget

By water budget is meant balance between the potential water resources available and developed, on this account even though substantial ground water resources are utilised .India's total surface water resources are 187 million hectares metre and it has also 43 million hectares metre of ground water potential, only about 69 million hectares metres can be used by conventional storage and diversional methods like for example dams canals, ponds .of these ground water potentials about one third of this potentials is being currently utilised. Though these ground water resources are replenishable there are heavy costs involved because of deep depth at which water is available. on the other side, the irrigational potential has increased from 22.60 million hectares in 1951 to about 85 million hectares (2000), not more than 50 per cent of the net sown area of about 1500 lakh hectares can be bought under irrigation. The constraints are (i) poor management of water supply resources (ii) technological and financial limitations (iii) deep depth of ground water (iv) absence of inter linkages between Himalayan and Peninsular rivers (v) poor flood control and river bank erosion measures. We will later discuss some of the measures being taken for the development and regulation of country's water resources.

Distribution and Utilisation

The water budget discussed above is extremely important for resource evaluation and management though we often regard water as a renewable resource, in essence it is finite like other resources unless we adopt measures and have proper man-environment relationship, it can be maintained or renewed with careful management.

Distribution of water is the first step in sound management. The distribution of water has two main aspects – Domestic use and Irrigation.

Domestic Use

Distribution of water for domestic use concerns chiefly making drinking water available to homes. Despite our best efforts, provision of drinking water to villages remains a major issue. At the meeting of the National Water Resources Council (NRWC) held in July 2000, under the chairmanship of the prime Minister it was decided to make provision for setting up River Basin organisations. So we will discuss this under irrigation. In the meantime a crisis like situation has developed in Delhi in respect of water for domestic use. Earlier while discussing groundwater-utilisation in the Union Territory of Delhi it has been said that there is over exploitation of ground water resources. It is presently more than 120 per cent. It means that more ground water is being used up than replenished b annual rainfall during the year Delhi presently uses about 120 percent of its ground water resources. Generally 90% under ground water resources can be used. This means that Delhi uses up 30% of its actual ground water resources annually. As a result the depth of water table goes deeper and deeper. There is danger of large scale subsidence of ground in many heavily inhabited areas. This is not to dramatise the situation but to suggest measures to overcome water crisis in the Union Territory. Some of these measures concern distribution and utilization to prevent over exploitation. The most important of all these measures is to give priority attention to revegetation. Many concrete areas and roads have destroyed the seed sources of plants as well as prevented water from going underground. Rainwater harvesting suggested as a water conservation measure may further expose Delhi to severe environmental conditions. In Delhi, Mumbai and Kolkata as well as in some other cities distribution of water for domestic use is the main concern.

Irrigation

The distribution and utilization of water-resources for industrial as well as agricultural use can best be described by irrigation. It involves used of water practically for all important purposes—agriculture, industrial uses, power generation, floods and droughts as well as construction of canals, dams and reservoirs. The same methods and sources of water can help solve drinking water problems of Indian villages. Here again catchment areas or drainage basins of rivers are an important consideration in management of water-resources for all the above mentioned different purposes.

Drainage basins: As we have learnt in the earlier class that the area drained by a single major river system is called a drainage basin or river basin. A look at the drainage basin map of India would reveal that even in the rocky plateau of peninsula where rainfall is highly seasonal a network of rivers carve out very complex drainage basins which need highly sophisticated engineering skills to undertake irrigation works on modern lines.

Methods of Irrigation

Various methods or irrigation are practiced in India. These methods differ according to surface or ground water, types of relief, soils and nature of crops. The canal irrigation is practiced in the alluvial Ganges plain: tank irrigation is used over Deccan plateau, wells are used in other parts of the country. The methods of irrigation can be divided into three major groups:

(i) Canals

(ii) Wells and Tubewells

(iii) Tanks

India has huge potential of water resources estimated at 1880 cubic kilometers, but these have not been fully utilized. India has an irrigation potential of 842 lakh hectares. Out of it 742 lakh hectares area is irrigated, so that about 42% of total sown area is irrigated.

Canals: Canals are the most important source of irrigation in India. India has one of the largest canal systems of the world. It extends for more than 1 lakh km and accounts for about 38% of the net irrigated area.

The canals are of two types: (i) Inundation Canals. These canals are taken out from the rivers directly without making any kind of barrage. These canals provide irrigation during the rainy season. (ii) Perennial Canals. These canals are taken from rivers by construction barrages across the rivers. These supply water throughout the year.

Most of the canal systems are found in the Northern plain and Eastern Coastal plain. About half of the net irrigated area lies in the states of U.P., Punjab, Haryana, Bihar, West Bengal. Most important penennial canals are Agra Canal, Sharda Canal, Eastern Yamuna Canal, Lower Ganga Canal in Uttar Pradesh, Haryan and Punjab, Damodar and Mayarakshi in Jharkhand, Bihar and Westt Bengal and Indira Gandhi Canal in Rajasthan. In the Peninsular India canals are foudnin the deltas of Andhra Pradesh, Orissa, Tamil Nadu. This has been due to snow-fed Himalayan rivers in the Northern Plains, perennial canals, fertile soils, gradual slope of the plains, demand for irrigation due to developed agriculture.

Wells and Tubewells. Wells are a over old means of irrigation. They constitute the most important source of irrigation in India. Approximately 358 lakh hectares of land in the country is irrigated by means of wells. There are about 50 lakh wells in our country. The largest number of wells in India are found in Uttar Pradesh. Wells irrigation is also in vogue in Punjab, Haryana, N.E. Rajasthan and Maharashtra. There are many reasons for the large number of wells in these areas:

(i) In these areas the cost of digging a well is low.

(ii) The soil is soft and well can be easily dug.

(iii) The water level is high.

Besides the wells, the tubewells are also used for irrigation in India. The first tubewell in India worked in 1930. But today there are about 5 lakh tubewells in different parts of the country. In addition to hydro-electricity diesel sets are also used for pumping out water for irrigation. The tubewells are largely found in U.P., Haryana, Punjab, Bihar, Rajasthan and Tamil Nadu.

Tanks: India about 24 lakh hectares on land is irrigated with the help of tanks. Andhra Pradesh leads in tank irrigation and is followed by Tamil Nadu, Uttar Pradesh, West Bengal and Karnataka. Many natural pits are found in these areas. These pits are turned into tanks by making embankments on their sides. The tanks are filled with water during the rainy season and the water thus stored is taken to the fields by drains.

Tank irrigation is the most widely practice method of irrigation all over the peninsula because:

(i) The hard rocks do not allow ground water.

(ii) The rivers are not snowfed, they flow only during the rainy season.

(iii) It is cheaper to build tanks; many small streams are dammed to form tanks. But these tanks depend on rainfall. When the rains fail, tanks fail.

Multipurpose Projects

Dams harness the surface water resources of rivers. There are 45,000 large dams in 140 countries of the world. Of these 22,000 are in China alone. Other leading countries are USA 6390, India 4291, Japan 1200, Spain 1000. In India, out of 4291 dams about 3596 or 73% are located in Western Agricultural states. 90% of the dams are for irrigation only. About 3 per cent of total dams are multipurpose dams. Only 1 percent are for drinking water supply. Construction of dams has come down from 1190 during 1971-80, 1066 during 19981-90 to 810 during 1991-2000.

The extension of irrigation and generation of power are two national priorities. The harnessing of river water resources for these two purposes is being realized through construction of dams across many rivers. These dams serve many needs like for example diversion of water through irrigation canals to where it is needed most, generation of hydro-electric power, control of floods, creation of lakes to serve as tourist sides, promote industrial development, afforestation, development of fisheries, make rivers navigable and above all encourage proper water management. For this reason they are known as Multipurpose River Valley Projects. Jawaharlal Nehru called these Projects "Temples of Modern India."

Projects:

Some of the Important river valley projects are the following:

1. Damodar Valley Corporation (DVC)
2. The Bhakra Nangal Project
3. The Indira Gandhi Canal Project
4. The Hirakud Project
5. The Tungabhadra Project
6. the Nagarjuna sager Project
7. The Rihand Project
8. The Chambal Project
9. The Narmada Valley (sardar sarover Project)
10. Farakka Barrage Project.

Damadar Valley Project: This project was the first to be started in 1948. It s design was based on Tennessee Valley Authority of USA. River Damodar flows from Chhotanagpur to West Bengal. River Damodar used to cuse devastating floods during the summer. Thousands of acres of land were flooded. It was known as river of sorrow.' In order to check these floods a series of dams have been built across river Damodar and its tributaries. The Damodar project is spread over the states of Jharkhand and west Bengal. The Corporation has built multi-purpose dams and power houses at four places—tilaya, Konar, Panchaet; and Maithon. A barrage 692 metres long and 11.58 metres high has been built at Durgapur, 2495 km long canals have been completed. Three thermal power stations at Bokaro, Chandrapur and Durgapur have been constructed. 137 km long navigation canal connects Durgapur with Kolkata. The D.V.C. Projects sets an example towards managing water resources on scientific lines. The total installed capacity of DVC in March 2001 was 2761.5 MW comprising2,535 of thermal capacity and 144 MW of hydel electricity and 82.5 MW by gas turbine station 5.5 lakh hectares of land are irrigated under this project. About 3.54 hectares of land has already been brought under irrigation. A total amount of Rs. 150 crores has been spent on this project. The DVC Project helps to utilize the mineral resources of Damodar valley i.e. coal and iron. It also helps provide power to major industries located at Jamshedpur Durgapur, Kulti etc. It also helps in flood control, power generation and development of irrigation.

Hirakud Project. This project was taken up in 1948 and was completed in 1957. It is world's longest mainstream dam. A total amount of 83 crores of rupees was spent on this project. Under this project a dam has been built across river Mahanadi at hirakud in Orissa. The dam is 4.8 km long and tourches the height of 61 metres. It forms a reservoir of 460 km^2. The dam stores about 810 lakh hectares of land. Nine power houses have been built under this project which produce abut 270 megawatt hydroelectricity. The project includes dams at Tikarara and Naraj also. The project will help in flood control, utilization of natural and forest resources of Orissa, provide irrigation to fertile land and power to different industries.

Tungghadra Project. This project was completed in 1966. this project is a joint venture of the Andhra Pradesh and Karnataka state governments. The Tungbhadra is a tributary of river Krishna. It is formed by joining Tung and the Bhadra streams. A dam has been built across this stream at Mallapuram in Bellary district of Karnataka. The dam is 2441 metres long and 49.33 metres high. A canal has been taken out form its left bank. The length of this canal is 225 km another canal which is 349 km long has been taken out from its right bank. These canals irrigate about 3.5 lakh hectares of land in Karnataka and Andhra Pradesh. Fourteen power houses have been built near this dam. Eight of them are located on the right and six on the left bank of the stream. These power houses generate 126 megawatts of hydro-electricity.

Rihand Project: This project has been built across river Rihand. It is a tributary of river Sone. The dam forms a reservoir over an area of 466 sq. km. with a storing capacity of 1060 crore cubic metres. This reservoir is known as Govind Ballabh Pant Sagar. An embankment has been built upto 160 km from Mirzaur. The dam is 90 metres high and 1020 metres long. The dam supplies water to many canals. The project has been completed at a cost of rupees thirty five crores. Abut 7 lakh hectares of land is irrigated in U.P. by the canals taken out from this dam. About 500 MW electricity is being generated from 6 units. The Rihand project is mainly a water power development project. It will provide power to aluminium industry at Renukoot, chemical industries at Pipri, cement industry at Churu and other industries.

The Bhakra-Nangal Project. This is the biggest multipurpose project of India it is now managed by Bhakra-Beas Management Board which also includes the water impounded at Pong river and that diverted at Pandoh. A dam has been built across the river Sutlej at Bhakra situated about 80 km upstream from Roper in Punjab. States of Punjab, Haryana, Himachal Pradesh and Rajasthan have benefited from this project. The project has four main features:

The Bhakra Dam. This dam is 226 metres high and 518 metres long. It is the highest gravity dam in the asia. A man-made lake created by this dam is known as Govind Sagar named (after Guru Govind Singh). This reservoir is 8 km wide and 80 km long and has storage capacity of 1000 crore cubic metres. Siwalik hills on either side of the Sutlej form this lake. It is located in the seismic zone.

The Nangal Dam. This dam is built at Nangal 13 km below the Bhkra dam. It is 29 metres high and 305 metres long. A canal known as Nangal Hydel channel has been developed from the left bank.

Power Houses. Two power houses have been built at Bhakra which produce 210 megawatts of hydroelectricity. On the Nangal Canal there are two other power-houses also. They have been built at Gangguwal and Kotla. The total installed capacity of BBMB powder plants is 2681.15 MW and the generation during 2001 was 10,424 MUs.

The Nangal Hydel Canal. This is a brick lined canal. It is 64 km long and has been developed at Nangal.

The water of the dam is taken to various states through canals. The chief canal of the network is known as Rajasthan Canal which is 640 km in length and originates from Sutlej at Harike. The canal carries water of Rajstahan where it will convert the desert into greenery when completed.

Benefits. The power houses under this project have a capacity to produce 1204 megawatts hydro-electricity, 1100 km long canals and 3400 km long distributaries developed under this project irrigate about 14.8 lakh hectares of land.

Kosi Project: This project has been built across Kosi river in Biharin co-operation with Nepal. River-Kosi is known as 'sorrow of Bihar: The main aim of the project is to control floods. The main canal has been taken off Hanuman Nagal barriage to irrigate 8,73,000 hectares of land.

Nagarjuna Sagar Project: It is built on the river Krishna is Andhra Pradesh. The dam had been named after the Buddhist scholar Nagarjuna. It is a 1.5 km long and 25 metres high measonary dam in Nalgonda district of Andhra Pradesh. The canals taken out of this river irrigate 8.67 lakh hectares of land. A power house has been constructed withtwo units of 50 MW each.

Chambal Project: This project is a joint venture of Madhya Pradesh and Rajasthan. Chambal is Southern Tribunary of Yamuna river. The project consists of Gandhi Sagar Dam. (Madhya Pradesh.) Kota barrage and Jawahar Sagar dam in Rajasthan and Rana Pratap Sagar Dam ear Rawat Bhata. The project canals will irrigate 5 lakh hectares of land.

Tehri Hyro Development Corporation Limited: it is a hydel power project. It was also mired in controversy for environmental reasons. Located in Tehri Garhwal in Uttaranchal, it will promote and organize hydroelectric projects in Bhagirathi and Bhilangana valley. It will generate 2400 MX of power and irrigate 27000 hectares. The project will also provide drinking water facilities for Delhi. It is expected to be completed by10th plan period.

Narmada Valley Project: Narmada is a major river on the western coast of India. It is a joint river of Madhya Pradesh, Gujarat, Rajasthan and Maharashtra. Sardar Sarowar dam has been set up under Narmada Control Authority. The project was conceived in 1946 but work started only in 1961. There are many problems of this dam regarding its ultimate height. A large number of tribal villages will be submerged. The rehabilitation of these tribals needs a sympathetic consideration. A Review committee headed by the Union Minister of Water Resources and with concerned Chief Ministers as members has been set up. Man problems of environment degradation have made it a controversial dam.

Indira Gandhi Canal Project: It is a major irrigation project which was earlier known as Rajasthan Canal Project. It is a bold project to irrigate a large part of Rajsthan desert. It was started in 1957. But in 1984, it was renamed as Indira Gandhi Canal Project in the memory of the late Prime Minister of India.

Aims of the project: (1) to provide water in the N.W. Rajasthan. (2) to provide drinking water in drought affected areas. (3) to provide irrigation. (4) to generate water power for industrial developments. (5) To increase foodgrains production. (6) to check the advance of Thar Desert.

Main outlines of the project:

Indira Gandhi feeder. This canal has been taken off from Harika barrage the confluence of river beas and Sutlej in Punjab. It is 205 km long. The first 150 km are in Punjab, 18 km in Haryana and the remaining 37 km are in Rajasthan. It is a fully lined masonary canal. It simply feeds the indira Gandhi Canal.

Main Indira Gandhi Canal. Its fully length is 445 km. It is 38 metres wide at the bottom and 67 metres wide at the top. It is 6.4 mts. Deep. In the first stage, 189 m long main canal has been completed.

Branches and distributaries. This canal has 9 branches and 21 distributaries. 2945 km long distribution system has been completed in the first stage.

Lift Canal. In higher areas water will be provided by a series of lift irrigation system. In the first stage 152 km long loon Karansar Bikaner lift canal has been completed. In the second stage 1680 km long lift canal will be constructed at Anoopgarh and Suratgarh on this canal with a capacity of 13 MW.

Cost of the Project. Rs. 1371 crores

Main features of Indira Gandhi Canal project.

Length of the feeder = 205 km.; Length of the main canal = 445 km.,; Length of distribution system = 7745km.; Irrigated Area = 11.81 lakh hectares.; Lift irrigation = 3.61 lakh hectares.; Foodgrains production = 37 lakh ton.; Total cost of construction = Rs. 1371 crore.

Growing Need for Water

Water is an inexhaustible gift of nature. However, its uneven distribution in space and time has often threatened human welfare, livelihood and economic development. The growing scarcity of water has been the result of rapidly growing population, rising demand for food and cashcrops, increasing urbanization and rising standard of living. These will increase the acuteness of the problem of water scarcity in future. There is an acute shortage of water in the arid tracts of western Rajasthan and the interior of the peninsular plateaus. In several villages and even in cities, the quality of water is degraded. It causes various kinds of waterborne diseases.

Drinking-water supply and sanitation are the basic needs of life. In spite of the concerted efforts made for increasing drinking water facilities, we have yawning gaps between demand and supply of water. Still eight per cent of the towns in India don't have potable water supply. About half of the villages in the country are yet to be provided with projected drinking water.

In spite of the fact that irrigation facilities in the country have improved considerably since independence, two-thirds of the cropped area is still rainfed. Increased use of tubewells and wells in recent years has lowered the water table and has caused depletion of under ground water resources. Excessive extraction of underground water in several states has present serious concern in the groundwater development programme in the country. Low availability and growing scarcity of water is another serious problem the country has been facing today. The quality of water available for various uses is not up to the mark. Major sources of water pollution are domestic water and industrial wastes.

6

FUNDAMENTALS OF WATER MANAGEMENT MEASURES

Evaluate potential water management improvements that might be applicable to your district. The average run-off in the river system of the coutnry has been assessed as 1,869 cubic kilometers. Of this,total utilisable water resource is estimated to be about 1122 km^3, surface water 690 km^3 and groudn water as 432 km^3. It will address the following:

* Describe a variety of types of water management problems and measures.
* Ask you questions about how these problems and measures are relevant to you.
* Help you think of water management measures that best fit you situation.

Reclamation has identified four fundamental water management measures that should be considered in any water management programme. They are:

1. Adequate Water Measurement and Accounting
2. Water Pricing Structure that Encourages Efficiency
3. Information and Education Services for Water Users
4. Designation of a Water Conservation Coordinator.

Water Measurement and Accounting Systems

Effective water measurement and accounting is necessary for developing a sound water management programme. A district's measurement and accounting systems should be capable of tracking the amount of water delivered to individual water users.

These systems are effective water management tools because they help inform both the water user and the district about the quantity, timing, and location of water use.

From the district's perspective, water measurement will help with:

* Assembling information needed for a detailed water budget.
* Identifying areas where additional efficiency can be achieved
* Implementing a billing system based on deliveries.

At the farm level, water measurement will help with application of the proper amount of water to meet crop requirements and therefore may help to:

* Reduce erosion.
* Reduce fertiliser leaching
* Reduce drainage problems

An effective water measurement and accounting system should accommodate some form of volumetric pricing and billing for individual users. The "ideal" water measurement system has flow measurements at all points in the diversion, conveyance and delivery system where flow division takes place, including farm turnouts and tailwater, drainage, and system spill locations. The actual number of flow monitoring stations required would depend on the size and complexity of the conveyance system. Where physical measurement capability at each agricultural turnout is determined to be infeasible, approaches can still be developed to provide individual user accountability and billing based on "blocks" or groups of users.

The ideal system would provide data on a real-time basis through use of automatic recording and data transmission devices. A comprehensive measurement programme provides all the delivery information needed to develop a detailed system-wide water budget.

To determine where measurement is most needed the following questions should be considered:

Do you know amounts of water diverted into the system, in terms of flow rates, volumes, timing, and location?

Do you know how much water was conveyed down major canals and laterals and turned out at individual farms?

Do you know the amounts, timing, and location of system spills?

Do you know the amounts, timing, and location of tailwater either leaving or returning to the system?

There are a variety of methods for measuring flows in canals, laterals, and drainageways and measuring on farm deliveries. Many of these techniques are discussed in detail in Reclamation's *Water Measurement Manual* and *supporting documents*.

Water use accounting systems will vary between districts, depending on the complexity of the district's conveyance system and the amount of water measurement data available. For example, in some districts, a simple ledger sheet might be used to track deliveries to a relatively small number of individual users or down a few canals or laterals. Other districts may use commercially available computer software or custom software developed to track deliveries through a complex system.

The appropriate accounting system must be determined at the district level, but in general, more detail is better. At a minimum, the accounting system should allow for tracking of water deliveries to individual users in order to accommodate a billing system based on deliveries.

Water Pricing Structure

To encourage efficient water use, a district's pricing and billing procedures should be based, at least in part on the quantity of water delivered. Quantity-based charges can be incorporated into various existing pricing structures to provide some degree of economic incentive for efficient water use. Fairness in water billing is an additional benefit of quantity-based pricing structures.

Disincentives to efficient water use include situations where the unit price of water declines as the volume of water used increases (declining block structure) or where a fixed charge per acre of irrigated land is assessed regardless of the quantity of water used. Both of these examples can lead to excessive water use. By contrast, pricing structures such as increasing block rates or fixed rates provide an economic incentive for more efficient use.

When evaluating water pricing structures, it is important to consider potential effects on revenues generated through water sales. Under the new pricing system, will there be sufficient revenues to cover district operating costs? Will modifications to the pricing structure result in supplemental revenues that could be used to develop more improvements?

Districts can encourage efficient water use by increasing the unit price of water as deliveries increase. With incentive pricing, a base price per unit of water is charged for all water deliveries upto a certain amount or block.

Water use in excess of this block is then charged at a higher unit price. One or more pricing levels (or "tiers") may exist within a pricing structure. The specific design of these structures will depend on individual district objectives.

The demand for water within an irrigation district is based on crop production and planning decisions made at the farm level. It also depends on crop selection, irrigation technique and land characteristics. The change in water demand in response to a change in water price is termed "demand elasticity." Factors affecting demand elasticity include:

* Crop values
* Crop tolerance to water shortages
* Ability to change crops
* Ability to change irrigation methods
* Availability of alternative water sources

Typically, changes in water prices lead to only small changes in the quantity of water demanded. Therefore, the water supply and demand relationship is fairly "inelastic." Water demand, price elasticity and potential changes in district revenues resulting from price changes are important considerations in evaluating the use of incentive pricing as a water management measure.

Incentive pricing programmes may be structured to optimise conjunctive use. For instance, a programme may be designed to encourage surface water deliveries and groundwater recharge in wet years by lowering the price to the grower. In dry years, the surface water price can be increased to encourage increased groundwater extractions.

Incentive pricing has successfully been implemented in California's Broadview Water District. The purpose of this structure is to motivate growers, to improve the efficiencies of their on-farm irrigation operations and to reduce the quantity of drainage water. The district's increasing block rate pricing structure has two components, crop-specific price levels and field-levels accounting of water deliveries. Crop-specific price levels are required because the volume of drain water generated from water application varies from crop to crop. Crops with higher ET rates are permitted to receive more irrigation water before reaching the higher price level. Without these concessions, growers could be limited in the kinds of crops they plant.

Field-level accounting of water deliveries encourages the growers to carefully monitor their irrigation supplies.

Incentive pricing may be an appropriate water management measure, if the district's existing pricing structure is based on a fixed rate or if water charges are not linked to the amount of water delivered.

Educational Programmes

An important component of any water management programme is providing information to irrigators about efficient water use and water management services available through the district or other organisations. Educational programmes can be effective because many water users are unaware of potential benefits from improvements in water use efficiency. Examples of educational programmes include irrigation system improvement programmes, on-farm irrigation scheduling programmes, real-time agricultural evapotranspiration (ET) information, school and community educational programmes and technical and financial assistance programmes. Information on the following topics could be made available to irrigators:

* Costs and potential water savings of water management measures.
* Best management practices for soil and water conservation.
* Irrigation method efficiencies.
* Soil characteristics.
* Day-to-day crop water requirements.
* Actual on-farm water use from delivery records.
* Actual district-wide water use and efficiencies.

There are a variety of ways, the district could convey this information to its water users. For example, a district could sponsor workshops covering topics such as weather, crop ET, soil moisture holding capacity, crop characteristics and the role these factors play in irrigation scheduling and water use planning. Educational workshops also can serve the district by providing a forum for irrigators to exchange ideas and experience. It might be appropriate to provide basic wise water use information to the general public residing within the district.

Educational programmes could include written publications, dial-in telephone services, or monthly water bills that provide water use data. Various local, state and federal agencies provide technical assistance for agricultural activities. Districts should take advantage of these resources when developing their own programmes.

Demonstration projects are another useful technique for educating water users. In these projects, specific measures are implemented in a controlled setting to allow precise determination of the effects. The results from monitoring demonstration projects are then presented to district water users, alongwith cost and implementation information.

Designating a Water Conservation Coordinator

Designating a district water conservation coordinator serves two primary functions: it allows the district to assign water conservation responsibilities and it provides a focal point through which all district water users and staff can consult. Responsibilities of a water conservation coordinator may include:

* Developing education and training progrmmes.
* Distributing data on soils, climate and crop water requirements.
* Providing technical assistance on irrigation techniques.
* Developing demonstration projects.
* Assisting with irrigation scheduling.

Reclamation and other agencies provide formal training in water conservation. Such resources allow conservation coordinators to keep up-to-date with conservation programmes, services and technological developments.

Institutional Water Management Measures

This section discusses water management measures which might be implemented through institutional changes, that is, by changing rules and policies. These measures include:

1. Water Shortage Contingency Planning
2. On-farm Conservation Incentives
3. Water Transfers
4. Land Management

Water Shortage Contingency Plan

Drought mitigation may most effectively be accomplished through a combination of water development, water conservation programmes and a drought preparedness or contingency plan. The basic objectives of a plan would include:

- Hydrologic forecasting to predict water supply.
- Definition of water allocation procedures to be used during drought periods.
- Identication of methods to increase reliability and use efficiency of existing water supplies
- Identification of alternative or supplemental water supplies.

Hydrologic forecasting to predict water availability can provide farmers with information that will help them prepare for a drought. For example, given a forecast, farmers can choose to irrigate less land or grow crops that require less water. Forecasting also will help the district assess the need for temporary operational changes or supplemental water supplies.

Water allocation procedures used during normal hydrologic conditions may not be appropriate during times of drought. For example, conveyance and delivery systems may not be designed for precisely targeted deliveries or there may be inequities related to either location of farms or types of crops grown. Water rationing techniques might include fixed allotments, percentage reductions, increased pricing or restrictions on specific cropping. Defining allocation procedures before drought conditions begin will provide farmers with fairly certain information as to what they can expect in terms of water deliveries and will allow them to plan accordingly.

An important component of a water shortage contingency plan is the identification of alternative or supplemental water sources to use in emergency situations. The plan should define "triggers" that would initiate use of these alternative sources. It should also estimate the amount and timing of supplies expected from these sources. Potential alternative sources or techniques that might be used to supplement a district's water supply during drought periods include:

* Interruptible supplies (temporary transfers or dry-year options)
* Intra-district transfers
* Exchange arrangements
* Water banks
* Storage hedging, carryover storage and conservation storage
* Integrated operations with other water suppliers.

If your district already has a plan, it may be necessary to review and update the plan to reflect changes in system operation, farming practices, forecasting technology or potential alternative water supplies. Some questions to consider when establishing, developing, or updating a water shortage contingency plan include:

1. Does your district have a water shortage contingency plan and is it up-to-date in terms of operating procedures, farming activities, water allocation schemes and forecasting methods?
2. Has a water shortage contingency plan ever been implemented due to drought conditions and if so, how severe was the drought? How well did the plan work?
3. Are water users in the district aware of existing drought contingency policies and water allocation procedures during drought periods?

On-farm Conservation Incentives

For some growers, the ability to implement efficient on-farm management practices and install modern water application equipment is hampered by the lack of capital. On-farm water management measures might include ditch lining, development of water reuse systems, installation of surge valves and gated pipes, sprinkler systems, field levelling, and soil treatments. Farmers may be willing to improve their irrigation efficiencies if long-term financing or other assistance is available from the district or other sources. Programmes to provide incentives for on-farm water management may include financing incentives, in-kind services and educational programmes.

Some financial incentives which may be made available by the district include:

* Tax incentives for adopting certain water management measures.
* Low interest equipment loans and leases.
* Equipment purchase subsidies.
* Water charge discounts or rebates for efficient water use.

An incentive programme may also consist of in-kind services to water users. For example, a district might establish a service to install on-farm soil moisture monitoring devices or provide climatic and crop water requirement data on a site specific basis. Such in-kind services may also be a part of efforts to improve district-wide irrigation scheduling.

Demonstration projects and educational programmes may act as water management incentives by making farmers aware of different measures and the potential benefits of their use. For example, districts might set up projects to demonstrate the effectiveness of using gated pipes and automatic surge valve controls to eliminate the time-consuming process of manually adjusting irrigation settings.

In developing on-farm programme incentives, the primary challenge faced by a district will be that of achieving good participation by water users. Financing opportunities, in-kind services and educational programmes may all be required to develop this participation.

For many districts, improvements in on-farm water use efficiencies offer the best opportunity for improving overall district water use efficiencies. Therefore, on-farm programme incentives will be an important water management measure for almost all districts.

Water Transfers

Water transfers generally try to move water from areas of surplus to areas of shortage. They may be an effective technique for meeting water demands and for managing the impacts of drought. The objective of the mechanisms discussed here is to facilitate voluntary transfers that do not unreasonably affect the district the environment, or third parties.

Water transfers can take many different forms and can serve a number of different purposes in the planning and operation of a district's irrigation system. The specific objectives of the district, in addition to certain legal or institutional constraints, will dictate which type of transfer mechanism is most appropriate. Types of transfers include:

* Permanent transfers
* Contingent transfers/dry year options.
* Tradeable shares or allotments
* Water banking
* Transfers of reclaimed, conserved or surplus water
* Water wheeling or other exchanges

A permanent transfer involves the acquisition nd change in ownership of water rights or allotments. Permanent transfers might be arranged on an intradistrict basis or between the district and water users outside of the district.

Contingent transfers and dry-year options are temporary arrangements. These transfers often define an "interruptible supply" that may periodically be used under certain conditions such as drought.

The simplest type of water transfer mechanism that a district might implement would be to set up a system of tradeable water shares. For example, the district might define shares or units representing fixed water allocations that could be bought and sold by irrigators within the district. In districts that are characterised by a wide range of crop values, such intra-district transfers would likely result in water allocations that maximise overall district economic benefit.

Water banking refers to arrangements whereby excess or unneeded water may be consigned to a "bank" by one user (or district). The water can then be purchased by another user who needs more. Water banks have been used to facilitate transfers to users outside irrigation districts and for uses other than irrigation.

Wheeling arrangements typically refer to cooperative agreements aimed at improving the storage or conveyance performance of a system. For example, an arrangement may call for water belonging to one district to be carried in a common canal with water from another district, thereby reducing overall canal seepage and evaporative losses. Losses might then be shared proportionally by both districts.

Transfers may also involve the right to use water that is made available by reclamation or reduction in water demands or through successful water conservation efforts. The right to use reclaimed or conserved water is a legal issue that will vary by state. In some areas, such water may simply revert back to the original source and become available to other users. In other areas, it may be possible for the entity responsible for the water savings to sell or lease the water to other users. Some districts have been able to finance conservation programmes through sale of the rights to conserved water.

Some of the questions you should consider in evaluating the relevance of water transfer measures to your district include:

1. Do state laws or district bylaws prohibit or encumber water transfers through specific restrictions or limits on transfers?
2. Would transfers involve federal water rights, storage or conveyance facilities or affect existing federal project operations and would a transfer be consistent with existing contractual agreements?
3. Are there unmet demands within the district or in the general area that might be served by a water transfer?
4. Are the district conveyance facilities sized and located favourably with respect to potential transfer opportunities?

Land Management

Land retirement, fallowing or conversion to dryland farming may be an appropriate water management measure if needed improvements in water ruse efficiency cannot be achieved on specific farms or fields. Land retirement refers to the permanent removal of irrigation supplies, while fallowing refers to a temporary removal of irrigation supplies. Conversion to dryland farming may be appropriate if local soils and climate conditions support production of alternative crops.

Lands within most irrigation districts have been classified by Reclamation according to their irrigability and potential productivity. The classification process considers soil characteristics, topography, drainage, water quality, economics of production and land development and climate. Class 1 lands are considered to have the most production potential and to be most easily irrigated within the project area. Higher class numbers are assigned to lands expected to be less productive and less efficiently irrigated or relatively expensive to develop for irrigation.

Land classifications often date to the time of original establishment of an irrigation district and may be outdated due to improvements in irrigation technologies and farming practices. For example, the availability of land-leveling techniques means that significant improvements could be made to the irrigability of some lands. It is important to consider if existing classifications are still accurate. First-hand knowledge of field situations is often the best information source for district-wide planning.

The decision to retire land, fallow it or convert to dryland farming may depend on many factors in addition to the lands' irrigability. These factors would include economic implications for both the farmers and the district and potential alternative uses of the lands. With regard to alternative land uses increased demand for recreational facilities has provided an opportunity for conversion of some agricultural lands in Arizona to parks, golf courses, and shooting ranges. Alternative uses may be permanent in nature or may be such that re-establishment of agricultural practices is possible at some point in the future. The permanence of the change will play an important factor in considering the economic viability of land management changes.

Once certain lands have been identified as potential candidates for land use changes, the district must encourage land owners to accept and make the changes. Some incentives include:

- Outright purchase of low Irrigability lands
- Modification of district boundaries to exclude low irrigability lands.
- Tax incentives for ceasing to irrigate certain lands.
- Payment in-kind programmes.
- Water pricing structures favourable to higher quality lands.
- Demonstration projects and education programmes on dryland farming.

Questions to help determine if this measure is relevant to your district include:

1. Are there lands within your district that would be candidates for retirement or fallowing because of poor irrigability or productivity?
2. Does your district have legal authority to acquire low irrigability lands through outright purchase or condemnation?
3. Does your district have legal authority to provide tax incentives for farming of lands with high irrigability?
4. Does your district have the legal authority or contractual flexibility to structure water prices based on irrigability of lands?

Operational Water Management Measures

This section discusses water management measures which would involve changes in system operations. These measures include:

1. Improved Operating Procedures
2. Improved Distribution Control
3. System-wide Irrigation Scheduling

4. On-farm Irrigation Scheduling
5. Conjunctive Use of Surface and Groundwater.

Improved Operating Procedures

Changes to a district's operating procedures may provide for increased delivery and storage flexibility. Some operating procedures which might be candidates for improvement are:

* Water ordering and delivery
* Canal/lateral operating practices
* Reservoir operations
* Integrated system operation.

Methods for scheduling water deliveries to individual farms vary depending on characteristics of the available water supply, diversion and conveyance facilities and irrigation water demands. The advantages and disadvantages of different water ordering and delivery scheduling methods must be considered from the perspectives of both the district and its water users. For example, schedules based on a fixed amount and fixed frequency of delivery may require the least capital investment and operating cost to the district. However, they can result in a severe mismatch between supply and demand at the farm level. Delivering water on demand requires very active participation by the district in demand forecasting and control of delivery facilities, but will usually reduce waste and under-deliveries. In general, schedules that allow for the most flexibility in both timing and amounts of water delivery will be the most expensive to operate. The costs associated with increasing this flexibility must be balanced with district objectives and expected benefits.

Closely related to a district's scheduling system are canal and lateral operating procedures. Some districts must run canals full in order to serve certain laterals or farm turnouts. During periods or reduced demand, this practice may result in significant spills at the ends of the canals. To avoid these spills, the district might institute a policy whereby canal levels would be more actively checked and would fluctuate seasonally. This might require modifications to some turnouts or siphons, but it could also provide substantial water savings.

Reservoir operations are another area where modifications can be made to improve efficiency. For example, releases made only in response to irrigation demand may greatly reduce the probability that storage water releases will go unused on farms. A policy which allows for carryover of storage water allotments, rather than "use it or lose it" policies may reduce the tendency for irrigators to use late season water even when it's not needed by crops. Policies also might be adopted to allow dedication of carryover storage to a water banking system.

Integrating the operations of several districts can improve water use efficiencies while at the same time improving overall system yield. Integrated operations have been particularly successful in areas where storage or delivery facilities are shared. For example, studies of the Colorado-Big Thompson/Windy Gap projects in northern Colorado have shown that integrated operations can increase the reliability of both systems.

To evaluate the relevance of improved operating procedures for your district, consider the following questions:

1. Does you district have flexibility, in terms of physical limitations and legal and contractual obligations, to modify its current operating practices and procedures?
2. Can your district adjust deliveries based on changes in demand?
3. What is your district's policy concerning carryover of water allotments within and between irrigation seasons?
4. Does you district allow water users to transfer portions of their allotments to other water users either inside or outside of the district?
5. Are there opportunities to integrate operations of the district's facilities with the facilities of other irrigation systems in the area?

Distribution Control

Distribution control refers to the ability of the district to control delivery rates and amounts of water. Of particular interest are the physical capacities of the system (diversion structures, canals and laterals), control mechanisms (gates, checks and weirs) and the ability of the district to operate these facilities in response to changes in water demands and hydrologic conditions. Limitations on physical features of the distribution system or difficulties responding to changes in hydrology and water demands may result in over-delivery to farm turnouts and system spills or under-deliveries, water shortages, crop stress and lower crop yields.

Measures to improve distribution control may be categorised as either facility-related, measurement-related or communication-related. Facility-related improvements include installation of new structures or improvements to existing structures to more precisely manipulate flow rates and head levels (check dams variable flow rate turnouts, automated controls). Regulatory storage and spill interceptor canals are two facility-related measures discussed in detail later in this section.

Improvements in flow measurement may be needed to help monitor and control water distribution. The use of a specific measuring technique will depend on hydraulic conditions and characteristics of the situation. Many measurement techniques may be used in conjunction with automatic recording and data transmission systems so that flow data may be available immediately and continuously at a central control point.

Timely information gathering, processing and dissemi-nation to facilities operators is essential to efficient system control and to minimising system waste. Operators must be kept informed of and be able to report changes in hydrologic conditions and diversion rates. Improving such communica-tions may be as simple as buying cellular phones for ditch riders.

Questions to help you evaluate if this measure is relevant to your district include:

1. Is the district distribution system or a portion of it, operated under pressurised water conditions?
2. Is your district able to modify the amount of water it receives through its diversion facilities? Are there contractual or legal obligations to divert at a fixed rate or a fixed volume?
3. Is your district able to modify flow rates in all parts of the distribution system in a timely manner to match localised demands?
4. Does the district experience frequent and significant operational spills or experience canal flooding when demands drop?

System-wide Irrigation Scheduling

System-wide irrigation scheduling attempts to schedule water deliveries to match irrigation requirements. System scheduling differs from on-farm scheduling in that, from a district perspective, the objective is to understand aggregated irrigation needs in district sub-areas, rather than on each individual farm. The district may then attempt to match deliveries to these sub-areas, subject to certain operating and distribution control constraints.

Much of the data needed for system scheduling is the same as for on-farm scheduling. In fact, one approach to system scheduling is to base it on actual water orders from farms. However, it may be more effective for the district to develop its own demand forecasts for specific crops and district sub-areas. Information required to develop irrigation demand forecasts includes:

- Types of crops grown.
- Acreages of each type of crop grown.
- Location of acreages (grouped into sub-areas by geographic location).

- Estimated ET for each crop type and sub-areas.
- Estimated soil moisture conditions within sub-area.
- Estimates of irrigation application efficiencies for each sub-area.
- Information on ground water and sub-surface return flows that may contribute to sub-irrigation.

Information about cropping patterns and acreages should only need to be gathered once a year, though the acreage, types of crops and on-farm water application methods will likely change from year to year. ET rates and soil moisture conditions, on the other hand, will change dramatically throughout the irrigation season and up-to-date information will be needed on a real-time basis. Therefore, the greatest challenge in irrigation system scheduling may be the collection and processing of continuous climate and soil moisture data to develop estimates of crop water requirements.

Techniques for estimating crop water requirements include direct field observation and measurement and theoretical calculation based on climatic conditions. The direct techniques include pan evaporation, visual inspection of plants and representative plot lysimeters. Recently, advances have been made in the use of infrared sensing of crop moisture levels. Theoretical equations for estimating water requirements include the Blarney-Criddle, Penman-Monteith, and Jensen-Haise methods.

Monitoring soil moisture provides information on the amount of water held within the root zone of the soil that is available to meet crop needs. It may be measured by neutron probes, tensiometers, electronic resistance blocks and by feel and appearance.

It may be possible to use one or a combination of these methods to estimate ET rates and soil moisture conditions. Because the objective of the district will be to forecast water needs for district sub-areas, data will not be necessary for each individual farm. Instead, data collection points should be located such that they provide information representative of the entire sub-area.

Processing information on climate and soil conditions in order to forecast irrigation needs may be facilitated by a computerised information management system (IMS). These systems have already been developed in some areas. The California Irrigation Management Information System (CIMIS), developed by the California Department of Natural Resources, uses an automated electronic weather station network to provide up-to-the-minute ET information. IMS's have also been developed that use soil moisture data collected by networks of neutron probe stations (rather than climate stations) to forecast irrigation requirements. These systems are usually developed for personal computers.

Irrigation application efficiencies may be estimated from application methods, characteristics of irrigated lands and soils, discussions with farmers and comparisons of calculated crop water requirements with historical farm deliveries. An understanding of the reliance on sub-irrigation in different sub-areas may be developed through discussions with individual farmers or through examination of the water budget.

The following questions should be considered to evaluate relevance of this measure to your district:

1. Do your water accounting records or comments from district water managers and individual farmers indicate a good match between supply and demand at a district-wide level?

2. Is there a method by which farmers can place water orders with the district based on need (i.e., irrigation requirements)?

3. Does your district support on-farm scheduling and is water requirement data available to and understood by farmers?

4. Do system spills often result from major laterals or canals because of changes in on-farm demands?

5. Will district distribution system facilities allow variable flows in different parts of the system without adversely affecting farmers' ability to take water through their turnouts?

On-farm Irrigation Scheduling

When to irrigate and how much water to apply are the two basic questions each irrigator must answer during the irrigation season. The answers will change throughout the irrigation season and will depend on crop type, climate conditions, soil types, application efficiencies and previous water applications. Improving on-farm scheduling to better match actual crop needs, thereby reducing over-application of water, may be a very effective water management measure.

On-farm irrigation scheduling can be based on the following methods:

- Crop and soil appearance and feel
- Water availability (often a fixed frequency)
- Theoretical ET calculations
- Allowable soil moisture depletion

The method chosen is usually a function of crop type and sensitivity to the timing of water application, availability of data, time constraints of the irrigator and system-wide water delivery flexibility.

Scientifically-based irrigation management considers soil characteristics, specifically the ability of soils to store irrigation water. The water holding capacity that is available to plants may be defined as the difference between the soil *field capacity* and the *wilting point*. The field capacity can be thought of as a full soil moisture reservoir, while the wilting point can be thought of as an empty one. Soil moisture holding characteristics vary by soil type. Characteristics are usually determined in a laboratory, although approximate holding capacities for various soil types are published.

The amount of water, that is available to the plants is termed the *available capacity*. A common objective of irrigation scheduling is to maintain soil moisture above some minimum refill point, such as 50% of the available capacity and to prevent soil moisture from decreasing to the wilting point, when crop stress occurs. This active soil moisture reservoir, between the field capacity and the refill point, is commonly referred to as the *allowable deplection*.

Figure 4.3 illustrates how these concepts apply to the scheduling of irrigations. At the beginning of the growing season, the root zone is assumed to be full (or soil moisture is at field capacity). ET from the crop steadily depletes the soil moisture over time. When the soil moisture level reaches the refill point, it is time to irrigate, and afterward irrigation soil moisture is again at field capacity. The *irrigation interval* is the time between subsequent irrigations.

The rates at which the soil moisture reservoir is depleted will depend on seasonally varying ET rates specific for each crop. Precipitation events will also affect soil moisture conditions and therefore the irrigation interval. For these reasons, real-time information on actual soil moisture conditions is essential for effective irrigation scheduling.

Irrigation scheduling using ET estimates and soil moisture data may offer excellent water management opportunities. Both of these methods are more quantitatively-based and allow a better estimate of true crop needs than simple visual inspection and will almost certainly result in meeting crop needs more effectively than irrigating on a fixed frequency. However, the difficulty in using these methods is that information must be collected and made available continuously throughout the irrigation season.

Numerous examples of data collection and information distribution programmes have shown these programmes to be feasible, affordable and to provide individual farmers with valuable information to assist them in on-farm scheduling. Often these programmes involve cooperative data collection efforts between Reclamation, the NRCS, other agencies and the farmers themselves. A variety of information distribution methods are possible including dial-in services, radio announcements, central literature postings and communication with a water conservation coordinator.

To evaluate the relevance of on-farm scheduling to your district, consider the following questions:

1. Do farmers have enough information about actual crop requirements to determine when to irrigate and how much to apply?
2. Is the district system flexible enough to adequately meet the farmers' needs in terms of amount and timing of water deliveries?
3. Based on the district's water budget, is there a reasonable match between water deliveries and crop water requirements on a district-wide basis?
4. Is crop stress due to over-or under-irrigation frequent in the district?

Conjunctive Use

Conjunctive use is the coordinated operation of surface water and groundwater resources to meet water requirements. Conjunctive use may provide an opportunity to increase the firm's water supply to a district or to more efficiently use the existing supply. In the former case, groundwater is used during periods when surface water supplies are less than demands. Such a situation may or may not result in a net depletion of the groundwater resources, depending on how the aquifer is recharged.

When conjunctive use is used to better regulate supplies, surface water available in excess of demands is intentionally used to recharge the underlying aquifer. This is followed by aquifer pumping when the surface supply is less than demands. In this case, the underlying aquifer effectively becomes a regulatory storage vessel. Recharge systems include injection wells, spreading basins, sump areas and recharge pits constructed in areas with high permeability. The feasibility of a groundwater pumping system will be a function of the local hydrogeology and specific water needs. A conjunctive use system may have automated controls to coordinate the groundwater component with flow conditions in the surface system and with water demands. A conjunctive use programme may also be appropriate in situations where it is more efficient to use a water supply nearer to the actual demands.

There are potential consequences associated with groundwater pumping that should be considered by the district. Groundwater mining may occur from pumping in excess of recharge rates, resulting in higher pumping costs, reduced water availability and aquifer depletion.

Pumping may also affect nearby surface water rights if the surface supplies are hydrologically connected to the groundwater. Groundwater pumping may affect the yields of other groundwater wells and salt-water intrusion may be a consequence in coastal areas.

Questions to help you evaluate the relevance of this measure to your district include:

1. Is suitable groundwater physically and legally available in the district?

2. Does the district experience periods of water shortages and are shortages due to limitations on diverted supply and/or distribution control?

3. Do problems with system losses, distribution control and system scheduling make it difficult to deliver water to specific areas in the district which might be served by close groundwater supplies?

4. If regulatory or carryover storage would improve distribution control, could groundwater storage offer the same benefits?

5. Is the geology of the aquifer and quality of the recharge water sufficient to make recharge and later use feasible?

Facilities-Related Water Management Measures

This section discusses some water management improvements achieved by constructing or modifying water delivery facilities. The topics include:

1. Construction of Regulatory Reservoirs
2. Lining of Canals and Reservoirs
3. Development of Water Reuse Systems.

Construction of Regulatory Reservoirs

Distribution system regulatory reservoirs can play an important role in helping the district match water deliveries to crop requirements. This may be especially true in systems that schedule deliveries on a rotation or fixed frequency. Regulatory reservoirs allow farmers to use their allocations at their convenience, both in terms of time of irrigation and the amount of water used. In addition to increasing water delivery flexibility, regulatory reservoirs may be used to:

* Reduce overall system spills
* Capture storm water runoff
* Capture tailwater runoff potentially available for re-use
* Help control desired groundwater levels to facilitate subirrigation.

Regulatory reservoirs should be strategically located in the district service area. Depending on the operational problems experienced, it may be most advantageous to locate a larger reservoir at the highest point in the system so that it may be used to regulate deliveries to all water users. If, on the other hand, distribution problems are more localised, a smaller reservoir constructed near the problem area might be in order.

The best indication of a need for additional regulation of water supply is a mismatch between water supply and demand. The demand for water may exceed supply because of a limitation in the available physical supply or because of bottlenecks in the conveyance facilities. The water supply may exceed demand at some times but be insufficient at others. In many systems, distribution control may be adequate overall but the speed at which a district can modulate supply to a particular area is inadequate to avoid shortages or system spills. A typical demand and supply relationship and the potential benefit in management flexibility and water conservation associated with regulatory storage.

The following questions will help the district evaluate relevance of this measure:

1. Does your district obtain its water at a constant or variable rate? How well do the rates match water demand?
2. Does your district already have regulatory reservoirs in its supply or distribution system that may be used to facilitate water delivery scheduling?
3. Is there a mismatch between water delivery rates and irrigation water demand on either a district-wise basis or in specific sub-areas?
4. Are there problems meeting demands in some areas of your district due to supply limitations or physical constraints of the conveyance facilities?
5. Do limitations on response time by district water managers result in demand shortages or over-deliveries?

Lining of Canals and Reservoirs

Canals, laterals and reservoirs may experience significant water losses due to seepage or evaporation. Installation of reservoir and canal linings or pipelines are effective methods to reduce these conveyance and storage losses. In addition to control of seepage and evaporation, lining and piping may provide the additional benefits of erosion control, reduced maintenance, increased safety and system pressurisation (piping only).

Factors affecting seepage or evaporative losses from conveyance and reservoir systems include:

- Bottom soils
- Capillary forces and gravity
- Silt deposition from operation
- Water depth and surface area
- Wetted area
- Water velocity
- Depth to groundwater

- Ground slope

Losses due to seepage from unlined canals may range from 10% to more than 50%. Lining activities commonly reduce losses to less than 10%, although the expected amount of water savings will depend on site characteristics and the type of lining used. A similar reduction in seepage losses can be achieved through piping with the additional benefit of reducing evaporative losses and possibly pressurising the system.

Significant seepage losses within the district may be indicated by the overall district water budget. Other general indications of seepage losses include phreatophyte growth adjacent to canals or reservoirs, water logging or pounding on adjacent lands, visible seepage faces on canal or reservoir embankments or return flow problems. While the district water budget may be used to develop a quantitative estimate of seepage losses, the latter indicators will provide a general idea of specific locations where seepage may be occurring.

Methods and materials used for canal lining include exposed linings (concrete, asphalt), buried membrances (plastic), earth linings (clay, soil sealants) and miscellaneous materials such as cast-in-place pipe. Methods and materials used for reservoir lining include earth compaction, earth blankets, bentonite, cement, chemical additives and flexible membranes.

Piping may be accomplished using a variety of materials including reinforced concrete, cast in place concrete, corrugated metal, PVC and other synthetics. Selection of materials for both lining and piping requires site-specific consideration of material availability, hydraulic requirements and costs.

There are many factors that influence the type of lining or pipeline chosen and no single lining type can be recommended to satisfy all situations. Numerous publications by Reclamation and others provide detailed information concerning material selection and design. These publications are listed in the Appendix.

Questions to consider to evaluate relevance of this measure include:

1. Does you district water budget indicate significant (greater than 10%) losses in the conveyance system?
2. Do lands adjacent to canals have excess vegetation or are they heavily vegetated with water loving plants?
3. Do lands adjacent to canals exhibit problems with water logging as evidenced by water ponding, phreatophyte growth and salt leaching in soils?

Water Re-use Systems

Water reuse systems may be an effective technique for improving irrigation system efficiencies and water management within a district. In addition to reducing the required diversion amount and increasing delivery flexibility, re-use systems may provide benefits in the areas of flood protection, erosion control and water quality of receiving waters. It may also be possible to locate and schedule crop irrigation to effectively take advantage of water re-use opportunities.

The purpose of re-use systems is to capture system spills, seepage, and drainage waters for immediate or later use. In the case of operational spills, a storage facility is usually required to hold water until demand increases once again. In contrast, it may be possible to use captured drainage water on a more immediate basis, and a storage reservoir may not be required. Re-use of water potentially reduces the required amount of diversion into he overall system. Reuse system will include a capture mechanism (a drainage canal or a diversion facility and reservoir) and the necessary pumping equipment and pipeline to deliver water from the capture location back into the application system. In some instances, it may be possible to use gravity for the delivery of the collected spills or drainage water.

In a system aimed at re-use of operational spills, it may be most efficient to capture spills at several locations in the conveyance system. Alternatively, the captured spills could be conveyed to a central storage location. The storage capacity required would typically depend on the flow rate in the service canal and the response time to changes in water demand.

Capture and re-use of operational spills as a conservation measure may be closely related to use of regulatory storage in the conveyance system. The use of regulatory reservoirs at higher ponts in the system may greatly improve the district's ability to respond to changing water demands and thus substantially reduce operational spills. It may also be more efficient to implement both measures and use the regulatory reservoirs for storage of pumped spill water.

In addition to capturing spilled water, capture and re-use of drainage water may be advantageous at more than one location in the system. Several drainage canals can be constructed at key locations in the service area to capture seepage from specific areas that exhibit the most significant drainage problems. This collected water is then conveyed to a central location.It may be possible to use common storage reservoirs for both captured spills and drainage waters.

7

OPTIONS OF CONSERVATION AND MANAGEMENT OF WATER RESOURCES

Protection, preservation and efficient utilisation of water resources is very important. For virtually every use of water in a building, facility managers can choose from a wide variety of water management options. Some options simply involve altering the water use of building occupants. Other options involve changing the way fixtures and equipments are operated and maintained. The most significant long-term savings, however, will probably require the retrofitting or replacement of fixtures and equipments. In some instances, one option alone might achieve the desired savings (such as replacing showerheads with low-flow models).

In others, a combination of options may be needed (for example, inserting flow restrictors and providing automatic sensor controls for bathroom faucets). A comprehensive water management plan should explore all water management options. This plan should recognise that a building's water system and changes to it, will have an impact on other systems in the building, such as heating. For example, installing a flow restrictor on a faucet not only will reduce the amount of water consumed, but also will lower energy costs associated with heating this water for use and lower sewerage costs based on consumption.

Some ways to reduce your current water consumption will be immediately apparent, such as fixing a leaky faucet. Others, such as determining how many and what types of toilets to install, will require some product research. It is important to evaluate each option not only on its ability to conserve water, but also on its practicality. For example, replacing a high-consumption fixture with a low-consumption fixture will enable you to realise the greatest amount of water savings over time, but where limited budgets prevent the initial high price of replacement, other interim measures, such as retrofitting toilets with displacement devices, may help save significant volumes of water.

Conservation Actions

Indoor uses of water will vary greatly from facility to facility. The person charged with the responsibility of implementing the water conservation plan should perform a detailed audit of each major water use, process, machine and position. Water management actions will then be chosen and evaluated to determine which are most cost-effective. The following discussion offers specific actions that you may want to evaluate to improve indoor water use at your facility. Generally these indoor uses of water fall into four major categories:

1. Domestic Plumbing
2. Cooling and Heating Systems
3. Landscape Water Uses
4. Kitchen and Cafeteria Water Uses
5. Laundry Water Uses
6. X-Ray and Photo Processing.

Outdoor water use (specifically, landscape water use) is often an area with significant conservation potential. Additional efforts should discussed with a landscaping consultant.

1. Domestic Water Uses

Domestic water use can include toilets, urinals, sinks, showers and other appliances used for human health and sanitation. Domestic water conservation opportunities in new and existing facilities are evaluated below.

Code Requirements

Most local plumbing codes require water-conserving toilets, faucets and shower heads in new construction. Federal requirements for water efficient plumbing took effect in 1992. The current state Construction Code requirements for toilets, urinals, lavatory faucets and showerheads are presented in the table below. All new fixtures sold must meet these requirements; however, replacement of existing fixtures is not generally required.

Federal Plumbing Fixture Standards

Toilets, gpf*	1.6
Urinals, gpf*	1.0
Lavatory Faucets, gpm+	2.5
Showerheads, gpm+	2.5

* gpf (gallons per flush)

\+ gpm (gallons per minute)

Several different approaches enable plumbing fixtures to be both effective and water-saving.

Toilets and Urinals

* Flush valves for toilets and urinals can be adjusted to reduce flow without reducing flushing effectiveness. Flow reducing devices can be installed.
* Toilets with individual tanks can be retrofitted by placing a dam or a water-filled plastic container in the tank to conserve a portion of the volume used by each flush.
* Retrofit devices of various types, such as toilet dams, displacement devices or early closing flappers, are available to reduce the volume of flushing.
* Toilets and urinals are now only available in ultra-low volume versions with improved bowl designs and flushing procedures. The models with the lowest water use typically incorporate either a siphon action or air or vacuum assistance.
* Check timing cycles and volumes for automatic water flushing systems in urinals and toilets. All automatic systems should be tied to operating hours and should not run 24 hours a day, 7 days a week.
* For tank-type toilets with 3.5 gallon or greater flush volumes, complete replacement of the fixture should have an economically feasible payback period, depending on usage. At the very least, toilet dams or low-flow flapper valves should be installed to decrease consumption per flush.

Faucets and Showerheads

* Faucets and showerheads can be retrofitted with aerators which add air to the flow stream, resulting in a spray-like flow and reducing water usage.
* Another approach is to replace the faucets and showerheads with reduced-flow models.
* Metering faucets deliver a measured quantity of water on demand.
* Spring-loaded faucets shut off immediately after use.
* An automatic sensor controlled system for faucets has been available for several years. It uses a beam of infrared light to detect the presence of the user and thereby starts and/or stops faucet flow. These devices deliver metered flows, only on demand, preventing running of water at faucets not in use. The controls are designed to prevent activation by passers-by and to reset after use to accommodate the next person.

Preventive Maintenance. A scheduled programme of leak detection and repair can provide considerable savings in water and energy costs for a small increase in maintenance effort. All tank toilets should be "dye-tested" to check for leaks. This simply involves placing a small tablet of dye in the tank, waiting 15 minutes, and checking the bowl to see if any water from the tank, coloured by the dye, has leaked into the bowl. Dye tablets are inexpensive. Alternatively, several drops of food colouring can be added to the tank instead of the dye. Metering faucets should be periodically checked to ensure that they do not run for excessive periods of time.

Down With the Clog

One of the major causes of clogged toilets and plumbing maintenance headaches is the misuse of toilets as trash cans. In traditional, high-volume flush gravity toilets, this practice did not seem to seriously impair the toilet's performance or harm the pipes, since the high volume of water made virtually any object flushable. With the 1.6 gpf models, however, even if waste appears to flush, there is less water to propel the waste through the pipes and clogs can form down the line, if there isn't supplemental water from other sources.

Cooling and Heating Systems

Cooling and heating may be used for both ambient climate control and cooling of equipment. Uses include, but are not limited to, cooling towers, boilers, chillers, air scrubbers, refrigeration equipment and evaporative coolers. For equipment, such as cooling towers that use large volumes of water, install submeters for both in fluent and bleed-off water. Small changes in operation can lead to great savings in water, energy and chemicals. Increase cooling tower cycles of concentration as equipment allows. Eliminate all single-pass water use. Investigate all possibilities of water reclamation and reuse.

Heating, ventilating and air-conditioning (HVAC) equipment can use a great deal of water to meet a facility's heating and cooling needs. This equipment often uses water inefficiently, either by not recycling it or by recycling fewer times than possible. For these reasons, improving the efficiency of HVAC equipment can produce considerable water savings in your facility.

Cooling Towers

Cooling towers are the site of significant water consumption in most large cooling systems. In the Phoenix area, most cooling towers are used as the mechanism for rejecting heat from air conditioning systems. Some serve the cooling needs for plant equipment with large heat loads. The thermal efficiency, proper operation and longevity of the water cooling system all depend on the quality of water and its re-use or recycling potential.

A free Cooling Tower Maintenance training video and workbook produced by the ADWR are available for on-site use. For a more detailed discussion of cooling tower water treatment and conservation or to obtain the video, contact your city's water conservation office.

In a cooling tower, a circulating stream of warm water contacts an air flow, causing evaporation of a portion of the water. When this water evaporates, the water which remains behind is cooled. The rate of evaporation from a typical cooling tower is approximately one percent of the rate of flow of the recirculating water passing through the tower for every 10°F decrease in recirculating water temperature achieved by the tower. The loss of heat by evaporation (latent heat) cools the remaining water. A small amount of cooling also takes place, when the remaining water transfers heat (sensible heat) to the air. The water which passes through a cooling tower then circulates through a cooling system, warms and returns to the tower.

A cooling tower consumes water in the following ways:

Evaporation. As noted above, cooling of the water stream is accomplished through the evaporation of a portion of that input water flow. The amount of evaporation that occurs is a function of the amount of cooling performed and the weather conditions. For these reasons, the amount of evaporation cannot be reduced without an unacceptable reduction in the performance of the cooling tower. A general guideline for estimating the rate of evaporation from a cooling tower is 3 gallons per minute (gpm) per 100 tons of cooling load.

Blow-Down. In addition to evaporation, water is lost from the cooling tower through "blow-down" or "bleed-off." Blow-down is the intentional release of some of the circulating water from the tower to remove suspended and dissolved solids left behind during the evaporation process. Without blow-down, dissolved minerals would continually increase in concentration and result in scale buildup in the system components.

Drift and Other Losses. Drift is the loss of water in the form of mist, driven by the air draft of the tower. Drift droplets contain suspended and dissolved solids, so this loss can be considered a part of blow-down. A typical rate of drift is 0.05 to 0.2 percent of the total water circulation rate. Other system losses, such as valve leaks or drawoff for other uses, can also be considered as part of total blow-down.

Make-Up Water. Water must be added ("made up") to the cooling tower to replace evaporation, blow-down and drift losses. The relationship of the quantities of make-up water and blow-down can be expressed in terms of the concentration ratio (CR), also known as the number of cycles of concentration. This value is the ratio of total dissolved solids (TDS) in the blow-down water to their concentration in the make-up water.

As the concentration ratio increases, the amount of blow-down decreases. This means that less water is discarded and the tower is more water efficient. Significant volumes of water can be conserved by reducing blow-down to the minimum level consistent with good operating practice. Reducing the amount of water lost as blow-down is usually accomplished by treating the cooling water by physical or chemical means.

The following equations express the relationships between the make-up water volume (M), evaporation volume (E), blow-down volume (B) and the concentration ratio (CR). Assume that drift, leaks and other losses are a part of the blow-down value.

$$M = B + E$$

$$CR = M \div B$$

By substitution, $CR = (B + E) - B$

Solve for B, $B = E \div (CR - 1)$

If you assume that evaporation is constant for a given set of conditions, then the following Figure 5.2 illustrates the relationship between concentration ratio and total make-up water consumption.

Water Quality Management Issues. The principal areas of concern with respect to the water circulating through the cooling tower are the prevention of scale, corrosion and biological fouling. Effective control of these potential problems prevents system failure, maintains energy efficiency and minimises system maintenance.

Scale. Scale is formed when minerals in the water precipitate and collect on the surfaces in contact with the water. The formation of scale is affected by pH, temperature and mineral concentration. Scale acts as an insulator, thereby reducing the heat transfer efficiency of equipment. Scale can also become an obstruction in piping, resulting in increased pumping costs. Scale can be controlled by several methods including addition of scale inhibiting chemicals, control of pH, make-up water softening and blow-down to reduce mineral concentrations.

Corrosion. The most common causes of corrosion are acid, oxygen, galvanic action and impingement. Aside from poorly controlled chemical feed systems, the primary source of acidity in cooling tower water is polluted air. Galvanic action can occur when dissimilar metals are in contact in the presence of water containing minerals (cooling tower water). Corrosion inhibiting chemicals can be added to the water to form protective films on the metal or otherwise stop corrosion.

Biofouling. Biofouling is the result of algae, bacteria and fungi growth. Biofouling causes plugging of tower water distribution systems, assists in scale and corrosion formation, decreases heat transfer efficiency and rots wooden tower components. Biofouling can be controlled by a number of chemical treatment including oxidising biocides such as chlorine.

State of Arizona Requirements. Water conservation requirements for cooling towers have been established by the Arizona Department of Water Resources for the Phoenix area since 1990. The Second Management Plan (1990 to 2000) affected all facilities defined as "new large cooling users," referring to industrial facilities whose aggregate cooling capacity exceeded 250 tons after the effective date of the plan. This plan required the affected facilities to achieve a minimum total dissolved solids concentration of 2,000 mg/1 in their tower water before blow-down. In its Third Management Plan, for the period 2000 to 2010, the requirements affect all facilities whose aggregate cooling tower capacity exceeds 1,000 tons (regardless of start date of operation). These users are required by the ADWR to achieve either a total hardness concentration of 1,200 mg/1 or a silica concentration of 120 mg/1 in the tower water prior to blow-down (whichever occurs first). The facilities are also required to use non-ground water for make-up water "where available and of suitable quality." Make-up and blow-down water volumes, as well as hardness and silica concentrations, must be measured and reported. These requirements may be waived if the facility reuses all of its blow down water in a beneficial manner, such as landscape watering. These requirements mean that facilities have to manage their cooling towers more water-efficiently than is currently achieved by many cooling tower users in the Valley.

Managing Your Cooling Tower System

* Prepare an inventory of each cooling tower you have, its cooling capacity and the equipment or processes that it serves. A Cooling Tower Water Survey Checklist is provided in Worksheet 5.1 to record this information.
* You may be able to have a credit for evaporation deducted from your sewerage bill, if you properly meter your cooling tower's water losses as previously described and if your provider offers this credit. If you wish to receive this deduction, be sure to set up your metering programme in accordance with your city's water services requirements.

Note: If you are a permitted Significant Industrial User (SIU), evaporation credits are *not* an option.

* If you purchase chemicals for the treatment of the recirculating cooling tower water, have the chemical vendor explain the purpose and action of each chemical.
* Have your chemical vendor provide a written report of each service call and be sure that the vendor explains the meaning of each analysis performed as well as the test results.
* Tell your chemical vendor that water conservation is a priority at your facility.

Ask your vendor to tell you about alternative programmes that could reduce the amount of water that is bled off from the towers. A performance contract for services is recommended.

Operation Modifications

* Improve the method of releasing the tower bleed-off. Most cooling towers are bled off automatically, when the conductivity of the water reaches a preset level. Try to operate the bleed-off on a more continuous basis, maintaining the conductivity of the tower closer to the limits, without wide fluctuations.

* Install flow submeters on the make-up and bleed-off lines. This practice enables the operator to verify the volume of water being used in the tower. Submeters should, at a minimum, be capable of totaling the flow. There are also submeters that display instantaneous flow. It is also important to read and record submeter data regularly. Submeters can be installed by your plumber and must meet AWWA specifications, if you wish to obtain deduction from your wastewater bill for evaporative losses (if this option is available to you). Worksheet 5.2 presents a Cooling Tower Water Consumption Logsheet which you may use to record the submeter data and estimate the tower's concentration ratio.

* Use sulfuric acid treatment for adjustment of alkalinity. When added to recirculating water, sulfuric acid can improve water efficiency be reducing scale buildup created from mineral deposits. This makes it possible to operate the tower at a higher concentration ratio. Sulfuric acid lowers the pH of the the water and is effective in converting a portion of the calcium bicarbonate, typically the primary cause of scale, to the more readily soluble calcium sulfate.

* Sulphuric acid treatment, however, is not for installations where the additive may be vulnerable to vandalism, such as schools or prisons and workers must be well trained in the handling and operation safety of this treatment. Contact your chemical vendor for further information.

* All water treatment, no matter what kind, must be strictly monitored and performed by qualified workers.

Retrofit Options

- If suspended materials are degrading the quality of your cooling tower water, use a sidestream filtration system composed of a rapid sand filter or a high-efficiency cartridge filter to cleanse the water. These systems draw water from the basin, filter out sediment and return the filtered water to the tower, enabling the system to operate more efficiently with less water. This system is particularly effective where the water is cloudy airborne contaminants are common or cooling water passages are small and susceptible to clogging. Removing particles or suspended solids in the recirculating water enables the system to operate more efficiently and with less maintenance.

- Consider an ozonation system for biological control. An ozonation system consists of an air compressor, ozone generator, diffuser or contractor and a control system. While it is a powerful oxidizing agent, ozone (a gas) has an effective life of less than an hour to a few minutes. Therefore, it must be generated at the site by passing cool, dry air (or pure oxygen gas) through a high voltage field between two electrodes (known as the *corona discharge method*).

Evaporative Coolers

The function of evaporative coolers is to decrease the temperature of incoming air being drawn into a building by increasing its humidity. Most evaporative cooling equipment is used to cool air flow for space cooling. The air's ambient or "dry bulb", temperature remains constant. After a short period of operation, recirculating water in an evaporative cooler assumes the wet bulb temperature of the entering air. This temperature is theoretically the lowest temperature to which the entering air may be cooled.

Most evaporative coolers are equipped with recirculation pumps and most coolers have a bleed-off to control concentrations of contaminants in the recirculating water and prevent damage to the cooler's pads. Water is used in some evaporative cooler's in "single-pass" fashion. This is not good practice for two reasons. Water consumption is unnecessarily high and the cooler does not cool as effectively, because the water does not cool to the wet bulb temperature. Evaporative coolers usually do require either a small amount of bleed-off or cleaning to operate effectively. Worksheet 5.3 presents an Evaporative Cooler Checklist to help you evaluate the condition and operation of your coolers.

— Replace the pads at the beginning of the season. Old pads will reduce the cooling efficiency and may thereby increase the water consumption.

— Be sure your coolers have pumps to recirculate the water through them.

— Check to make sure you are not bleeding off an excessive amount of water. For a typical small cooler, anything more than a few gallons per hour may be excessive.

— Pipe the bleed-off from your coolers to help water a landscaped area.

- Consider installation of thermostats to control the operation of coolers.
- Consider the use of chemical additives to allow the cooler to efficiently operate with reduced bleed-off volume.

Once-Through Cooling

Many facilities in Arizona have equipment cooled by a single-pass flow of water. After passing through and cooling the equipment, the water is discarded. This is prohibited by many city codes. Equipment which might be cooled by once-through water includes: ice-making machines, air conditioners, air compressors, degreasers, rectifiers, hydraulic equipment, x-ray machines, condensers, hydraulic presses, welders and vacuum pumps. The ADWR prohibits the use of once-through cooling water by industrial users supplied by their own wells. The discharge of this uncontaminated water to the sanitary sewer may be prohibited by your city's municipal sewerage ordinance.

More efficient water use can be achieved through alternatives to single-pass cooling, including:

- Replace the existing water-cooled equipment with new air-cooled equipment.
- Remote air-cool, the condenser fluid (applicable to air conditioners, ice machines etc.).
- Connect the water cooled equipment to chilled water or cooling tower piping.
- Re-use the single-pass cooling water as make-up water for other process needs or for landscape irrigation.

Boilers/Steam Generators

Boilers and steam generators are commonly used in large heating systems, in cooling or in facilities where large amounts of processed steam are used. This equipment consumes varying amounts of water depending on the size of the system and the amount of water that has not evaporated (called condensate return).

Maintenance Modifications

- Check steam traps and lines for leaks, which should be repaired as soon as possible. These are very costly energy-wasters as well as water-wasters.
- Provide proper insulation on piping and on the central storage tank.

Retrofit Options

- Install a condensate return system. By recycling condensate for re-use, water supply and operating costs for this equipment canbe reduced upto 70 percent. A condensate return system also helps to lower energy costs since the condensate water is already hot.

Landscape Water Uses

Landscaping provides many benefits to industrial, commercial and institutional properties. These include enhanced aesthetics, shading and climate mitigation, pleasant outdoor spaces. for employees and clientele, as well as greater property value.

More than half of the water provided by Valley cities is used outdoors to water lawns and landscape plants. For this reason, it is very important to plan and install landscapes carefully and to plan for proper maintenance. With good planning, we can have beautiful, colour landscapes that are water efficient and easy to maintain.

A good design will include desert-adapted plants that are thoughtfully placed for attractive and functional landscapes and ease of maintenance. The ADWR has established a list of recommended low-water-use plants, which is included in the appendix and is available on ADWR's web site, http://water.az.gov/. The irrigation design should segregate the site into zones based on exposure, provide the most efficient types of irrigation system components for different plant needs and include products that minimise water waste.

A well-planned, well-installed design will avoid future maintenance problems and expense. Watering costs alone can be cut by one-half to two-thirds by installing a Xeriscape instead of turf or other types of water-thirsty landscapes.

The term "Xeriscape" comes from the Greek word "xeros," meaning dry, but should not be confused with barren "zero-scapes." Xeriscape describes a philosophy that includes sound horticultural practices and a common-sense approach to landscaping. The following seven Xeriscape principles serve as guidelines to successful landscaping.

Good landscape planning and design. Selecting the right size and type of plant for the location, grouping plants with similar needs together and creating attractive, functional areas will help ensure a long-lasting and enjoyable landscape.

Appropriate turf areas. Grass lawns should be placed where they can be used and enjoyed. Wall-to-wall turf is unnecessary. Small, irregular areas may be inefficient and hard to maintain. High-foot traffic areas may be better served with hardscape instead of turf.

Efficient irrigation. Good water management practices, alongwith an efficient system, help maintain a healthy landscape without wasting water.

Soil improvements. Some soil may need to be aerated or amended to improve water absorption and the water-holding capacity of the soil.

Use of mulches. Organic or inorganic mulches protect the soil from being baked in direct sun; help retain water; and control weeds, dust and mud.

Use of low-water-use plants. The wide variety of plants available provide year-round colour in many forms and functions. They can create almost any look and help reduce energy costs, when placed for shade and insulation. Desert-adapted plants usually require less maintenance.

Proper maintenance of plants and irrigation systems. The natural look of many plants is enhanced with occasional pruning, fertilising, weeding and pest control. Proper maintenance means less waste going to the landfills; healthy, long-lasting landscapes; and protection of your investment. Checking your irrigation system regularly can prevent costly repairs.

Proper plant selection and placement reduces water use. Low-water-use, drought-tolerant plants can be used to create a variety of looks, from Sonoran to tropical, formal or casual. Many other groundcovers, flowers, shrubs, and grasses can be used instead of turf. Trees and shrubs in planters can provide shade, privacy screening, noise reduction, area definition, as well as attractive foliage, colourful flowers and pleasant fragrances.

Low-and high-water use plants should not be planted together in the same area to avoid overwatering the low-water-use plants. High-water-use plants can be planted in low-lying areas or swales to intercept runoff from hardscape or pavement and decrease the need for supplemental watering. Group high-water-use plants together in a mini-oasis near the building for energy savings or in areas where they can be enjoyed up close, such as a courtyard. The lowest-water-using plants should be placed farthest away from the building in the arid zone. Desert-adapted trees are more tolerant of the harsh conditions of parking lots. The area in between the arid zone and the mini-oasis or turf area is called the transition zone. This zone has low-to moderate-water use plants that blend the lush areas with the more arid ones. For an example of the Xeriscape zone concept, see the following diagram.

Proper Landscape Water Management Saves Money

Potential financial impacts of landscape water management include water cost, maintenance cost, plant loss and replacement cost and property value. Recent local studies show that many landscapes are over-watered by as much as 100%, while others are deficit watered. Over-watering encourages excessive growth, disease and other maintenance problems. Other common problems are shallow watering or poorly applied water. Deep, periodic watering encourages strong, healthy root systems that can better tolerate periods of drought.

There are a number of ways to conserve water used for landscape irrigation. Proper irrigation system design, installation and maintenance are important. Be sure to hire contractors who have experience and knowledge with water management. You may wish to hire a company to provide water management training to your current staff or contractors.

Irrigation systems should be designed to avoid unnecessary sprinklers and blockage of the spray stream by obstacles. Sprinklers should serve only the required turf areas and not spray on buildings or non-landscaped areas. Excess water on sidewalks and pavement causes damage, increases liability and wastes water. The irrigation system should have a timer and/or moisture sensors to activate the system, and watering should be done before sunrise or after sunset to reduce evaporation losses. Turf areas, planters, trees and shrubs should be watered separately to meet differing needs. The amount of solar exposure, wind and soil types also affect irrigation needs. Take into consideration, the surrounding plantings that may have overlapping watering schedules. Always irrigate the entire depth and width of the root zone regardless of the time of year. Once or twice a year, water twice as long to leach out salts that build up.

Proper system maintenance is essential to irrigation water conservation. Sprinkler heads should be inspected regularly; and damaged, worn or broken heads should be replaced promptly. Sprinkler heads should be cleaned periodically to remove mineral deposits and maintain hydraulic efficiency. The system should be inspected for leaks in pipes, couplings and faucets and should be repaired as necessary. All irrigation timing cycles should be adjusted monthly to meet varying seasonal demands. Large turf areas should be watered according to the evapotranspiration (ET) rate, which can be found in the weather section of your daily newspaper.

Proper Landscape Practices Checklist

* Adjust irrigation programme frequency monthly. This requires effort and persistence, but results in healthier, more attractive landscapes and lower water bills.
* Automate landscape irrigation systems.
* Schedule irrigation for early morning or late evening.
* Water only as frequently as necessary. In the Phoenix area, turf should be watered no more than every third day in summer and less frequently in fall and spring. Dormant Bermuda grass needs no supplemental winter watering.
* Drip irrigation should run for two or three hours to provide deep watering. Frequency of operation should vary according to plant needs. Variables are based on temperature, solar exposure, rainfall, soil conditions, plant types and maturity, density of plantings, number and placement of emitters and emitter application rate. Use the watering guide in your local newspaper or the

watering recommendations using the ET rate found on the Internet at http://ag.arizona.edu/azmet.

* Segregate valves by plant needs and exposure. For example: water turf and seasonal flowers separately. Solar exposure is more significant to water needs than temperature. The north side of a building has the least sun exposure.
* Place enough drip emitters around the root zone (at the canopy edge) of trees to encourage roots to spread further from the trunk.
* Add or move drip emitters as plants mature. Cap emitters if no longer needed.
* Install rain or moisture sensors to reduce scheduling requirements.
* Decrease or eliminate turf areas. Keep only those that are used for active recreation. Myoporum uses only $^1/_{10}$ of the amount of water required for turf. Groundcovers reduce maintenance requirements, too.
* Landscape with drought-tolerant Xeriscape plants. A list of these plants is included in the Appendix.
* Use mulches, such as decomposed granite, around plants to help retain moisture.
* Keep turf at the proper height. Grass that is too short uses more water. Keep at $^3/_4$ to 1 inch for warm season grass, 1½ to 2 inches for cool season grass.
* Dethatch or aerate lawns annually to improve water infiltration.
* Remove weeds that compete with desired plants for water.
* Follow the principles of Xeriscape to ensure a long-lasting, water and energy efficient landscape.
* Only prune as needed. Heavily sheared spheres and cubes are less healthy and much more wasteful of resources than plants with a natural form.
* Keep your irrigation system running as efficiently as possible (see Irrigation System Tune-Up Checklist below).

Irrigation System Tune-Up Checklist

Identify Equipment

* Make an irrigation system map that shows the location of all water lines, sprinklers, bubblers, emitters and valves.

Check for Leaks

* Turn off all water and read the meter. After 15 minutes, read it again. If the

meter hand has moved, you may have a leak inside or outside the building.

* Leaks outdoors can often be located by looking for overly green or muddy areas, but sometimes they are undetectable without special equipment.

Check Controllers

* Make sure that all valves are turning on. If the controller has a battery backup, check the charge on the battery.
* Replace electro-mechanical clocks with electronic models, which are much more accurate and allow more flexible watering schedules.
* Make a list of where all of the stations water. Place the list in the controller box.

Irrigation System

* Repair or replace broken or missing sprinkler heads, bubblers and drip emitters.
* Check seals between the neck and base of the sprinkler heads. Water will squirt out of the base if worn. Make sure all heads pop up all the way and fully retract when water is turned off.
* Check for sprinkler spray blocked by weeks or grass. If the spray is blocked, lower the mowing height or raise the sprinkler level.
* Make sure sprinklers are vertical and flush with soil grade. Soil should be tightly compacted around the sprinklers.
* Check for low system pressure. Water will stream out of the sprinkler instead of forming a spray. Consult an irrigation supplier for advice.
* Clean or replace clogged nozzles. Clean the sprinkler's trash screen, if it has one.
* Check the rotation and direction of spray. Adjust the radius and arc to avoid spraying sidewalks and buildings.

Irrigation Scheduling

* Water at night or in the early morning. Between 2 a.m. and 6 a.m. is best.
* Do not water turf more than once every three days. Sandy soils and hybrid (Tiff) Bermuda grass may need to be watered more often.
* If water runoff is a problem, irrigate two or three times per night at

½ to 1/3 the normal watering times, respectively. Wait an hour between waterings.

* Change the watering schedule about once a month according to prevailing conditions. Use ET as a guide.

The following schematic shows the basic components and general layout of a drip irrigation system. Backflow prevention devices must be installed in compliance with local ordinances.

Proper Maintenance Protects Landscape Investment

Good maintenance practices will help increase property value and attract clientel. Poor maintenance practices detract from the building's appearance and become costly to repair.

If a tree is pruned improperly or staked so long that the bark has grown around the support wires, you can probably consider the tree a loss. Remember the investment you have in that tree: the initial cost of the tree, planting cost, watering cost and any other maintenance time. With a chainsaw, a landscaper without the proper pruning knowledge can destroy a tree in minutes. A tree that has been topped often becmes a liability, as well as an eyesore. Proper pruning is done for three reasons: the health of the plant, safety, and aesthetics. Excessive pruning increases water needs, contributes to landfill waste, is hard on the plant, and is costly in terms of maintenance. With proper plant selection (the right plant for the right place), much of the need for pruning can be eliminated. Many plants have attractive natural forms that need little or no pruning.

Turf should be kept to the proper height: ¾ to 1 inch for warm season grasses such as Bermuda and 1½ to 2 inches for cool season grasses such as rye. Dethatching turf annually in April or October increases aeration and water infiltration, which leads to healthier turf and decreased water consumption. Drought resistance is assisted by decreasing nitrogen fertilisers and increasing potassium levels. Weeds should be removed regularly so that don't compete with desired plants for water and nutrients.

Landscape maintenance can be one of the most difficult areas to manage on your property, especially if you are unfamiliar with proper maintenance techniques. Like many other services that are contracted out, it is important to hire a company that employs highly trained, skilled individuals.

When choosing a landscape or lawn care contractor, there are many important questions to consider. The checklist below will help guide you in selecting a contractor.

Contractor Selection Checklist

References: Call them and look at quality an condition of projects.

Education: Owner or crew supervisor should have some training. There are several local training and certification programmes. See the following list.

Licensed and Bonded: Check registrar of contractors for status and type of license.

Customer Service: Do they return phone calls promptly? Are they friendly and courteous? Is someone available at all times? Will they provide records or plan-of-work reports tailored to your project? Are they willing to have meetings or inspections with you?

Water Management Philosophy: Do they practice seasonal scheduling and watering to promote deep roots? Can they develop water budgets?

Irrigation System Maintenance: What is their frequency of inspection and how do they handle repairs?

Pruning Philosophy: Have they had special training in pruning? Do they believe in minimal or heavy pruning? Do they prefer natural or formal pruning? If plants require pruning constantly because of location, would they prefer to replace them with something more appropriate? Do they have knowledge of plant material and understand its natural form? Is equipment sharp, in good condition and appropriate for the job?

Weed and Pest Control Philosophy: Do they have an Arizona Structural Pest Control Certification Card? What is their philosophy on weed control in turf and/or in desert landscape areas?

Fertiliser Regime: How often do they recommend fertilising desert plants and/or tropical plants? How often for turf?

Turf Management Philosophy: At what height do they cut the grass? How often do they dethatch and aerate the soil? What is their over-seeding philosophy?

Titles or Certifications in the Landscape Industry

The list below includes a description of titles or certifications that are common in the landscape industry. Don't hesitate to ask your landscape contractor about his or her training and level of expertise. Anyone who has had the training will be proud to show you his or her credentials.

Arizona Certified Landscape Professional: A landscaper who has received certification by the Arizona Landscape Contractors Association. Testing required.

Certified Arborist: An arborist who has received certification by the International

Society of Arboriculture. An exam on tree identification and care is required. Thirty hours of continuing education are required in every three years.

Certified Landscape Irrigation Auditor, Contractor, Designer or Manager: An irrigation specialist who has received certification by the Irrigation Association. The four certifications listed above represent different levels of certification. A Landscape Irrigation Auditor is at the beginning level and an Irrigation Manager is the advanced level.

Certified Tree Worker: A tree worker trained to prune and climb properly and certified by the International Society of Arboriculture. Requires an oral test on tree care and practical exam covering climbing skills. Requires eighteen (18) months or experience. Continuing education is required.

Consulting Arborist: No license or certification is required. Typically it is a person who offers advice on tree selection and care.

Desert Landscaper Certification: A programme administered by the Desert Botanical Garden consisting of thirty (3) workshops over a ten (10) months period which include basic training, hands on experience and a final comprehensive landscaping project.

Horticulturist: Anyone with a two-years, four-years or advanced degree in horticulture.

Landscape Contractor: The Arizona Landscape Contractor's Association certifies a landscape installation and maintenance contractor. Testing and insurance are required.

Master Gardener: A volunteer who has gone through sixteen (16) weeks of specialised horticultural training from the University of Arizona Cooperative Extension.

Pesticide Applicator Certification: A pesticide applicator who has been tested and certified by the Arizona Structural Pest Control Commission. Anyone spraying chemicals on commercial property must have this certification.

Smartscape Certified: Smartscape is a training programme for nursery and landscape professionals designed to encourage consistent horticultural practices compatible with the Sonoran Desert. Participants must complete a series of eight (8) two-and-a-half (2½) hours workshops.

If you oversee a landscape maintenance contractor and especially if you are responsible for the landscape maintenance directly, it is advisable to get some basic landscape maintenance training. The Arizona Municipal Water Users Association offers a four-week landscape programme two times a year called *smartscape*. Call (602) 248-8482 for more information.

The Irrigation/Pruning Connection

Irrigation affects pruning and vice versa. When landscape plants are given excessive water, they grow much more rapidly. More plant growth means more pruning, increasing maintenance time and expense. This is a good example of why water management is one of the most important components of your maintenance programme. Not only can water management save a great deal of money on water budgets, but it also saves on maintenance, overall plant health and landscape longevity.

Pruning can also affect how much water landscape plants use. Poor pruning removes shade protection on the branches, trunks, and roots. It also removes leaves, buds, and stored energy which are needed for healthy growth. Removing too many branches also increases susceptibility to pests, slows growth, undermines health, and stimulates excessive sprouting. Plant stress, higher temperature, open wounds and excessive sprouting can cause a plant to require more water than normal.

Tree Pruning

Pruning is both a skill and an art. The skill is in making cuts that heal and callus properly and minimise the chance for decay. The art is in making cuts in the right places, so that the plant takes on an attractive, natural form.

Reasons for Pruning

* To remove dead, weakened, diseased or insect-damaged branches.
* To improve safety by eliminating hazards such as branches in walkways or paths.
* To remove crowded or crossing limbs.
* To direct growth of the tree.
* To improve stability by reducing wind resistance.

Trees allowed to grow to their natural form and with the most of their lower branches intact are stronger and less likely to be wind damaged. Some thinning of top-heavy trees may be necessary. Pruning should rarely drastically change the height or shape of the plant but should enhance its natural form and character.

For the Healthiest Trees

- Do not top trees.
- Do not remove tree branches unless necessary.
- Always cut back to a branch; do not tip back.
- Leave lower branches on as long as possible.
- Tree workers should be highly skilled.

Shrub Pruning

Shrubs and groundcovers used in landscapes should be permitted to grow and develop into their natural shapes. They may require pruning periodically to control size, remove die-back or for rejuvenation. Designing and selecting a plant with the mature size in mind reduces the need for frequent or heavy pruning. You can prune shrubs to stay within limited bounds without shearing into contrived shapes that increase maintenance costs and shorten the life of the plant.

"Remember that pruning is a dwarfing process, because it removes food producing leaves. Pruning is also a wounding process, allowing dessication of the plant and openings to insects and disease."

- Do not shear back shrubs.
- Do not cut back cold-damaged branches until new growth emerges.
- Use thinning cuts to reduce size.
- Remove shrubs that are too big for the area and replace with more appropriate plants.

Make sure that your landscape maintenance contractor is knowledgeable about pruning. You may want to consider hiring a Certified Arborist under a separate contract for your tree care.

For further information on Xeriscape, appropriate plant materials, proper irrigation, and water management, contact your city water conservation office or read some of the publications listed below. The "Low Water Using Plant List" for the Phoenix Active Management Area is in the Appendix. Updated versions and an extensive bibliography are available from the Arizona Department of Water Resources and on its website, http://water.az.gov.

Kitchen and Cafeteria Water Uses

Many facilities have kitchens and cafeterias. Most of these kitchens are equipped with dishwashing machines, garbage disposers and ice makers. These typically are the major water-using items in kitchens.

Dishwashers

Commercial spray-type dishwashers are designed to clean dishes, flatware and glassware by washing with detergent and water and to sanitise the dishes by the application of hot water or chemical solutions. There are several types of commercial dishwashers for different volumes of dishes and utensils to be cleaned. In a stationary rack machine, dishes are loaded into a rack that fits inside the machine; complete wash and rinse cycles average from 1 to 3 minutes. In a conveyor-type machine, dishes are loaded onto a conveyor belt that travels through the machine. The final dishwashing rinse is accomplished with either hot fresh water or with a chemical sanitising agent that is mixed with water. Dishwashing machines that use chemical sanitising agents for the final rinse use approximately the same amount of water as machines using only hot water for the final rinse.

Water Use Requirements. Minimum wash and rinse requirements for dishwashers are established by the National Sanitation Foundation (NSF). Typical water use requirements are 4.5 to 6.0 gallons per cycle of wash and rinse for stationary rack machines using water for the final rinse and 2 to 6 gallons per cycle for conveyor-type machines. Commercial dishwashing machines typically re-use the final rinse water in wash steps for the succeeding racks of dishes.

Water Conservation Opportunities. The way in which a dishwasher is operated affects its water efficiency. Higher efficiency can be achieved by operating the equipment properly, washing full loads and limiting water flow rates to those specified by the manufacturer. Pressure and flow regulators are available to maintain the desired flow during periods of high water supply pressure.

- Check your dishwasher to be sure that it is not using an excessive flow of water. Experiment with a modest reduction (about ten percent) in the flow rate of water to your dishwasher to see if any problem result. If no problem occur, continue to operate at the reduced flow rate. Consult with the equipment manufacturer or your service contractor before making major changes.
- Re-use waste-water from your dishwasher for a low-grade purpose such as prewashing and garbage disposers. Final rinse water may be reused in the following wash cycle.
- Be sure that the flow of water through the dishwasher stops when the flow of items being washed stops. Conveyor-type dishwashers should be equipped with an automatic shutdown device to deactivate the rinse water when dishes are not passing through the system.
- Reduce or eliminate the amount of fresh water used for prewashing before the dishwasher.

Garbage Disposers

Commercial garbage disposers grind solid wastes into small particles so that they can be disposed of and conveyed through a sewer system. The ground garbage is passed into a mixing chamber, where it is mixed with water for disposal. In larger systems, the garbage disposer is often preceded by a scrapping and preflushing system that uses water to carry garbage to the disposer. For some larger systems, a conveyor can be used instead of a scrapper to transport waste to the disposer using less water.

Water Use. Typical water consumption rates for various garbage disposers combined with scrapers or conveyors equipment are as follows:

Equipment	*Typical flow rate, gallons per minute (gpm)*
Disposer	4 to 8
Scrapper/disposer	7
Conveyor/disposer	10

Water Conservation Opportunities. Because it is not necessary to dispose of food wastes to a sewer, the use of garbage disposers could be eliminated entirely. In fact, some facilities do not use garbage disposers because they frequently require repair or replacement. Consider eliminating garbage disposers and disposing of wastes by other means.

Garbage Strainers. One method of eliminating garbage disposers is installation of a garbage strainer. A strainer-type waste collector passes a recirculating stream of water over food waste held in a basket, reducing the waste volume by as much as 40 per cent by washing soluble materials and small particles to the sewer. The holding basket is periodically emptied. The water consumption rate for these units is approximately 2 gpm, considerably less than the 5 to 8 gpm requirement of garbage disposers. This water could be provided by wastewater from the dishwasher, eliminating any additional fresh water consumption by the strainer

If use of the disposer is deemed necessary, there are still opportunities for conservation.

- Use waste-water from other kitchen operations (such as the dishwasher) for garbage disposer and trash trough flushing.
- Be sure that the flow of water through the garbage disposer stops, when the disposer motor stops.
- Many disposers have two water supply lines, one to the bowl and one to the grinding chamber. Be sure to check both.

3 Experiment by gradually reducing the flow rate of water through the disposer. If no problem arise, continue to operate at the reduced flow rate.

Ice-Making Machines

Ice-Making Equipment. Ice-making equipment can be divided into two different groups: ice cube machines and ice flake machines. The methods used to produce ice cubes and flaked ice are different. Descriptions of the machines and their use of water are presented below.

Ice Cube Machines. Ice cube making usually is a batch process. The goal of ice cube machines is to produce clear ice cubes. Cloudy ice cubes can be caused by minerals or other substances frozen in the ice. Most ice cube machines are designed to wash the frozen surface of the cube as it forms. The dissolved contaminants are more soluble in the slightly warmer run-off water (which does not freeze) and are therefore carried off by the run-off water. The frozen water in cube ice, therefore, typically is purer than the source water.

Ice Flake Machines. Flake ice production is a continuous process, operated with less concern for the quality of the ice. The flakes are thin, randomly shaped and mostly white or cloudy. Flake ice is typically produced on a rotating evaporation drum. Ice is broken off the drum by an ice cutter and scraped to produce the flakes.

Uses of Water. There are uses of water in ice-making machines other than the water that is frozen as ice. As noted above, in cube ice makers, where the frozen water quality is important, a continuous water bleed-off is used to remove dissolved contaminants. In batch processes a batch dump may be used instead. According to information from manufacturers of cube ice-making equipment, approximately 20 to 25 gallons of water is required to produce 100 pounds of clear ice cubes. Because 100 pounds of ice is equal to approximately 12 gallons of water, it is evident that approximately half of the water used to produce ice is not frozen, but is drained from the ice cube maker. There also is wide variation in the amount of water required for ice production because of the different ways that cube ice can be made. Some manufacturers require upto 90 gallons of water to produce 100 pounds of cube ice.

Water is also used by some ice makers to cool the refrigeration condenser. Other condenser cooling options are air cooling, cooling by the plant's chilled water system or remote air-cooled condensers. Water-cooled ice makers are popular because they are less expensive than remote-cooled units and do not generate heat in the kitchen, as air-cooled units do.

Water-cooled ice makers also generally use slightly less electricity than the other two types. Most water-cooled ice makers do not recirculate the cooling water. For typical ice makers, ranging in capacity from 400 to 1,200 pounds of ice per day, approximately 130 to 180 gallons of cooling water are required for per 100 pounds of ice produced.

Water Conservation Opportunities. There are two sources of water consumption for ice makers: the ice-making process itself and the cooling of the refrigerant condenser (for water-cooled models).

* **Ice-Making Water.** Conservation potential for water used in ice making depends on the bleed rate. Ice makers that produce ice flakes generally use the potable water source with no bleed-off. Ice cube makers have a large variation in the amount of water bled off per unit of ice produced. Some units recirculate the

water until it is frozen, with a set bleed rate. Other units use once-through water flow. Pretreatment of the ice-making water to remove hardness could be used as a way to reduce water consumption without sacrificing the quality of the ice.

Condenser Water. Most water-cooled ice makers use cooling water on a once-through basis. Possible conservation technologies and practices for once-through cooling water are discussed in the once-through cooling section of this report. Another water-conserving option is replacement of water-cooled units with air-cooled ones. These units require slightly more electricity for operation and do not produce as much ice as water-cooled units. Requiring the installation of only air-cooled ice makers in new facilities is technologically and economically feasible. Under some conditions, ice makers often have a useful life of only about five years. This implies that replacement of existing water-cooled ice makers with air-cooled models is also feasible and could be done when the water-cooled units require replacement.

Eliminate the use of once-through ("single-pass") cooling of ice-making machines. Consider replacing water-cooled units with air-cooled models or supply cooling water for the ice maker from the plant's recirculating chilled water system. Otherwise, re-use the cooling water for some other purpose such as landscape watering.

Other Kitchen Uses

Additional kitchen water uses can include food preparation, thawing frozen food, rinsing vegetables, steam tables and leaking faucets.

* Repair leaks in steam, hot water and cold water lines.
* Do not thaw frozen foods with a running stream of water unless absolutely necessary; plan ahead and thaw in a refrigerator. If water-thawing is necessary, a running stream of water should be used for health reasons, but use a slow flow.

Laundry Water uses

Some facilities operate large laundry operations for linens, uniforms and other washable items. Water conservation for laundries can involve simple options using existing equipment or more sophisticated approaches requiring new or additional equipments. The easiest, operational-oriented conservation approach is to consistently load the washing equipment to its maximum capacity.

Water reclamation equipment may be added and used in conjunction with existing equipment. Although water reclamation equipment is now commercially available for laundries, most laundries in Arizona have not installed it. If new or replacement

Watering Schedule Guidelines

Plant Type		*Spring (Mar.-May)*	*Summer (May-Oct.)*	*Fall (Oct.-Dec.)*	*Winter (Dec.-Mar.)*	*Watering Depth*
Trees	Desert-adapted	14-30 days	7-21 days	14-30 days	30-60 days	3-4 feet
	High-water-use	7-12 days	7-10 day	7-12 days	14-30 days	3-4 feet
Shrubs	Desert-adapted	14-30 days	7-21 days	14-30 days	30-45 days	2-3 feet
	High-water-use	7-10 days	5-7 days	7-10 days	10-14 days	2-3 feet
Groundcovers	Desert-adapted	14-30 days	7-21 days	14-30 days	21-45 days	1 foot
	High-water-use	7-10 days	2-5 days	7-10 days	10-14 days	1 foot
Cacti and Succulents		21-45 days	14-30 days	21-45 days	if needed	1 foot
Annual		3-7 days	2-5 days	3-7 days	5-10 days	1 foot
Warm Season Grass	7-10 days	3-5 days	7-10 days	30- days	6-8 inches	
Cool Season Grass		3-5 days	none	3-5 days	5-10 days	8-10 inches

Guidelines for established plants (2 years for shrubs 5 years for trees). More water is required for new plantings, sandy soils, and extremely hot, dry weather. Water as deep as the root zone and 1½ times the canopy width.

washing equipment is to be purchased, the equipment now available is more water efficient than those used in the past.

Re-use Systems. Some existing laundry equipments can be set upto recycle water used in the rinse cycle into water used in subsequent wash cycles. This requires the installation of a holding tank for the rinse water. Ideally, the washing machine will have two separate drain ports; one for draining the wash water to the sewer, and one for draining the rinse water to the holding tank. Likewise, two supply ports may be used to separate the fresh water and recycle water supply. Some machines will already be equipped with the additional piping required for this approach. However, a machine which does not already have this built-in capability may be retrofitted with actuated valves on the supply and drain piping.

Reclamation Systems. Several different systems have been developed to reclaim wastewater from commercial laundries. These systems can be cost-effective due to savings in water, laundry chemicals, energy for heating and sewerage fees.

One system specifically designed to require little maintenance consists of a mixed media filter containing plastic beads, anthracite coal and silica; an activated carbon column; and an ion exchange unit. The ion exchange unit requires frequent regeneration; and the activated carbon must be replaced monthly. The system provides approximately

75 per cent re-use and is available as a packaged unit.

Another reclamation system uses settling, high-rate ultrafiltration and fixed bed carbon adsorption processes. Pretreatment with hydrated lime in dry powder form is used to assist the ultrafiltration treatment.

Additionally, a commercially available package treatment system claims savings in water costs of 70 percent; in water heating, 50 percent; in softening chemicals, 70 percent; and in alkali-chemicals, 35 per cent. The system is patented and includes dissolved air flotation (DAF), flow equalisation, filtration (macro and micro) and flocculation.

These systems can include one or more of various treatment processes including filters, ion exchanges, settling tanks, ultrafiltration and dissolved air flotation.

Continuous-Batch Washers. The continuous-batch wisher or "tunnel" washer, has been in use for a number of years in Europe and is now being installed in many large U.S. laundries. The conventional washer-extractor found at most laundries has a chamber which is filled and emptied each time a new step in the wash cycle begins. In contrast, a continuous-batch washer has one or more modules for each process step and the laundry items pass automatically from one module to the next. Significant water conservation is achieved by these tunnel washers due to the use of counter-current flows. Properly operated installations can save 60 to 70 percent of the volume of water and steam required by washer-extractors. Additional benefits include energy savings due to recovery of heat from the laundry itself during the rinse cycles, savings in labour costs because the process is automated, and reduced maintenance costs. Chemical usage can also be reduced in some cases. Disadvantages of continuous-batch machines include the need to carefully schedule loads to minimise the need for resetting of equipment controls.

Additional Water-Conserving Ideas for Laundry Water Users

- Be sure to launder full loads only.
- Work with your laundry chemical supplier to reduce water consumption. Inform your chemical soupier supplier water conservation is a priority in you laundry operations.
- Consider recycling rinse water for use in wash cycle.
- Investigate laundry water reclamation systems for applicability to your facility.
- Consider the use of continuous-batch washers for new laundries or major expansions of existing laundry operations.

X-ray and Photo processing

Many facilities utilise X-ray or photo processing equipments. Processing is done using automated equipment. Water-conserving technologies related to X-ray processing have been researched and developed due in part to regulatory requirements pertaining to silver in waste water discharges. Water savings may realised through modifications in operation and equipment and use of reclamation and recovery systems.

X-ray processing is a series of complex chemical transformations. In general, these processes must develop, stop, fix, harden, wash, bleach and dry the film. Some of these steps are repeated, omitted or combined in the various specific types of processing that are performed. Automatic processing equipment contains tanks and dryers which operate in series to provide the necessary process steps. A transport system is responsible for moving the film from one tank to the next.

Most modern automatic processing equipment has solenoid valves which open to feed water for wash purposes only when film is being processed. This is a water-saving feature, but these valves must be properly maintained to perform as designed. Regulating valves are also available to limit the flow rate of the wash water to a set quantity. The most advanced machines offer automatic control of flows, chemicals and other process variables which are adjusted as the equipment monitors the product passing through the processing sequence. This type of control may provide the highest quality product for the least water consumption.

Proper Operation. The first step for water conservation in X-ray processing operations is to ensure that the facilities and equipment in place are being operated as water-efficiently as possible. Many hospitals have the flow rates through X-ray film processors set higher than necessary. In many cases, a flow rates of 2 gallons per minute (gpm) or less is sufficient for effective processing, but the actual rates being used are 3 to 4 gpm or even higher. This can be corrected by simply adjusting a valve to reduce the flow rate to the minimum rate that still provides for quality processing results. One approach to this would be to install an inexpensive flow rate meter on the water line feeding each processor. This would enable staff to verify that the appropriate flow rate of rinse water is being received by the processor.

Squeegees. One water saving feature available is the squeegee. This device physically removes the liquid from the product surface as it travels from one tank to the next. This serves to reduce carryover of processing solutions and thus wash water requirements. The degree of carryover reduction depends on squeegee type, product area and the speed with which the product travels through the machine. Carryover reduction due to squeegee typically ranges upto 95 per cent.

REFERENCES

Arizona Municipal Water Users Association (AMWUA). *Converting to Xeriscape: Renovate Your Landscape with Style*. Phoenix, AZ: AMWUA, 1997, 16 pp.

AMWUA, *Xeriscape Gardens: Plants for the Desert Southwest*. Phoenix AZ: AMWUA, 1998, 32 pp.

AMWUA, *Xeriscape: A New Look for Arizona Gardens*. Phoenix, AZ: AMWUA. 1997, 16 pp.

AMWUA, *Visions of Xeriscape*, Phoenix, AZ: AMWUA, 1997, 24 pp.

Brookbank, George, *Desert Landscaping*. Tucson, AZ: University of Arizona Press, 1992, 253 pp.

Duffield, M. and Warren D. Jones. *Plants for Dry Climates*. 2nd Edition. Tucson, AZ: H.P. Books, 1992, 192 pp.

Johnson, Eric A. *Pruning, Planting and Care*. Tucson, AZ: Ironwood Press, 1997, 160 pp.

Johnson, Eric A. and Scott Millard. *The Low-Water Flower Gardener*. Tucson, AZ: Ironwood Press. 1993. 144 pp.

McPherson, E. Gregory and Charles Sacamano. *Southwestern Landscaping that Saves Energy and Water*. Tucson. AZ: College of Agriculture, University of Arizona. 1989, 64 pp.

McPherson, E. Gregory and Gary C. Woodard. "Cooling the Urban Heat Island with Water-and-Energy Efficient Landscapes" in *Arizona Review*. Tucson, AZ: College of Business and Public Administration, University of Arizona. Spring 1990.

Mielke, Judy, *Native Plants for Southwestern Landscapes*. Austin, TX: University of Texas Press, 1993, 310 pp.

Miller, George O. *Landscaping with Native Plants of Texas and the Southwest*. Still Water, MN: Voyageur Press, 1991, 128 pp.

Perty, Robert. *Landscape Plants for Western Regions*. Claremont, CA: Land Design Publishing Co. 1992, 318 pp.

Phillips, Judith, *Southwestern Landscaping with Native Plants*, Santa Fe, NM: Museum of New Mexico Press. 1987, 140 pp.

Shuler, Carol. *Low Water Use Plants for California and the Southwest*. Tucson, AZ: Fisher Books, 1993, 138 pp.

Sunset Magazine and Books. *Waterwise Gardening*. Menlo Park, CA: Lane Publishing, 1995, 624 pp.

Sunset Magazine and Books. *Sunset Western Garden Book*. 6th Edition. Menlo Park, CA: Lane Publishing Co. 1995, 624 pp.

Sunset Magazine and Books. *Sunset Western Landscaping*. Menlo Park, CA: Sunset Books, Inc. 1997, 416 pp.

8

PUBLIC PARTICIPATION IN WATER MANAGEMENT

Public participation involves the rights of persons to take part in decision-making that affects them and gives concrete benefits to decision-making. It does so through the guarantee of rights on access to information, public participation in decision-making and access to justice in environmental matters. This improves decision-making through greater information and enhances respect for decisions and assists in the development of democracy, civil society and the rule of law. Public participation contributes to the endeavours of public authorities to protect the environment, to learn about the concerns of the public, including the various users of the water resources and to take due account of such concerns. Public participation in the field of water management should lead to an improvement in the quality and implementation of, and commitment to decisions, as well as increased accountability, transparency and public awareness of water management issues. This in turn will help to achieve water management goals and improve the environment. Principle 10 of the Rio Declaration on Environment and Development (United Nations Conference on Environment and Development, Rio de Janeiro, 1992) emphasises that environmental issues are best handled with the participation of all concerned citizens, at the relevant level.

Other widely recognised international policy documents emphasise the need for an adequate role of the public, including non-governmental organisations (NGOs), in environmental and water management. Examples are the Dublin Statement on Water and Sustainable Development (International Conference on Water and the environment, Dublin, 1992), Agenda 21 (United Nations Conference on Environment and Development, Rio de Janeiro, 1992), the Noordwijk Political Statement and Action Plan (Ministerial Conference on Drinking-Water and Environmental Sanitation, Noordwijk, 1994) and the Guidelines on Access to Environ-mental Information and Public

Participation in Environmental Decision-Making (Environment for Europe Conference, Sofia, 1995).

In the pan-European region, there are a number of international legal documents which are important for public participation in water management. The Convention on Access to Information, Public Participation in Decision-Making and Access to Justice in Environmental Matters (Aarhus, 25 June 1998; Aarhus Convention) guarantees the rights of access to information, public participation in decision-making and access to justice in environmental mattes. The Convention on the Protection and Use of Transboundary Watercourses and International Lakes (Helsinki, 17 March 1992; UN/ ECE Water Convention) and the Protocol on Water and Health to the 1992 Convention on the Protection and Use of Transboundary Watercourses and International Lakes (London, 17 June 1999; Protocol on Water and Health) form a legal framework for the pan-European region in the field of water management and the protection of human health and safety. The UN/ECE Water Convention covers, among other things, public information, while the Protocol stipulates broader rights on public information and public participation. In addition, the Convention on Environmental Impact Assessment in a Transboundary Context (Espoo, 25 February 1991; Espoo Convention) and the Convention on the Transboundary Effects of Industrial Accidents (Helsinki, 17 March 1992) are relevant for the management of transboundary watercourses and international lakes in the pan-European region as both Conventions include provisions on public information and public participation.

As concerns transboundary waters, article 3, paragraph 7 of the Aarhus Convention is relevant which provides that each Party shall promote the application of the principles of this Convention in international environmental decision-making processes and within the framework of international organisations in matters relating to the environment. In addition, article 6, paragraph 5(b), of the Protocol on Water and Health is relevant. It stipulates that in the development of water management plans - including plans to be drawn up in a transboundry context- the Parties to the Protocol shall make appropriate practical and/or other provisions for public participation, within a transparent and fair framework and shall ensure that due account is taken of the outcome of the public participation.

Furthermore, the Espoo Convention provides that the Party of origin shall provide [Y] an opportunity to the public in the areas likely to be affected to participate in relevant environmental impact assessment procedures regard-ing proposed activities and shall ensure that the opportunity provided to the public of the affected party is equivalent to that provided to the public of the Party of origin (article 2, paragraph 6). It also provides that the concerned Parties shall ensure that the public of the affected Party in the areas likely to be affected be informed of and be provided with possibilities for making comments or objections on the proposed activity and for the transmittal of these comments or objections to the competent authority of the Party of origin, either directly to this authority or, where appropriate, through the Party of origin (article 3, paragraph 1 (8)).

It follows from the above, that these draft guidelines are intended to assist Governments and joint bodies throughout the world in developing and implementing procedures to enhance public participation in water management. They are particularly intended to assist Governments and joint bodies in the UN/ECE region. The draft guidelines draw on the experience of experts from Governments, joint bodies and NGOs from the pan-European region.

General Recommendations

Public participation in the field of water management should take place in a manner that takes full account of the rights and responsibilities of the public and the public authorities.

At the national level, States are encouraged to guarantee legal rights for the public on access to information, public participation indecision-making and access to justice in environmental matters, so that the public may enjoy these rights during decision-making processes relating to water management. For that purpose, States should adapt their national legal systems, as necessary.

Public Participation in Water Management in England and Wales

The Environment Agency is producing 131 Local Environment Agency Plans (LEAPs) covering all river catchments in England and Wales. LEAPs are five year plans of action for improvements to local environments by the Agency and other organisations working in partnership.

LEAPs take an integrated approach to local environmental issues, managing on a whole catchment basis. Public participation and the building of local consensus for action is seen as a prime advantage of the LEAPs process. The agency aims to produce a Consultation Draft LEAP in partnership with key stakeholders such as local authorities, industry and environmental NGOs. These stakeholders may be directly involved in the process of drafting the plan or may have an oversight role through their membership of Area Environment Groups which are local advisory bodies established by the Agency.

The Consultation Draft Plan is then published for public consultation. It is sent to all local organisations with significant environmental interests and is available to the general public on request. Ample time is given for representations and at the end of the consultation period, the Agency publishes a report on consultation, indicating the views received and the Agency's response. The Agency then publishes the adopted LEAP for the river catchment. The LEAP is reviewed each year by the

Agency in consultation with the local Area Environment Group and an Annual Review Report is published. Initiatives aimed at promoting public participation in LEAPs include use of the Internet and CDs for publishing, use of focus groups to prioritise local issues and consultation on local authority boundary basis.

At the international level, States should further cooperate, as appropriate, with a view to adapting international instruments accordingly.

It is important that the public has access, at an early stage, to all relevant information and that the public becomes involved in decision-making on water management as early as possible, while all options are still open, in order to provide for effective public participation.

Access to information is a prerequisite for public participation. States and joint bodies are encouraged to ensure that access to information on transboundary water management and other environmental information is provided to all members of the public, within and beyond international borders, without having to state an interest.

To provide for effective access to information, it is important that States guarantee the right to information through adequate legislation. States are encouraged to provide that public authorities should make information available to the public.

Public participation is important for the protection and sustainable use of catchment areas. It may contribute to resolving problems of water pollution and problems of water sharing and distribution among riparian States and interested sectors of water use.

Public participation is important for the protection and sustainable use of catchment areas. It may contribute to resolving problems of water pollution and problems of water sharing and distribution among riparian States and interested sectors of water use.

When taking decisions regarding water management, States should ensure that the outcomes of public participation are properly taken into account by public authorities and joint bodies.

Aral Sea Basin

The water sector plays a vital role in the region and the professional level of the mangers and decision makers within the sector was very high. After the collapse of the Soviet Union, lack of qualified staff was among the reasons for environmental detoriation. To increase human resources, especially at the level of policy making in the water sector, public awareness campaigns and NGO involvement have a crucial role.

The principal institutions which are in charge of water resources management and development in the Aral Sea Basin are the Ministries of Agriculture and Water-Resources in all five countries (Kazakhstan, Kyrgyzstan, Tadjikistan, Turkmenistan, Uzbekistan). Real-time water management is predominantly concerned with managing supplies to meet allocation objectives at different levels of water management. Common to such activities are issues related to water conservation, allocation of water under scarcity conditions and other techniques to ensure that water demands are managed to correspond to water availability. Implementing agencies never were accountable to the public for their activities. In most cases, the public was hardly involved. The growing importance of public opinion and NGO activities have only been recognised in the past 5-7 years.

In 1998, the International Fund for Saving the Aral Sea initiated the project A Water Resources and Environmental Management in the Aral Sea Basin supported by GEF and World Bank. The central element of this project is the public awareness component. Its objective is to educate the public to conserve water. There will be two steps. First, education of decision-makers who are still ignoring public opinion about water resources management and development. At the second stage, governmental institutions and implementing agencies should provide public access to information about policies and strategies.

The Pan-European Region

The secretariat of the UN/ECE Water Convention should play an important role in the dissemination of information and relevant agreements about rivers and lakes in the pan-European region. For that purpose, use should be made of electronic means of information dissemination.

The Context of Transboundary Waters

If not specifically stated, the following recommendations are addressed to riparian States bordering the same transboundary waters.

Access to Information

Where the public interest is served by the disclosure of information contained in working documents (documents in the course of completion) and comments thereon, riparian States and joint bodies should consider granting the public access to these documents.

Riparian States and joint bodies are encouraged to publish specific information or documents on transboundary waters. The following information should be actively disseminated:

(a) Treaties, protocols and rules of procedure;

(b) Plans and programmes.

NGOs as Observers in the Meuse Commission

In the Walloon region in Belgium, the river Meuse was long time considered as a shipping route and as a channel for municipal and industrial waste waters. Being an industrial area in decline, the Walloon region considered investments in waste-water treatment a waste of money, as the profits of such investments would largely end up downstream in the Netherlands, which for 25 years tried unsuccessfully to establish cooperation to clean the river Meuse.

After the adoption of the UN/ECE Water Convention, the Walloon delegation agreed to create an International Commission for the Protection of the Meuse (ICPM), but expressed its disagreement with the proposals to lay down precise waste-water treatment targets within the Agreement on the Protection of the Meuse Convention, signed on 26th April 1994, by France, the Netherlands, the Brussel's Capital Region and the Walloon Region. The development of and agreement on, such targets was seen by the Walloon delegation a task of the ICPM. NGOs in the Netherlands threatened Walloon=s industry with liability suits and took samples close to industrial sewage outlets in the Walloon region. On these grounds, the Walloon delegation nearly withdrew from the negotiation table. Even after the adoption of the Meuse Convention, the Walloon region=s disagreement on the involvement of NGOs in plenary meetings of the ICPM remained - still considering the taking of water samples an illegal action of NGOs.

In the meantime, the Walloon region has developed a large-scale waste-water treatment programme. Moreover, another commission - the International Commission on the Protection of the Rhine - agreed on the observer status of NGOs. Thus, Walloon agreed to request one ICPM member to make a comparative assessment of different options for involving NGOs in ICPM=s work. This assessment contained five options: NGO participation at preparatory meetings of delegations, consultation of NGOs by ICPM prior to its meetings, NGOs participation at ICPM meetings as members of a delegation, NGOs participation at ICPM meetings as observers, NGOs participation at ICPM meetings as full members.

In the meantime, the Walloon region had developed a large-scale waste-water treatment programme. Moreover, another Commission—the International Commission on the Protection of the Rhine - agreed on the observer status of NGOs. Thus, Walloon agreet to request one ICP Mmember to make a comparative assessment of different options for involving NGOs in ICPM=s work. This assessment contained five options: NGOs participation at preparatory meetings of delegations, consultation of NGOs by ICPM prior to its meetings, NGOs participation at ICPM meetings as members of a delegation, NGOs participation at ICPM meetings as observers, NGOs participation at ICPM meetings as full members.

These options were assessed as to their transparency, advantages and disadvantages. The result was that the fourth option - observer status for NGOs - was considered to be preferable; it was also stressed that such NGOs should have an international character.

Its till took a number of meetings of the ICPM, but finally a Ministerial meeting agreed that NGOs can participate as observers in meetings of the ICPM.

Riparian States and joint bodies should grant access to the following information covering a wide spectrum;

(a) Conditions of the transboundary waters and results of monitoring there of including floods and ice drifts, as well as transboundary impact;

(b) Measures taken to prevent, control or reduce transboundary impact, including water saving measures and assessment of the effectiveness of the measures;

(d) Measures taken in the field of water-quantity management, including flood management and the effectiveness of those measures;

(e) Water-quality objectives, and results of checking compliance with the water-quality objectives;

(f) Permits issued and the conditions to be met;

(g) Results of water effluent sampling;

(h) Results of checking compliance with permit conditions;

(i) Drafts of plans and programmes, including comments by NGOs;

(j) Lay-persons-guides to these documents.

Lake Peipsi

The border in the Lake Peipsi area between Estonia and the Russian Federation was established in 1991. It became necessary to formulate an international legal framework for joint management of transboundary waters.

Created in 1993, NGO Lake Peipsi Project (LPP) promoted communication and information exchange across the border. At that time, the legal basis for cooperation was still under negotiation. LPP organised meetings that gave an opportunity to Estonian and Russian environmental experts to meet informally and to discuss their future cooperation.

As a part of an environmental monitoring project supported by the Swedish

Environmental Protection Agency, LPP has set up an Internet server, developed the Lake Peipsi's regional web site and established an e-mail network that jointed officials and NGOs involved in water protection of Lake Peipsi.

LPP submitted its proposals for the text of an Estonian and Russian draft agreement on management of transboundary waters shared between both countries aimed at promoting public participation as well as participation of NGOs and local authorities in the protection of Estonian and Russian transboundary waters. Most of these proposals were incorporated into the text of the agreement signed by the Estonian and Russian Governments in 1997. The agreement established a Joint Commission on Transboundary Waters. Both Estonian and Russian State officials stressed the importance of developing cooperation between the two countries on intergovernmental as well as local levels. The Commission established a working group on cooperation with NGOs, local governments and international organisations, that incorporated also representatives of NGOs and local governments.

In 1998, the Centre for Transboundary Cooperation was established as an NGO umbrella organisation. In accordance with the work plan of the Estonian and Russian Transboundary Water Commission, the Centre implements the transboundary water agreement in the Lake Peipsi catchment area and involves public and local stakeholders.

Riparian States and joint bodies should consider granting access to meeting documents, including:

(a) Agendas of meetings of the joint body and its subsidiary organs, if any;

(b) Minutes of such meetings;

(c) Drafts of treaties, protocols, rules of procedure - including comments from NGOs - relevant for the area of application of the UN/ECE Water Convention or for specific transboundary waters;

(d) Other documents to be discussed.

Wherever practicable, the information should be available and effectively accessible for inspection free of charge. This could be done among others through the establishment of documentation centres, libraries, databases and web-sites of, for example, the secretariat of the joint body.

As one of the means to inform the public, electronic forms of communication should be used. This is valuable tool, especially in an international context, to make information accessible.

Baltic Sea

The Baltic Marine Environment Protection Commission (Helsinki Commission) has 31 governmental, inter-governmental and non-governmental observers. At present, the observer status has been granted to 17 non-governmental organisations which have full rights to participate in all meetings and which are provided with all meeting documents.

In 1992, the Diplomatic Conference approved a 20 years programme of action, the Joint Comprehensive Baltic Sea Environmental Action Programme (JCP). It consists of six components: policies, laws and regulations, institutional strengthening and human resources development, investment activities, management programmes for coastal lagoons and wetlands, applied research and public awareness and environmental education. The Programme Implementation Task Force (PITF) was also established to initiate, facilitate and monitor coordination of the implementation of the JCP. Seven non-governmental organisations participate in the PITF, in addition to the 14 countries of the Baltic Sea catchment area, the European Community, regional intergovernmental organisations and international financial institutions. One of those NGOs, the World Wide Fund of Nature (WWF) coordinates the implementation of the programme element "Management Programmes for Coastal Lagoons and Wetlands." Five Integrated Coastal Zone Management Plans on the Baltic Sea Coast have been finalised covering environmentally sensitive and economically valuable areas in Estonia, Germany, Latvia, Lithuania, Poland and the Russian Federation. The implementation phase now started. WWF has shown that NGOs can effectively be entrusted with the tasks of a Lead Party.

Public Participation

States and joint bodies should promote public participation in decision making on environmental matters at all levels of decision making, including the level of transboundary catchment areas. Therefore, riparian States should develop - through joint bodies - ways and means to enhance public participation at the transboundary level. This should include public participation in environmental impact assessment procedures in a transboundary context following the principles and approaches of the Espoo Convention.

Riparian States and joint bodies should provide for the participation of NGOs as non-voting participants in meetings of joint bodies. They should also consider NGO participation in meetings of subsidiary organs of joint bodies. They should encourage NGOs to organise themselves for effective participation in such meetings.

Conditions for inviting NGOs to participate as observers in meetings of a joint body and its subsidiary organs must be based on transparent and reasonable criteria, which should be clear to the public.

Riparian States and joint bodies should establish procedures so that the public can have an oversight role in the conduct of transboundary cooperation to protect and use transboundary waters and their catchment areas including the fulfilment of obligations arising from bilateral and multilateral agreements.

The development of international documents, plans and programmes for specific catchment areas should be open to public participation, including programmes for monitoring the conditions of transboundary waters.

Riparian States are encouraged to provide for public participation, including NGOs, in the preparation and development of international water agreements. NGOs could be invited to participate in intergovernmental negotiation meetings. They could be requested to comment on draft texts. Due account could be taken of such comments.

Public Participation in the Process of Implementing the 1992 Bucharest Convention on the Protection of the Black Sea against Pollution.

The following steps were taken to implement the Convention=s provision:

(a) Black Sea NGOs Forum established in the framework of the Black Sea Environmental Programme (BSEP);

(b) Analysis and involvement of active NGOs in forum events like the International Black Sea Day, Info-bus campaigns, seminars, environmental lessons, public debates on the environment, beach clean-ups and tree-planting in all the Black Sea Countries;

(c) Introduction of legislative measures to guarantee public participation in the decision-making process for the Black Sea region;

(d) Establishment of Black Sea Environment Information, Education and Resource Centres in Bulgaria and Romania;

(e) GEF/NGO Small Grants Programme for better environmental management;

(f) Organisation of Black Sea country's national NGO-Forums;

(g) Establishment of the Black Sea NGOs Network;

(h) Training in public participation and organisational management for Black Sea NGOs;

(i) Public information in the Black Sea region through newsletters, leaflets, seminars, exhibitions and libraries.

Joint bodies should open up their work for the public, including NGOs, so that the public and the joint bodies can work as partners in decision making and implementation.

Therefore, the joint bodies should have the opportunity to receive and consider information from the public. To this end, the secretariat of a joint body should play a crucial role in receiving and handling information and transmitting it to the plenary or an appropriate subsidiary organ of the joint body. In addition, the public should be given the opportunity to submit inquiries in writing to the joint body, in order to oversee the work of the joint body and to establish an open dialogue.

Joint bodies - or riparian States jointly - should develop a public communication strategy and establish a focal point for liaison with non-governmental entities regarding specific transboundary catchment areas. Such a communication strategy should include the access to information systems, allow to compare data from different riparian countries and pay attention to multimedia use.

Riparian States should jointly provide for public participation in the preparation and implementation of decisions on the protection and use of their transboundary waters, particularly on such issues as:

(a) Development of harmonised policies, programmes and strategies covering the relevant catchment areas;

(b) Measures to prevent, control and reduce transboundary impact, including water saving measures;

(c) Ecological rehabilitation projects;

(d) Water-quantity management;

(e) Flood protection;

(f) Policies to reduce inputs of nutrients and hazardous substances from industrial and municipal sources;

(g) Policies to reduce inputs of nutrients and hazardous substances from non-point sources, including those in agriculture;

(h) Emission standards for discharges from point sources into surface waters;

(i) Developing water-quality objectives;

(j) Environmental impact assessment and other means of assessment;

(k) Specific measures to prevent the pollution of groundwaters;

(l) Licensing of waste-water discharges and monitoring and control of authorised discharges;

(m) Contingency planning.

Riparian States and joint bodies should consider the role which the public should have in the process of monitoring compliance with obligations under international water agree-ments.

The National Context

In as far as Governments have not yet ratified, accepted, approved or acceded to the Aarhus Convention, the following is recommended:

Access to Information

To provide for effective access to information, it is important that States guarantee the right to information through adequate legislation. States should ensure that public authorities make information available to the public. Thus, all information relevant to the protection and sustainable use of waters and other environmental information, should be made available to the public, unless it falls within a finite list of exempt categories.

As far as national legislation contains restrictions on access to environmental information, such exemptions should be clearly defined and construed narrowly, taking into account the public interest served by the disclosure and taking into account whether the information relates to emissions into the environment.

It is important that States guarantee the right of any natural or legal person to request information on water management issues without having to show an interest and on a non-discriminatory basis. A request for information on water management issues should not be refused.

The public should be actively informed on specific occasions, such as (threat of) flooding, water pollution due to accidents, water scarcity, groundwater depletion, if there is a danger to human health and safety.

Environmental impact assessment is an important tool to be considered in the management of catchment areas. Adequate procedures for public information and public participation should be drawn up.

Public Participation in Water Management: A Challenge for Armenia

There are no special laws or regulations on public participation in water management in the system of the Armenian Legislation. However, in existing laws there are some provisions regarding public participation. These provisions include article 11 of the fundamentals or Armenian Legislation on Nature Protection (1991) and articles 6, 8 and 10 of the Armenian Law on Environmental Impact Expertise (1995). These articles acknowledge the right of the public to participate in decision making, but they do not contain implementation mechanisms.

Regretfully, there is no much public participation in hearings on activities to be carried out, through the law On Environmental impact Expertise calls for it. A procedure, adopted by the Government, on how to conduct public hearings is still missing. This means that environmental decision-making is still performed without publicparticipation.

Public participation is the more important as catchment areas - especially the catchment area of Lake Sevan which is of national importance and attracts public attention - are in bad conditions.

When informing the public, use can be made of the media, including electronic forms of communication.

Public Participation in Decision-Making

States should provide for effective public participation rights in their national legal systems.

Public participation in the preparation of plans, programmes and policies relating to water management at different levels of Government should be ensured through the national legal system.

The public should be informed about and involved in, standard setting (*e.g.*, minimum quality standards for waste water, emission standards).

The procedures for the granting of permits (*e.g.*, groundwater withdrawal, discharge of waste water) should provide for significant public information and public participation.

States should provide for public participation procedures concerning decisions on specific activities (*e.g.*, the construction of a dam) on a non-discriminatory basis.

States should consult the public, when preparing their national positions to negotiate international agreements of relevance to transboundary waters.

It is vital to inform the public about the procedures for public participation. Education and training programmes for officials involved in managing public participation procedures should be organised to promote public awareness and to teach the members of the public how to use public participation procedures.

States should carry out capacity building measures to improve public participation for water management.

Sweden

In Sweden, several forms of cooperation between stakeholders in catchment areas have been tested. The most common form of formalised cooperation is the water protection association. At present, almost 60 associations exist. The main task of a water protection association is environmental monitoring, complementing the monitoring conducted by the authorities. Some associations have shown an interest in a more profound involvement in the management of the catchment area, but the lack of formalised procedures to involve these associations seems to hinder this development.

Today, major attention is given to the proposal for a EC Directive establishing a framework for Community action in the field of water policy. Its forthcoming adoption and entry into force will drastically affect the management of catchment areas and also the involvement of stakeholders. Several projects have been initiated to study the administrative implications of this directive.

In Sweden, much attention is now given to curbing pollution from diffuse sources, such as agriculture and forestry. The traditional way of tackling pollution through the authorities that regulate work in these sectors has not always proven to be the most efficient one—as regards both the costs as well as the ways and means of combatting pollution deriving from diffuse sources. Today there is an ever increasing interest in combining regulations from the authorities and promoting specific locally adapted measures. This opens up for and encourages, new forms of cooperation between stakeholders and the participation of the public.

One recently initiated project is project Orsbaken, involving stakeholders in 13 local communities, in the area of Nykoping, south of Stockholm. Project Orsbaken aims to mobilise both the public and the authorities in the environmental work. This board cooperation is expected to give additional positive effects apart from a cleaner environment. The approach is to actively inform all stakeholders, not least the public. The idea behind the project is that all stakeholders are willing and interested in sharing the responsibility for their local environment. To succeed with this, there has to be an openness and willingness to share ideas and discuss different options. Free and open access to information as well as a broad participation in decision making processes are prerequisites.

The difficulties encountered so far may be summarised as follows: The administrative system is too complex and not adapted to the management of catchment areas; the present legislation is somehow contradictory; there are many stakeholders with conflicting interests; among the persons involved, there is a fear of change.

The project group furthermore concluded that society should seek new forms of cooperation in catchment areas. Promoting local initiatives is highly recommended to achieve quicker anymore efficient results in the environment.

Access to justice

States should guarantee the right of the public, including NGOs, to seek judicial or administrative review, to challenge the acts and commissions of public authorities and private persons in water management and the protection of waters and to invoke the right to compensation for damage caused by an unlawful act. Such legislation should include rules on liability in appropriate cases.

It is important to make the public aware of the possibilities to invoke their rights in court.

To minimise barriers to access to justice, the adoption of mechanisms on legal and financial assistance for citizens can be considered.

The capacity should be built to make the right of access to justice effective, including the training of judges and attorneys. Effective public access to justice in the field covered by these draft guidelines will contribute to improved compliance with the relevant legislation. States should ensure effective access to justice in the field covered by these draft guidelines to improve compliance with the relevant legislation.

9

IMPACT OF POPULATION GROWTH ON WATER RESOURCES

Water resources are sources of water that are useful or potentially useful to humans. Uses of water include agricultural, industrial, household, recreational and environmental activities. Virtually all of these human uses require fresh water. 97.5% of water on the Earth is salt water, leaving only 2.5% as fresh water of which over two thirds is frozen in glaciers and polar ice caps. The remaining unfrozen freshwater is mainly found as groundwater, with only a small fraction present above ground or in the air. Fresh water is a renewable resource, yet the world's supply of clean, fresh water is steadily decreasing. Water demand already exceeds supply in many parts of the world, and as world population continues to rise at an unprecedented rate, many more areas are expected to experience this imbalance in the near future. The framework for allocating water resources to water users (where such a framework exists) is known as water rights.

Water and Conflict

The only known example of an actual inter-state conflict over water took place between 2500 and 2350 BC between the Sumerian states of Lagash and Umma. Yet, despite the lack of evidence of international wars being fought over water alone, water has been the source of various conflicts throughout history. When water scarcity causes political tensions to arise, this is referred to as water stress. Water stress has led most often to conflicts at local and regional levels.

Water stress can also exacerbate conflicts and political tensions which are not directly caused by water. Gradual reductions over time in the quality and/or quantity of fresh water can add to the instability of a region by depleting the health of a population, obstructing economic development, and exacerbating larger conflicts.

Conflicts and tensions over water are most likely to arise within national borders, in the downstream areas of distressed river basins. Areas such as the lower regions of China's Yellow River or the Chao Phraya River in Thailand, for example, have already been experiencing water stress for several years. Additionally, certain arid countries which rely heavily on water for irrigation, such as China, India, Iran, and Pakistan, are particularly at risk of water-related conflicts. Political tensions, civil protest, and violence may also occur in reaction to water privatization. The Bolivian Water Wars of 2000 are a case in point.

Surface water

Surface water is water in a river, lake or fresh water wetland. Surface water is naturally replenished by precipitation and naturally lost through discharge to the oceans, evaporation, and sub-surface seepage.

Although the only natural input to any surface water system is precipitation within its watershed, the total quantity of water in that system at any given time is also dependent on many other factors. These factors include storage capacity in lakes, wetlands and artificial reservoirs, the permeability of the soil beneath these storage bodies, the runoff characteristics of the land in the watershed, the timing of the precipitation and local evaporation rates. All of these factors also affect the proportions of water lost.

Human activities can have a large impact on these factors. Humans often increase storage capacity by constructing reservoirs and decrease it by draining wetlands. Humans often increase runoff quantities and velocities by paving areas and channelizing stream flow.

The total quantity of water available at any given time is an important consideration. Some human water users have an intermittent need for water. For example, many farms require large quantities of water in the spring, and no water at all in the winter. To supply such a farm with water, a surface water system may require a large storage capacity to collect water throughout the year and release it in a short period of time. Other users have a continuous need for water, such as a power plant that requires water for cooling. To supply such a power plant with water, a surface water system only needs enough storage capacity to fill in when average stream flow is below the power plant's need.

Nevertheless, over the long term the average rate of precipitation within a watershed is the upper bound for average consumption of natural surface water from that watershed.

Natural surface water can be augmented by importing surface water from another watershed through a canal or pipeline. It can also be artificially augmented from any of the other sources listed here, however in practice the quantities are negligible. Humans can also cause surface water to be "lost" (i.e. become unusable) through pollution.

Canada is the country estimated to have the largest supply of fresh water in the world, followed by Brazil and Russia.

Sub-surface water

Sub-Surface water, or groundwater, is fresh water located in the pore space of soil and rocks. It is also water that is flowing within aquifers below the water table. Sometimes it is useful to make a distinction between sub-surface water that is closely associated with surface water and deep sub-surface water in an aquifer (sometimes called "fossil water").

Sub-surface water can be thought of in the same terms as surface water: inputs, outputs and storage. The critical difference is that due to its slow rate of turnover, sub-surface water storage is generally much larger compared to inputs than it is for surface water. This difference makes it easy for humans to use sub-surface water unsustainably for a long time without severe consequences. Nevertheless, over the long term the average rate of seepage above a sub-surface water source is the upper bound for average consumption of water from that source.

The natural input to sub-surface water is seepage from surface water. The natural outputs from sub-surface water are springs and seepage to the oceans.

If the surface water source is also subject to substantial evaporation, a sub-surface water source may become saline. This situation can occur naturally under endorheic bodies of water, or artificially under irrigated farmland. In coastal areas, human use of a sub-surface water source may cause the direction of seepage to ocean to reverse which can also cause soil salinization. Humans can also cause sub-surface water to be "lost" (i.e. become unusable) through pollution. Humans can increase the input to a sub-surface water source by building reservoirs or detention ponds.

Water in the ground are in sections called aquifers. Rain rolls down and comes into these. Normally an aquifer is near to the equilibrium in its water content. The water content of an aquifier normally depends on the grain sizes. This means that the rate of extraction may be limited by poor permiability.

Desalination

Desalination is an artificial process by which saline water (generally sea water) is converted to fresh water. The most common desalination processes are distillation and reverse osmosis. Desalination is currently expensive compared to most alternative sources of water, and only a very small fraction of total human use is satisfied by desalination. It is only economically practical for high-valued uses (such as household and industrial uses) in arid areas. The most extensive use is in the Persian Gulf.

Several schemes have been proposed to make use of icebergs as a water source, however to date this has only been done for novelty purposes. Glacier runoff is considered to be surface water.

The concept of water stress is relatively simple: According to the World Business Council for Sustainable Development, it applies to situations where there is not enough water for all uses, whether agricultural, industrial or domestic. Defining thresholds for stress in terms of available water per capita is more complex, however, entailing assumptions about water use and its efficiency. Nevertheless, it has been proposed that when annual per capita renewable freshwater availability is less than 1,700 cubic meters, countries begin to experience periodic or regular water stress. Below 1,000 cubic meters, water scarcity begins to hamper economic development and human health and well-being.

Population growth

In 2000, the world population was 6.2 billion. The UN estimates that by 2050 there will be an additional 3 billion people with most of the growth in developing countries that already suffer water stress. Thus, water demand will increase unless there are corresponding increases in water conservation and recycling of this vital resource.

Increased affluence

The rate of poverty alleviation is increasing especially within the two population giants of China and India. However, increasing affluence inevitably means more water consumption: from needing clean fresh water 24 hours a day, 7 days a week and basic sanitation service, to demanding water for gardens and car washing, to wanting jacuzzis or private swimming pools.

Expansion of business activity

Business activity ranging from industrialization to services such as tourism and entertainment continues to expand rapidly. This expansion requires increased water services including both supply and sanitation, which can lead to more pressure on water resources and natural ecosystems.

Rapid urbanization

The trend towards urbanization is accelerating. Small private wells and septic tanks that work well in low-density communities are not feasible within high-density urban areas. Urbanization requires significant investment in water infrastructure in order to deliver water to individuals and to process the concentrations of wastewater – both from individuals and from business. These polluted and contaminated waters must be treated or they pose unacceptable public health risks. In 60% of European cities with more than 100,000 people, groundwater is being used at a faster rate than it can be replenished. Even if some water remains available, it costs more and more to capture it.

Climate change

Climate change could have significant impacts on water resources around the world because of the close connections between the climate and hydrologic cycle. Rising temperatures will increase evaporation and lead to increases in precipitation, though there will be regional variations in rainfall. Overall, the global supply of freshwater will increase. Both droughts and floods may become more frequent in different regions at different times, and dramatic changes in snowfall and snowmelt are expected in mountainous areas. Higher temperatures will also affect water quality in ways that are not well understood. Possible impacts include increased eutrophication. Climate change could also mean an increase in demand for farm irrigation, garden sprinklers, and perhaps even swimming pools.

Depletion of aquifers

Due to the expanding human population, competition for water is growing such that many of the worlds major aquifers are becoming depleted. This is due both for direct human consumption as well as agricultural irrigation by groundwater. Millions of small pumps of all sizes are currently extracting groundwater throughout the world. Irrigation in dry areas such as northern China and India is supplied by groundwater, and is being extracted at an unsustainable rate. Cities that have experienced aquifer drops between 10 to 50 meters include Mexico City, Bangkok, Manila, Beijing, Madras and Shanghai.

Pollution and water protection

Water pollution is one of the main concerns of the world today. The governments of many countries have striven to find solutions to reduce this problem. Many pollutants threaten water supplies, but the most widespread, especially in underdeveloped countries, is the discharge of raw sewage into natural waters; this method of sewage disposal is the most common method in underdeveloped countries, but also is prevalent in quasi-developed countries such as China, India and Iran.

Uses of fresh water

Uses of fresh water can be categorized as consumptive and non-consumptive (sometimes called "renewable"). A use of water is consumptive if that water is not immediately available for another use. Losses to sub-surface seepage and evaporation are considered consumptive, as is water incorporated into a product (such as farm produce). Water that can be treated and returned as surface water, such as sewage, is generally considered non-consumptive if that water can be put to additional use.

Agricultural

It is estimated that 69% of world-wide water use is for irrigation, with 15-35% of irrigation withdrawals being unsustainable.

In some areas of the world irrigation is necessary to grow any crop at all, in other areas it permits more profitable crops to be grown or enhances crop yield. Various irrigation methods involve different trade-offs between crop yield, water consumption and capital cost of equipment and structures. Irrigation methods such as most furrow and overhead sprinkler irrigation are usually less expensive but also less efficient, because much of the water evaporates or runs off. More efficient irrigation methods include drip or trickle irrigation, surge irrigation, and some types of sprinkler systems where the sprinklers are operated near ground level. These types of systems, while more expensive, can minimize runoff and evaporation. Any system that is improperly managed can be wasteful. Another trade-off that is often insufficiently considered is salinization of sub-surface water.

Aquaculture is a small but growing agricultural use of water. Freshwater commercial fisheries may also be considered as agricultural uses of water, but have generally been assigned a lower priority than irrigation (see Aral Sea and Pyramid Lake).

As global populations grow, and as demand for food increases in a world with a fixed water supply, there are efforts underway to learn how to produce more food with less water, through improvements in irrigation [1] methods [2] and technologies, agricultural water management, crop types, and water monitoring.

Industrial

It is estimated that 15% of world-wide water use is industrial. Major industrial users include power plants, which use water for cooling or as a power source (i.e. hydroelectric plants), ore and oil refineries, which use water in chemical processes, and manufacturing plants, which use water as a solvent.

The portion of industrial water usage that is consumptive varies widely, but as a whole is lower than agricultural use.

Household Drinking water

It is estimated that 15% of world-wide water use is for household purposes. These include drinking water, bathing, cooking, sanitation, and gardening. Basic household water requirements have been estimated by Peter Gleick at around 50 liters per person per day, excluding water for gardens.

Recreation Whitewater rapids

Recreational water use is usually a very small but growing percentage of total water use. Recreational water use is mostly tied to reservoirs. If a reservoir is kept fuller than it would otherwise be for recreation, then the water retained could be categorized as recreational usage. Release of water from a few reservoirs is also timed to enhance whitewater boating, which also could be considered a recreational usage. Other examples are anglers, water skiers, nature enthusiasts and swimmers.

Recreational usage is usually non-consumptive. Golf courses are often targeted as using excessive amounts of water, especially in drier regions. It is, however, unclear whether recreational irrigation (which would include private gardens) has a noticeable effect on water resources. This is largely due to the unavailability of reliable data. Some governments, including the Californian Government, have labelled golf course usage as agricultural in order to deflect environmentalists' charges of wasting water. However, using the above figures as a basis, the actual statistical effect of this reassignment is close to zero.

Additionally, recreational usage may reduce the availability of water for other users at specific times and places. For example, water retained in a reservoir to allow boating in the late summer is not available to farmers during the spring planting season. Water released for whitewater rafting may not be available for hydroelectric generation during the time of peak electrical demand.

Environmental Impact

Explicit environmental water use is also a very small but growing percentage of total water use. Environmental water usage includes artificial wetlands, artificial lakes intended to create wildlife habitat, fish ladders around dams, and water releases from reservoirs timed to help fish spawn.

Like recreational usage, environmental usage is non-consumptive but may reduce the availability of water for other users at specific times and places. For example, water release from a reservoir to help fish spawn may not be available to farms upstream.

World water supply and distribution

Food and water are two basic human needs. However, global coverage figures from 2002 indicate that, of every 10 people:

- roughly 5 have a connection to a piped water supply at home (in their dwelling, plot or yard);
- 3 make use of some other sort of improved water supply, such as a protected well or public standpipe;
- 2 are unserved;
- In addition, 4 out of every 10 people live without improved sanitation.

At Earth Summit 2002 governments approved a Plan of Action to:

- Halve by 2015 the proportion of people unable to reach or afford safe drinking water. The Global Water Supply and Sanitation Assessment 2000 Report (GWSSAR) defines "Reasonable access" to water as at least 20 liters per person per day from a source within one kilometer of the user's home.
- Halve the proportion of people without access to basic sanitation. The GWSSR defines "Basic sanitation" as private or shared but not public disposal systems that separate waste from human contact.

Projected water distribution in 2025

As the picture shows, in 2025, water shortages will be more prevalent among poorer countries where resources are limited and population growth is rapid, such as the Middle East, Africa, and parts of Asia. By 2025, large urban and peri-urban areas will require new infrastructure to provide safe water and adequate sanitation. This suggests growing conflicts with agricultural water users, who currently consume the majority of the water used by humans.

Generally speaking the more developed countries of North America, Europe and

Russia will not see a serious threat to water supply by the year 2025, not only because of their relative wealth, but more importantly their populations will be better aligned with available water resources. North Africa, the Middle East, South Africa and northern China will face very severe water shortages due to physical scarcity and a condition of overpopulation relative to their carrying capacity with respect to water supply. Most of South America, Sub-Saharan Africa, Southern China and India will face water supply shortages by 2025; for these latter regions the causes of scarcity will be economic constraints to developing safe drinking water, as well as excessive population growth.

Economic considerations

Water supply and sanitation require a huge amount of capital investment in infrastructure such as pipe networks, pumping stations and water treatment works. It is estimated that OECD nations need to invest at least USD 200 billion per year to replace aging water infrastructure to guarantee supply, reduce leakage rates and protect water quality.

International attention has focused upon the needs of the developing countries. To meet the Millennium Development Goals targets of halving the proportion of the population lacking access to safe drinking water and basic sanitation by 2015, current annual investment on the order of USD 10 to USD 15 billion would need to be roughly doubled. This does not include investments required for the maintenance of existing infrastructure.

Once infrastructure is in place, operating water supply and sanitation systems entails significant ongoing costs to cover personnel, energy, chemicals, maintenance and other expenses. The sources of money to meet these capital and operational costs are essentially either user fees, public funds or some combination of the two.

But this is where the economics of water management start to become extremely complex as they intersect with social and broader economic policy. Such policy questions are beyond the scope of this article, which has concentrated on basic information about water availability and water use. They are, nevertheless, highly relevant to understanding how critical water issues will affect business and industry in terms of both risks and opportunities.

Business response

The World Business Council for Sustainable Development in its H2OScenarios engaged in a scenario building process to:

- Clarify and enhance understanding by business of the key issues and drivers of change related to water.
- Promote mutual understanding between the business community and non-business stakeholders on water management issues.
- Support effective business action as part of the solution to sustainable water management.

It concluded that

- Business cannot survive in a society that thirsts
- You don't have to be in the water business to have a water crisis.
- Business is part of the solution, and its potential is driven by its engagement.
- Growing water issues and complexity will drive up costs.

REFERENCES

1. Scientific Facts on Water: State of the Resource. GreenFacts Website. Retrieved on 2008-01-31.
2. Rasler, Karen A. and W. R. Thompson. "Contested Territory, Strategic Rivalries, and Conflict Escalation." International Studies Quarterly. 50. 1. (2006): 145-168.
3. Wolf, Aaron T. "Water and Human Security." *Journal of Contemporary Water Research and Education*. 118. (2001): 29
4. Postel, S. L. and A. T. Wolf. "Dehydrating Conflict." *Foreign Policy*. 126. (2001): 60-67.
5. http://www.worldwater.org/data.html The World's Water 2006-2007 Tables, Pacific Institute.
6. World population to reach 9.1 billion in 2050, UN projects
7. Groundwater – the processes and global significance of aquifer degradation
8. http://reports.eea.europa.eu/92-826-5409-5/en Europe's Environment: The Dobris Assessment]
9. Groundwater in Urban Development
10. WBCSD Water Facts & Trends

11. "The World's Water: The Biennial Report on Freshwater Resources" (Island Press, Washington DC)

12. WBCSD Water Facts & Trends

13. The cost of meeting the Johannesburg targets for drinking water

14. Financing Water for All

- UN World Water Development Report
- Water Resources of the United States
- International Water Resources Association
- Canadian Water Resources Association
- American Water Resources Association
- Institute for Water Resources - USACE
- Water Resource Research Center
- "Threats to water resources" by the *Environment Agency*
- Ancient Irrigation from the *University of California, Geology Department*
- Mining Water from the *University of California, Geology Department*
- Selected World Water Data
- Uses for Water...
- Future Sources of Fresh Water
- World Water Supply and Demand: 1995 to 2025 from the International Water Management Institute
- *Addressing Our Global Water Future*PDF (3.71 MiB) from the Center for Strategic and International Studies (CSIS) / Sandia National Laboratories
- Porous cities, new directions in urban water usage.
- Water and the Future of Life on Earth
- Water and Cities: Acting on the Vision
- FAO Water Portal Food and Agriculture Organization of the United Nations

10

RECYCLED WATER STRATEGY

Recycled Water Strategy

Recycled water is a valuable resource and we must find ways to harness its potential. Today we use only 20 per cent of our city's recycled water. Our aim is to increase this amount to approximately 80 per cent by 2056.

To reach this target, Council and a community-driven advisory committee are developing a ground-breaking, 50-year recycled water strategy for the city. This strategy may include piping recycled water to:

- existing suburbs and new developments for outdoor use and toilet flushing
- industry, for manufacturing and industrial uses
- farms, sports fields, parks and recreation areas for irrigation.

They are also considering purified recycled water for water supply replenishment as well as a number of recycled water storage and release options.

There are four strategies being assessed by the Recycled Water Strategy Advisory Committee at present. They have been developed as a result of over 10 months of detailed work by the Advisory Committee with assistance from the Gold Coast Water project team.

A complex multi criteria analysis will be used to assist in determining the preferred strategy. Some of the important criteria to be assessed are potable water substitution, recycled water use, security of water supply, greenhouse gas emissions and the impact on the community.

Council and the Advisory Committee are working towards preparing a draft strategy by October this year. Once this is completed, the strategy will be made available to the community to gain their feedback and input before it is finalised in early 2008.

Recycled Water

Recycled water is wastewater that has been treated according to stringent environmental and health guidelines. Rather than releasing it into the ocean, it is put to good use. Currently around 20 per cent of our wastewater is recycled, with use of recycled water increasing in recent years.

Recycled water has been an important and safe resource for the Gold Coast for over thirty five years and its use is vital to manage our precious water resource into the future.

Wastewater is water that has already been used in homes and businesses. Examples include water from showers, washing machines, kitchen sinks and toilets. Recycled water can be treated to different qualities, depending on its intended use.

What is recycled water used for?

Recycled water is currently used for a range of non-drinking purposes including:

- Irrigating agricultural crops
- Irrigating parks, gardens, golf courses and other open space areas
- Development sites for dust suppression and landscaping. The use of potable (drinking) water is banned on building sites with exceptions by absolute necessity.

Why recycle?

Gold Coast Water's objective is to manage water resources by following the hierarchy of:

1. Reduce (consumption)

2. Use/Recycle (water and recycled water)

3. Release (recycled water)

Recycling water is important because we live on the driest continent on earth and we need to reduce pressure on our precious drinking water reserves. Recycled water is a resource, not a waste.

Recycled water is not harmful to plants, which is why so many parks and golf courses use it to irrigate.

How is wastewater recycled?

Wastewater is collected from homes and businesses via the wastewater network. It is then treated at Wastewater Treatment Plants through a range of purification processes in accordance with national recycled water quality standards.

After leaving the Wastewater Treatment Plant, the recycled water is either transported to a Class A+ Recycled Water Treatment plant for further treatment or released into the ocean at the Gold Coast Seaway. All wastewater on the Gold Coast receives secondary treatment, with some wastewater receiving advanced nutrient removal and tertiary treatment.

What is a Water Efficiency Management Plan (WEMP)?

A Water Efficiency Management Plan (WEMP) is a document that is to be submitted by a business or other non-residential water user to demonstrate that water usage has been assessed and best practices for water efficiency practices have been identified for implementation.

Suspension of water restrictions

The Queensland Waster Commission has announced the temporary suspension of water restrictions on the Gold Coast commencing Saturday 9 February 2008. The suspension of water restrictions will occur until the Hinze Dam drops below 95%. Odd and even watering days do not apply.

Non-residential:

While the suspension of outdoor watering restrictions also applies to non-residential users, there is no relaxation of those business restrictions which relate to Water Efficiency Management Plans (WEMPS), installation of water efficient devices and other permanent water conservation measures.

NEW Guidelines for Sport and Recreation Clubs, Schools and Childcare Centres

The Queensland Water Commission has recently released new guidelines on the irrigation of playing surfaces used for sport and recreation activities and in schools and child care centres. These users need to register with Gold Coast Water by 30 November 2007. Find out more about Active Playing Surfaces irrigation ...

- Frequently asked questions - Active Playing Surfaces (PDF 83kb)

Who is required to submit a WEMP?

- Premises using 1ML or more per annum
- Any non-residential premise with a urinal system
- Any business with a cooling tower for air conditioning
- Specific outdoor water use categories such as active sports fields, nurseries and turf farms, fixed location car washes and outdoor public swimming pools.

WEMP Guidelines

Water Efficiency Management Plans (WEMP) Guidelines have been developed by the Queensland Water Commission and aim to help businesses better manage water use, save on water costs, improve efficiency and reduce business water consumption – by a minimum of 25% or best industry practice – in line with regionally agreed water reductions.

Further Information

Access WEMP guidelines and forms

There are 5 documents or parts to a WEMP. Refer to the below table to identify which parts apply to your business.

- WEMP Part 1A: Taps and Showers
- WEMP Part 1B: Toilets and Urinals
- WEMP Part 2: Evaporative Cooling Systems
- WEMP Part 3: Outdoor Water Use
- WEMP Part 4: Process and Other Water Use

To assist business implement these measures, the Queensland Government has allocated $40 million for the Business Water Efficiency Program (BWEP) – an incentive scheme providing financial and technical support.

SEQWater advises that due to the overwhelming response to the Business Water Efficiency Program in South East Queensland, based on the applications received to date, the program funding of $40 million is close to being allocated to water efficiency projects.

BWEP funding will continue to be allocated until the $40 million is fully committed. Once the funding has been committed, any further applications will be progressively approved only if funds become available due to previously approved applications being withdrawn or projects not being completed on time.

Council will continue to accept BWEP applications from businesses until Monday 28 January 2008. Should funds become available, these applications will be assessed as a pool against the BWEP criteria, based on the best return on investment to the State.

As advised since the program began and in line with the published BWEP guidelines, in the event that funding is fully allocated, there is no guarantee that eligible applications will receive funding.

BWEP projects must be completed by 30 April 2008. Projects with expected water savings of more than 200,000 litres a day may be granted an extension to 30 September 2008.

11

WATER PURIFICATION

Sustainable Development Portal

Water Portal

Water purification is the process of removing contaminants from a raw water source. The goal is to produce water for a specific purpose with a treatment profile designed to limit the inclusion of specific materials; most water is purified for human consumption (*drinking water*). Water purification may also be designed for a variety of other purposes, including to meet the requirements of medical, pharmacology, chemical and industrial applications. Methods include, but are not limited to: *ultraviolet light, filtration, water softening, reverse osmosis, ultrafiltration, molecular stripping, deionization, and carbon treatment.*

Water purification may remove: particulate sand; suspended particles of organic material; parasites, Giardia; Cryptosporidium; bacteria; algae; virus; fungi; etc. Minerals calcium, silica, magnesium, etc. and toxic metals (lead, copper, chromium etc). Some purification may be elective in the purification process, including smell (hydrogen sulfide remediation), taste (mineral extraction), and appearance (iron incapsulation).

Governments usually dictate the standards for drinking *water quality*. These standards will require minimum / maximum set points of contaminants and the inclusion of control elements that produce drinking water. Quality standards in many countries require specific amounts of *disinfectant* (such as *chlorine or ozone*) in the water after it leaves the water treatment plant (WTP), to reduce the risk of re-contamination while the water is in the distribution system.

It is not possible to tell whether water is safe to drink just by looking at it. Simple procedures such as *boiling* or the use of a household *activated carbon* filter are not sufficient for treating all the possible contaminants that may be present in water from an unknown source. Even natural spring water - considered safe for all practical purposes in the 1800s - must now be tested before determining what kind of treatment, if any, is needed. Chemical analysis, while expensive, is the only way to obtain the information necessary for deciding on method of purification.

Sources of drinking water

Water Supply

1. *Groundwater:* The water emerging from some deep ground water may have fallen as rain many decades, hundreds, thousands or in some cases millions of years ago. Soil and rock layers naturally filter the ground water to a high degree of clarity before it is pumped to the treatment plant. Such water may emerge as springs, artesian springs, or may be extracted from boreholes or wells. Deep ground water is generally of very high bacteriological quality (i.e., pathogenic bacteria or the pathogenic protozoa are typically absent), but the water typically is rich in dissolved solids, especially carbonates and *sulfates* of *calcium* and *magnesium*. Depending on the *strata* through which the water has flowed, other ions may also be present including *chloride,* and *bicarbonate.* There may be a requirement to reduce the *iron* or *manganese* content of this water to make it pleasant for drinking, cooking, and laundry use. *Disinfection* may also be required. Where groundwater recharge is practised, it is equivalent to lowland surface waters for treatment purposes.

2. *Upland lakes and reservoirs:* Typically located in the headwaters of river systems, upland reservoirs are usually sited above any human habitation and may be surrounded by a protective zone to restrict the opportunities for contamination. Bacteria and pathogen levels are usually low, but some bacteria, *protozoa* or *algae* will be present. Where uplands are forested or peaty, humic acids can colour the water. Many upland sources have low pH which require adjustment.

3. *Rivers, canals and low land reservoirs:* Low land surface waters will have a significant bacterial load and may also contain algae, suspended solids and a variety of dissolved constituents.

4. *Atmospheric water generation* is a new technology that can provide high quality drinking water by extracting water from the air by cooling the air and thus condensing water vapour.

5. *Rainwater harvesting* or *fog collection* which collect water from the atmosphere can be used especially in areas with significant dry seasons and in areas which experience fog even when there is little rain.

Pre-treatment

1. *Pumping and containment* - The majority of water must be pumped from its source or directed into pipes or holding tanks. To avoid adding contaminants to the water, this physical infrastructure must be made from appropriate materials and constructed so that accidental contamination does not occur.

2. *Screening* - The first step in purifying surface water is to remove large debris such as sticks, leaves, trash and other large particles which may interfere with subsequent purification steps. Most deep *groundwater* does not need screening before other purification steps.

3. *Storage* - Water from rivers may also be stored in *bankside reservoirs* for periods between a few days and many months to allow natural biological purification to take place. This is especially important if treatment is by *slow sand filters*. Storage reservoirs also provide a buffer against short periods of *drought* or to allow water supply to be maintained during transitory *pollution* incidents in the source river.

4. *Pre-conditioning* - Many waters rich in hardness salts are treated with soda-ash *(Sodium carbonate)* to precipitate *calcium carbonate* out utilising the *common ion effect*.

5. *Pre-chlorination* - In many plants the incoming water was chlorinated to minimise the growth of fouling organisms on the pipe-work and tanks. Because of the potential adverse quality effects, this has largely been discontinued.

Widely varied techniques are available to remove the fine solids, micro-organisms and some dissolved inorganic and organic materials. The choice of method will depend on the quality of the water being treated, the cost of the treatment process and the quality standards expected of the processed water.

pH adjustment

Distilled water has an average pH of 7 (neither alkaline nor acidic) and sea water has an average pH of 8.3 (slightly alkaline). If the water is acidic (lower than 7), lime or soda ash is added to raise the pH. Lime is the more common of the two additives because it is cheap, but it also adds to the resulting water hardness. Making the water slightly alkaline ensures that *coagulation* and *flocculation* processes work effectively and also helps to minimize the risk of *lead* being dissolved from lead pipes and lead *solder* in pipe fittings.

Flocculation

Flocculation is a process which clarifies the water. Clarifying means removing any turbidity or colour so that the water is clear and colourless. Clarification is done by causing a precipitate to form in the water which can be removed using simple physical methods. Initially the precipitate forms as very small particles but as the water is gently stirred, these particles stick together to form bigger particles - this process is sometimes called flocculation. Many of the small particles that were originally present in the raw water absorb onto the surface of these small precipitate particles and so get incorporated into the larger particles that coagulation produces. In this way the coagulated precipitate takes most of the suspended matter out of the water and is then filtered off, generally by passing the mixture through a coarse sand filter or sometimes through a mixture of sand and granulated anthracite (high carbon and low valoatiles coal). Coagulants or flocculating agents that may be used include:

1. Iron (III) hydroxide. This is formed by adding a solution of an iron (III) compound such as iron (III) chloride to pre-treated water with a pH of 7 or greater. Iron (III) hydroxide is extremely insoluble and forms even at a pH as low as 7. Commercial formulations of iron salts were traditionally marketed in the UK under the name *Cuprus*

2. *Aluminium hydroxide* is also widely used as the flocculating precipitate although there have been concerns about possible health impacts and mis-handling lead to a severe poisoning incident in 1988 at *Camelford* in south-west UK when the coagulant was introduced directly into the holding reservoir of final treated water.

3. Aluminium Hydroxychloride is an artificially produced polymer and is one of a class of synthetic polymers that are now widely used. These polymers have a high molecular weight and form very stable and readily removed flocs but tend to be more expensive in use compared to inorganic materials.

Sedimentation

Water exiting the flocculation basin may enter the *sedimentation basin,* also called a clarifier or settling basin. It is a large tank with slow flow, allowing floc to settle to the bottom. The sedimentation basin is best located close to the flocculation basin so the transit between does not permit settlement or floc break up. Sedimentation basins can be in the shape of a rectangle, where water flows from end to end, or circular where flow is from the centre outward. Sedimentation basin outflow is typically over a weir so only a thin top layer-furthest from the sediment-exits.The amount of floc that settles out of the water is dependent on the time the water spends in the basin and the depth of the basin. The retention time of the water must therefore be balanced against the cost of a larger basin. The minimum clarifier retention time is normally 4 hours. A deep basin will allow more floc to settle out than a shallow basin. This is because large particles settle faster than smaller ones, so large particles bump into and integrate smaller particles as they settle. In effect, large particles sweep vertically though the basin and clean out smaller particles on their way to the bottom.

As particles settle to the bottom of the basin a layer of sludge is formed on the floor of the tank. This layer of sludge must be removed and treated. The amount of sludge that is generated is significant, often 3%-5% of the total volume of water that is treated. The cost of treating and disposing of the sludge can be a significant part of the operating cost of a water treatment plant. The tank may be equipped with mechanical cleaning devices that continually clean the bottom of the tank or the tank can be taken out of service when the bottom needs to be cleaned.

Filtration

After separating most floc, the water is filtered as the final step to remove remaining suspended particles and unsettled floc. The most common type of filter is a rapid sand filter. Water moves vertically through sand which often has a layer of *activated carbon* or *anthracite coal* above the sand. The top layer removes organic compounds, which contribute to taste and odour. The space between sand particles is larger than the smallest suspended particles, so simple filtration is not enough. Most particles pass through surface layers but are trapped in pore spaces or adhere to sand particles. Effective filtration extends into the depth of the filter. This property of the filter is key to its operation; if the top layer of sand were to block all the particles, the filter would quickly clog.

To clean the filter, water is passed quickly upward through the filter, opposite the normal direction (called *backflushing* or *backwashing*) to remove embedded particles. Prior to this, compressed air may be blown up through the bottom of the filter to break up the compacted filter media to aid the backwashing process; this is known as *air scouring*. This contaminated water can be disposed of, along with the sludge from the sedimentation basin, or it can be recycled by mixing with the raw water entering the plant.

Some water treatment plants employ pressure filters. These work on the same principle as rapid gravity filters, differing in that the filter medium is enclosed in a steel vessel and the water is forced through it under pressure.

Advantages:

Filters out much smaller particles than paper and sand filters can.

Filters out virtually all particles larger than their specified pore sizes.

They are quite thin and so liquids flow through them fairly rapidly.

They are reasonably strong and so can withstand pressure differences across them of typically 2-5 atmospheres.

They can be cleaned (back flushed) and reused.

Membrane filters are widely used for filtering both drinking water and sewage (for reuse). For drinking water, membrane filters can remove virtually all particles larger than 0.2 um—including Giardia and cryptosporidium. Membrane filters are an effective form of tertiary treatment when it is desired to reuse the water for industry, for limited domestic purposes, or before discharging the water into a river that is used by towns further downstream. They are widely used in industry, particularly for beverage preparation (including bottled water). However no filtration can remove substances that are actually dissolved in the water such as phosphorus, nitrates and heavy metal ions.

Slow sand filters

Slow sand filters may be used where there is sufficient land and space as the water must be passed very slowly through the filters. These filters rely on biological treatment processes for their action rather than physical filtration. The filters are carefully constructed using graded layers of sand with the coarsest at the top and finest at the base. Drains at the base convey treated water away for disinfection. Filtration depends on the development of a thin biological layer on the surface of the filter. An effective slow sand filter may remain in service for many weeks or even months if the pre-treatment is well designed and produces water with a very low available nutrient level which physical methods of treatment rarely achieve. Very low nutrient levels allow water to be safely sent through distribution system with very low disinfectant levels thereby reducing consumer irritation over offensive levels of chlorine and chlorine by-products. Slow sand filters are not backwashed; they are maintained by having the top layer of sand scraped off when flow is eventually obstructed by biological growth.

Lava filters

Lava filters are similar to sand filters and may also only be used where there is sufficient land and space. Like sand filters, the filters rely on biological treatment processes for their action rather than physical filtration. Unlike slow sand filters however, they are constructed out of 2 layers of lava pebbles and a top layer of nutrient-free soil (only at the plants roots). On top, *water-purifying plants* (as *Iris pseudacorus* and *Sparganium erectum)* are placed. Usually, around 1/4 of the dimension of lavastone is required to purify the water and just like slow sand filters, a series of herringbone drains are placed (with lava filters these are placed at the bottom layer). [1]

Ultrafiltration

Ultrafiltration membranes are a relatively new development; they use polymer film with chemically formed microscopic pores that can be used in place of granular media to filter water effectively without coagulants. The type of membrane media determines how much pressure is needed to drive the water through and what sizes of micro-organisms can be filtered out.

Other mechanical and biological techniques

In addition to the many techniques used in large-scale water treatment, several small-scale, *less (or non)-polluting techniques* are also being used to treat polluted water. These techniques include techniques based on mechanical and biological processes. An overview:

- mechanical systems: *sand filtration,* lava filter systems and systems based on UV-radiation)
- biological systems:
- *plant systems* as *constructed wetlands* and *treatment ponds* (sometimes incorrectly called reedbeds) and *living walls*) and
- compact systems as *activated sludge systems, biorotors, aerobic* and *anaerobic biofilters, submerged aerated filters, biorolls*

In order to purify the water aduquatly, several of these systems are usually combined to work as a whole. Combination of the systems is done in 2 to 3 stages, knowingly a *primary* and a *secundary purification*. Sometimes a tertairy purification is also added.

Disinfection

Disinfection is accomplished both by filtering out harmful microbes and also by adding disinfectant chemicals in the last step in purifying drinking water. Water is disinfected to kill any *pathogens* which pass through the filters. Possible pathogens include *viruses, bacteria,* including *Escherichia coli, Campylobacter* and *Shigella,* and protozoans, including *G. lamblia* and other Cryptosporidia. In most developed countries, public water supplies are required to maintain a residual disinfecting agent throughout the distribution system, in which water may remain for days before reaching the consumer. Following the introduction of any chemical disinfecting agent, the water is usually held in temporary storage - often called a *contact tank or clear well* to allow the disinfecting action to complete.

1. *Chlorination-* The most common disinfection method is some form of *chlorine* or its compounds such as *chloramine* or *chlorine dioxide*. Chlorine is a strong oxidant that rapidly kills many harmful micro-organisms.

Because chlorine is a toxic gas, there is a danger of a release associated with its use. This problem is avoided by the use of *sodium hypochlorite,* which is a relatively inexpensive solution that releases free chlorine when dissolved in water. Chlorine solutions can be generated on site by electrolyzing common salt solutions. A solid form , calcium hypochlorite exists that releases chlorine on contact with water. Handling the solid, however, requires greater routine human contact through opening bags and pouring than the use of gas cylinders or bleach which are more easily automated. The generation of liquid sodium hypochlorite is both inexpensive and safer than the use of gas or solid chlorine. All forms of chlorine are widely used despite their respective drawbacks. One drawback is that chlorine from any source reacts with natural organic compounds in the water to form potentially harmful chemical by-products *trihalomethanes* (THMs) and *haloacetic acids* (HAAs), both of which are *carcinogenic* in large quantities and regulated by the *United States Environmental Protection Agency* (EPA). The formation of THMs and haloacetic acids may be minimized by effective removal of as many organics from the water as possible prior to chlorine addition. Although chlorine is effective in killing bacteria, it has limited effectiveness against protozoans that form cysts in water. (*Giardia lamblia* and *Cryptosporidium,* both of which are pathogenic).

2. Chlorine dioxide is another faster-acting disinfectant. It is, however, relatively rarely used, because in some circumstances it may create excessive amounts of chlorite, which is a by-product regulated to low allowable levels in the USA. Chlorine dioxide is made in water and added/used in water to avoid gas handling problems; chlorine dioxide gas accumulations may spontaneously detonate.

3. *Chloramines* are another chlorine-based disinfectant. Although chloramine is not as strong of an oxidant it does provide a longer lasting residual than free chlorine, and it not form THMs or haloacetic acids. It is possible to convert chlorine to chloramine by adding ammonia to the water after addition of chlorine: The chlorine and ammonia react to form chloramine. Water distribution systems disinfected with chloramines may experience *nitrification,* wherein ammonia is used a nutrient for bacterial growth, with nitrates being generated as a byproduct.

4. *Ozone* (O_3) is a relatively unstable molecule "free radical" of oxygen which readily gives up one atom of oxygen providing a powerful oxidising agent which is toxic to most water borne organisms. It is a very strong, broad spectrum disinfectant that is widely used in Europe. It is an effective method to inactivate harmful protozoans that form cysts. It also works well against almost all other pathogens. Ozone is made by passing oxygen through ultra-violet light or a "cold" electrical discharge. To use ozone as a disinfectant, it must be created on site and added to the water by bubble contact. Some of the advantages of ozone include the production of relatively fewer dangerous by-products (in comparison to *chlorination)* and the lack of taste and odour produced by ozonation. Although fewer by-products are formed by ozonation, it has been discovered that the use of ozone produces a small amount of the suspected carcinogen *Bromate,* although little *Bromine* should be present in treated water. Another one of the main disadvantages of ozone is that it leaves no disinfectant residual in the water. Ozone has been used in drinking water plants since 1906 where the first industrial ozonation plant was built in *Nice, France*. The U.S. Food and Drug Administration has accepted ozone as being safe; and it is applied as an anti-microbiological agent for the treatment, storage, and processing of foods.

5. *UV radiation (light)* is very effective at inactivating cysts, as long as the water has a low level of colour so the UV can pass through without being absorbed. The main disadvantage to the use of UV radiation is that, like ozone treatment, it leaves no residual disinfectant in the water.

   Because neither ozone nor UV radiation leaves a residual disinfectant in the water, it is sometimes necessary to add a residual disinfectant after they are used. This is often done through the addition of chloramines, discussed above as a primary disinfectant. When used in this manner, chloramines provide an effective residual disinfectant with very little of the negative aspects of chlorination.

6. *Hydrogen peroxide* is another disinfectant. It works similar to ozon, yet activators as *formic acid* are to be added to increase the working of this chemical substance. It also has the disadvantage that it is slow working; *phytotoxic* (in high dosage) and that it decreases the PH of the water it purifies.

Additional treatment options

1. *Fluoridation* -in many areas *fluoride* is added to water for the purpose of preventing *tooth decay*. This process is referred to as *water fluoridation*. Fluoride is usually added after the disinfection process. In the United States, fluoridation

is usually accomplished by the addition of *hexafluorosilicic acid,* which decomposes in water, yielding fluoride ions.

2. *Water conditioning:* This is a method of reducing the effects of hard water. Hardness salts are deposited in water systems subject to heating because the decomposition of bicarbonate ions creates carbonate ions which crystalise out of the saturated solution of calcium or magnesium carbonate. Water with high concentrations of hardness salts can be treated with soda ash (*sodium carbonate*) which precipitates out the excess salts, through the *Common-ion effect,* producing calcium carbonate of very high purity. The precipitated calcium carbonate is traditionally sold to the manufacturers of *toothpaste.* Several other methods of industrial and residential water treatment are claimed (without general scientific acceptance) to include the use of magnetic or/and electrical fields reducing the effects of hard water.

3. *Plumbosolvency reduction*: In areas with naturally acidic waters of low conductivity (i.e surface rainfall in upland mountains of *igneous* rocks), the water may be capable of dissolving *lead* from any lead pipes that it is carried in. The addition of small quantities of *phosphate* ion and increasing the pH slightly both assist in greatly reducing plumbo-solvency by creating insoluble lead salts on the inner surfaces of the pipes.

4. *Radium Removal:* Some groundwater sources contain *radium,* a radioactive chemical element. Typical sources include many groundwater sources north of the *Illinois River* in *Illinois.* Radium can be removed by ion exchange, or by water conditioning. The back flush or sludge that is produced is, however, a low-level *radioactive waste.*

5. *Fluoride Removal:* Although fluoride is added to water in many areas, some areas of the world have excessive levels of natural fluoride in the source water. Excessive levels can be *toxic* or cause undesirable cosmetic effects such as staining of teeth. One method of reducing fluoride levels is through treatment with *activated alumina.*

Other water purification techniques

Other popular methods for purifying water, especially for local private supplies are listed below. In some countries some of these methods are also used for large scale municipal supplies. Particularly important are distillation (de-salination of seawater) and reverse osmosis.

1. *Boiling:* Water is heated hot enough and long enough to inactivate or kill *micro-*

organisms that normally live in water at room temperature. Near sea level, a vigorous rolling boil for at least one minute is sufficient. At high altitudes (greater than two kilometers or 5000 feet) three minutes is recommended. In areas where the water is "hard" (that is, containing significant dissolved calcium salts), boiling decomposes the *bicarbonate* ions, resulting in partial precipitation as *calcium carbonate*. This is the "fur" that builds up on kettle elements, etc., in hard water areas. With the exception of calcium, boiling does not remove solutes of higher boiling point than water and in fact increases their concentration (due to some water being lost as vapour). Boiling does not leave a residual disinfectant in the water. Therefore, water that has been boiled and then stored for any length of time may have acquired new pathogens.

2. *Carbon filtering: Charcoal,* a form of *carbon* with a high surface area, absorbs many compounds including some toxic compounds. Water passing through *activated charcoal* is common in household water filters and fish tanks. Household filters for drinking water sometimes contain *silver* to release silver ions which have an anti-bacterial effect.

3. *Distillation* involves boiling the water to produce water *vapour*. The vapour contacts a cool surface where it condenses as a liquid. Because the solutes are not normally vaporised, they remain in the boiling solution. Even distillation does not completely purify water, because of contaminants with similar boiling points and droplets of unvaporised liquid carried with the steam. However, 99.9% pure water can be obtained by distillation. Distillation does not confer any residual disinfectant and the distillation apparatus may be the ideal place to harbour *Legionnaires' disease*.

4. *Reverse osmosis*: Mechanical pressure is applied to an impure solution to force pure water through a *semi-permeable membrane*. Reverse osmosis is theoretically the most thorough method of large scale water purification available, although perfect semi-permeable membranes are difficult to create. Unless membranes are well-maintained, algae and other life forms can colonise the membranes.

5. *Ion exchange*: Most common ion exchange systems use a *zeolite* resin bed to replace unwanted Ca^{2+} and Mg^{2+} ions with benign (soap friendly) Na^{+} or K^{+} ions. This is the common water softener.

6. *Electrodeionization:* Water is passed between a positive electrode and a negative electrode. Ion selective membranes allow the positive ions to separate from the water toward the negative electrode and the negative ions toward the positive electrode. High purity deionized water results. The water is usually passed through a *reverse osmosis* unit first to remove non-ionic organic contaminants.

7. The use of iron in removing arsenic from water. See *Arsenic contamination of groundwater.*

8. Direct contact membrane distillation (DCMD). Applicable to desalination. Heated seawater is passed along the surface of a *hydrophobic* polymer membrane. Evaporated water passes from the hot side through pores in the membrane into a stream of cold pure water on the other side. The difference in vapour pressure between the hot and cold side helps to push water molecules through.

Portable water purification

Main article: Portable water purification

Portable techniques for purifying water are used for hiking, camping etc. or for use in rural areas or emergency situations. Common techniques include boiling, disinfection with tablets or ultra-filtration using a small hand pump.

In addition to this "portable water purification" may also include residential, commercial or industrial water treatment systems that are regenerated off site (by others). These systems are most commonly used for deionization in industrial applications or softening for residential applications. Also known as Service Deionization (SDI), industrial companies use these portable systems for a variety of reasons. Most commonly, the user has a small application and can not justify the expense of having regenerant chemicals such as sulfuric or hydrochloric acid and sodium hydroxide on site for safety and or manpower reasons. There may be waste water discharge limitations that make owning and operating an in-house deionizer (also known as a demineralizer) too expensive in comparison to the outsourcing of regeneration.

In residential applications a water treatment company delivers portable softener exchange tanks to a household. These softener tanks treat all or some of the water entering the household and remove hardness minerals. They are exchanged on a predetermined schedule so the household has softened water on a on a continual basis. Although not as cost effective as owning a water softener, portable water softeners require no maintenance by the home owner; furthermore there is no discharge of brine to septic or municipal waste treatment systems.

Water purification for hydrogen production

For the small scale *production of hydrogen,* water purifiers are installed to prevent formation of minerals on the surface of the electrodes and to remove organics and chlorine from utility water. First, the water passes through a 20 micrometre interference (*mesh* or *screen filter)* filter to remove sand and dust particles, then a *charcoal filter* using *activated carbon* to remove organics and *chlorine* and, finally, a *de-ionizing filter* to remove metallic ions. Testing can be done before and after the filter to verify the proper removal of *barium, calcium, potassium, magnesium, sodium and silicon.*

Safety and controversies

There has been *controversy over the fluoridation of water* since the 1930s, when the benefits to dental health were first claimed. There is evidence that excessive concentrations of fluorides can make teeth, and bones, more brittle and easily damaged / broken. Fluoridation is banned in many countries.

Water supplies have sometimes been the subject of concerns over terrorism or actual *terrorist threats.*

Accidents have also been known to happen. In April, 2007, the water supply of *Spencer, Massachusetts* became contaminated with excess *sodium hydroxide* (lye) when its treatment equipment malfunctioned.

REFERENCES

1. *Pictures and small overview of lavafilters* (in dutch)

2. *Overview of biological systems with pictures*

3. US EPA emergency disinfection recommendations

- Masters, Gilbert M. Introduction to Environmental Engineering. 2nd ed. Upper Saddle River, NJ: Prentice Hall, 1998.

- United States EPA Ground and Drinking Water Homepage. *EPA Ground and Drinking Water Homepage* Visited 12/13/05

12

IMPORTANCE OF WATER

Water is our lifeline that bathes us and feeds us. In ancient cultures water represented the very essence of life. The Romans were the first to pipe water into their growing cities, especially with their aqueducts. They also realized that sewage water could cause damage to their people, and needed to be removed from large areas of people.

Water has played a role not only in the history of countries, but in religion, mythology, and art. Water in many religions cleanses the soul through holy water. For example, the water at Lourdes, France is thought by many religions to be sacred water with healing powers. In Egyptian mythology, the Nu was the beginning of everything and represented water. It brought life to their people, but in drought, produced chaos.

Water has always been perceived as a gift from the gods as it rained from the heavens. The water or hydrologic cycle explains interactions between the atmosphere, hydrosphere, and lithosphere. The water or hydrologic cycle is a major driving force on our planet. Water is in constant motion, evaporating into the atmosphere from oceans, lakes, rivers and streams. When the atmosphere can no longer support the moisture within the clouds, we experience rain, snow, hail, or sleet. Some water is locked in the form of ice at the polar caps and in glaciers. Water melts in the spring, producing runoff, that percolates through the Earth as groundwater (subsurface) or makes its way back to the sea (surface). The oceans contain most of the water, but it is salt water which is unusable by most organisms. Only pure H2O (water) can interact with organisms.

The movement of the oceans also has a direct effect on the atmosphere. The atmosphere is that envelope of gas that keeps organisms living on this planet. Oceans and atmosphere interact to give us weather.

Water provides the Earth with the capacity of supporting life. An organism doesn't have to be told how important water is to their existence. An amphibian knows to lay their eggs in water or else there will be no new born. Even flies know to lay their eggs in fresh water.

The only organism that doesn't understand the importance of water is humans, especially in industrialized countries. Children in those societies turn on the water in a sink and never think about the trouble someone has gone for that "miracle" to occur.

In the United States it is mandated by law that its citizens should be given clean and abundant water. Dams, reservoirs, filtering plants, and pipes all bring clean water when the facet is turned on. Sewage water is only mixed with recycled water supplies after the water goes through rigorous cleaning methods. Water borne diseases do not effect the U.S. population like in other countries that do not treat their water supply.

Water borne diseases are any illnesses caused by drinking contaminated water. Diseases can include infection from bacteria (Salmonella), viruses, or by small parasites (Cryptosporida, Giardia, and Toxoplasma). These organisms and viruses cause diseases like cholera, typhoid fever, malaria, botulism, polio, dysentery, giardia, and hepatitis A. One of the first symptoms of these diseases is diarrhea, which cause about three million deaths throughout the world, mainly in India, Africa, and South America.

Sewage is sometimes discharged into rivers, where children downstream might be taking a bath or using the water to drink. The simplest treatment method is boiling. Just bring the water to a boil for at least one minute, then allow it to cool. But this is not always effective in heavily chemical polluted water supplies.

Without water, organisms could not exist. Water is a resource that should not be taken for granted. It needs to be conserved, just as we save other valuable resources.

Water is one of the weirdest compounds known to humans. The difference between the boiling point and freezing point of water is one of the largest ranges of any compound. It is this span of temperature that mirrors the range of where life can exist, from bacteria to humans. Water also has a very high specific heat, which means that it can absorb or lose much heat before its temperature changes. This is important in maintaining body heat in mammals. It also takes a lot of energy before vaporization can occur. For this reason, water evaporates slowly from ponds and lakes, where many life forms are dependent on a stable, warm environment.

Water is less dense in its solid state than in its liquid state, so that ice floats instead of sinking. This property permits life to develop in polar and subpolar regions where ice floats and allows life to continue living below the surface. If ice were heavier than water, it would sink, and more ice would form on top of it. As a result, all life in the waters would be trapped in the ice in the many areas of the world where it gets cold enough to freeze water.

Water is a remarkable solvent, where most elements and compounds can dissolve in its powerful molecular structure. Gases such as oxygen and carbon dioxide, can also dissolve, making it readily available for photosynthetic and nonphotosynthetic organisms to use.

Resistance of water to a disturbance.

Water also exhibits viscosity. One can observe the effects of viscosity alongside a stream or river with uniform banks. The water along the banks is nearly still, while the current in the center may be swift. This resistance between the layers is called viscosity. This property allows smaller fish to live near the shore, while larger fish are able to swim efficiently in strong currents. Viscosity is also responsible for the formation of eddies, creating turbulence that leads to good mixing of air in the water and more uniform distribution of microscopic organisms.

How water provides all these properties are complex, but only emphasizes the importance of water to every organism on Earth.

Water is a fundamental part of our lives. Human survival is dependent on water — water has been ranked by experts as second only to oxygen as essential for life. The average adult body is 55 to 75% water. 2/3 of your body weight is water (40 to 50 quarts). A human embryo is more than 80% water. A newborn baby is 74% water. Everyday your body must replace 2 1/2 quarts of water.The Water you drink literally becomes you! Since such a large percentage of our bodies is water, water must obviously figure heavily in how our bodies function. We need lots of fresh water to stay healthy. Aside from aiding in digestion and absorption of food, water regulates body temperature and blood circulation, carries nutrients and oxygen to cells, and removes toxins and other wastes. This "body water" also cushions joints and protects tissues and organs, including the spinal cord, from shock and damage. Conversely, lack of water (dehydration) can be the cause of many ailments. In his book, Your Body's Many Cries for Water, Dr. Fereydoon Batmanghelidj noted that chronic dehydration may cause certain problems for the body, including hypertension, asthma, allergies, and migraine headaches.

Every process in our body occurs in a water medium. We can exist without food for 2 months or more, but we can only survive for a few days without water.

Most people don't drink enough water. The body responds to this water deficiency in a variety of ways, which we frequently see as illnesses. When, many symptoms decrease. Ongoing dehydration may cause actual disease as the body struggles to maintain itself with insufficient water.

Concern About the Nation's Drinking Water

Although water covers more than 70% of the Earth's surface, only 1% of the Earth's water is available as a source of drinking water. Unfortunately, Americans are finding that our limited supplies are often polluted with contaminants such as Asbestos, Cysts (like Cryptosporidium and Giardia), Lead, Mercury, Trihalomethanes, Turbidity, Endocrine Disrupters and Volatile Organic Chemicals

Consumers are taking matters into their own hands and are now determining the quality of the water they and their families will drink by installing a drinking water system that will give them clean, refreshing, and healthier water.

Hard Water vs. SoftWater

Soft water (water with the minerals removed) appears to contribute to a higher incidence of hypertension and heart disease. Hypertension, more commonly known as high blood pressure, is an adaptive process to a gross body water deficiency. According to an article Good Housekeeping, nutritionists have determined that the amount of minerals in your tap water can make a significant difference to your health. The article cited a recent study in the Journal of the American Dietetic Association that found that drinking "hard" water (water with the minerals left in) may actually reduce your risk of heart disease.

According to Whitney and Hamilton's Nutrition, "soft water appears to contribute to a higher incidence of hypertension and heart disease in areas where it is used. Hard water may oppose these conditions."

Metabolism

Water is the medium for various enzymatic & chemical reactions in the body. It moves nutrients, hormones, antibodies, & oxygen through the blood stream & lymphatic system. The proteins & enzymes of the body function more efficiently in solutions of lower viscosity. Water is the solvent of the body & it regulates all functions, including the activity of everything it dissolves & circulates.

Water and Weight Loss

Among its other benefits, water plays a major part in weight loss. Since water contains no calories, it can serve as an appetite suppressant, and helps the body metabolize stored fat, it may possibly be one of the most significant factors in losing weight. In the article "Water Bearers", (Shape magazine) Elizabeth Austin notes that "water is the single most important nutrient you take in every day. It's fat -free, cholesterol-free, low in sodium, and completely without calories." Also, drinking more water helps to reduce water retention by stimulating your kidneys. Studies have recommended that if you are overweight according to average height and weight comparison charts, you should add one glass of water to your daily requirement (of eight glasses) for every 25 pounds over your recommended weight.

Dehydration leads to excess body fat, poor muscle tone & size, decreased digestive efficiency & organ function, increased toxicity, joint & muscle soreness, & water retention. Water works to keep muscles and skin toned.

Digestive System

The digestion of solid foods depends on the presence of copious amounts of water. Acids & enzymes in the stomach break the food down into a homogenized fluid state which can pass into the intestine for the next phase of digestion.

An "acid stomach" will respond to hydration.

Constipation is a frequent symptom of dehydration. Increased water, along with increased fiber, will usually totally eliminate a problem.

Gastritis, duodenitis, pain from ulcers (as long as the ulcer is not perforated), & heartburn all decrease with increased water intake. Water eliminates toxins & waste from the body.

Water Loss

Adults lose nearly 6 pints (12 cups) of water every day. We lose 1/2 cup to 1 cup a day from the soles of our feet. Another 2 to 4 cups is lost from breathing. Perspiration accounts for another 2 cups. Another 3 pints (6 cups) are lost in urine.

Dehydration

When the body is dehydrated, a form of rationing & distribution goes into play to ration the available water. Since the body has no reserve system, it operates a priority distribution system for the amount that has been made available by intake.

The body's signals of dehydration are frequently joint pain, stomach pain & ulcers, back pain, low energy, mental confusion & disorientation. Numerous disease symptoms respond to increased water intake.

Water Retention

If you're not drinking sufficient water, your body starts retaining water to compensate for this shortage. To eliminate fluid retention, drink more water, not less. If you don't drink enough water to maintain your body's fluid balance, you can impair every aspect of your body's physiological function.

The Thirst Reflex

The "dry mouth" signal is the last outward sign of extreme dehydration. As our bodies try to adjust to being deprived of water, our thirst mechanism becomes disabled. The only time we receive the "dry mouth" signal is as the last outward sign of extreme dehydration. In addition, the thirst sensation gradually decreases with age. The result is increasing dehydration. As we start to give our bodies more water, the thirst mechanism begins to work again, but doesn't become fully apparent until our bodies are fully hydrated. When we are getting sufficient water, we're often thirsty.

Body Temperature

Water helps regulate our body temperature through perspiration, which dissipates excess heat & cools our bodies.

Breathing

We even need water to breathe! As we take in oxygen & excrete CO2, our lungs must be moistened by water. We lose about 1 to 2 pints of water each day just exhaling.

Asthma is frequently relieved when water intake is increased. Histamine plays a key role in regulating the way the body uses & distributes water & helps control the body's defense mechanisms. In asthmatics, histamine level increases with dehydration. Our defense for the body is to close down the airways.

Kidneys

The kidneys remove wastes such as uric acid, urea & lactic acid, all of which must be dissolved in water. When there isn't sufficient water, those wastes are not effectively removed, which may result in damage to the kidneys.

Joints

Water lubricates our joints. The cartilage tissues found at the ends of long bones

& between the vertebrae of the spine hold a lot of water, which serves as a lubricant during the movement of the joint. When the cartilage is will hydrated, the two opposing surfaces glide freely, & friction damage is minimal. If the cartilage is dehydrated, the rate of "abrasive" damage is increased, resulting in joint deterioration & increased pain.

The actively growing blood cells in the bone marrow take priority over the cartilage for the available water that goes through the bone structure.

Rheumatoid joint pain frequently decreases with increased water intake & flexing exercises to bring more circulation to the joints.

75% of the upper body weight is supported by the water volume that is stored in the spinal disc core. 25% is supported by the fibrous materials around the disc. The spinal joints are dependent on different hydraulic properties of water which is stored in the disc core. Back pain is frequently alleviated with hydration.

The Brain

Brain tissue is 85% water. Although the brain is only 1/50th of the body weight, it uses 1/20th of the blood supply.

With dehydration, the level of energy generation in the brain is decreased. Depression & chronic fatigue syndrome are frequently results of dehydration.

Migraine headaches may be an indicator of critical body temperature regulation at times of "heat stress." Dehydration plays a major role in bringing on migraines. Dehydration causes stress & stress causes further dehydration.

Pregnancy

Morning sickness is a thirst signal of both the fetus & the mother. During the intrauterine stage of cell expansion, water for the fetus' cell growth has to be provided by the mother. One of the first indicators for water needs of the fetus & the mother seems to be morning sickness during the first trimester of pregnancy.

1. Water helps carry nutrients through blood to the baby.

2. Water helps prevent bladder infections, constipation, and hemorrhoids, which are common during pregnancy.

3. The more water you drink, the less water you retain.

4. Dehydration can trigger contractions and early labor.

5. Amniotic fluid (mostly water) is replaced continuously throughout the day, so more water is needed to replenish the body.

6. Hydration is essential to good breast milk production.

Not only is it important to drink enough water, the quality of the water consumed is of paramount concern. Many studies have shown that water contamination risks are greatly increased in infants, due to their size and stage of development, with their brains and bodies being formed.

Water vs. Other Beverages

There is a difference between drinking pure water & beverages that contain water. Fruit juice, soft drinks, coffee, etc., may contain substances that are not healthy, & actually contradict some of the positive effects of the added water. Caffeinated beverages stimulate the adrenal glands and act as diuretics, robbing your body of necessary water. Soft drinks contain phosphorus which can lead to depletion of bone calcium. Soda contains sodium. Fruit juices contain a lot of sugar & stimulate the pancreas. These drinks may tax the body more than they cleanse it. A 12 ounce can of regular soda contains the equivalent of 9 teaspoons of sugar and loads of empty calories.

Other Beverages also contain dehydrating agents. They may actually reduce the water reserves in the body! Drinking other beverages to the exclusion of water also causes you to lose your taste for water. This is particularly true with children as they become dependent on Sodas & juices.

How much water should you drink?

A non active person needs a half ounce of water per pound of body weight per day. That is ten 8 ounce glasses a day if your weight is 160 pounds. For every 25 pounds you exceed your ideal weight, increase it by one 8 ounce glass.

An active, athletic person needs 2/3 ounce per pound which is 13-14 8 ounce glasses a day if you're 160 pounds. The more you exercise the more water you need. Spread out your water intake throughout the day. Do not drink more than 4 glasses within any given hour. After a few weeks your bladder calms down & you will urinate less frequently, but in larger amounts.

Tailoring Water Management Solutions

Recent researches suggests government and donor efforts to transfer water management institutions and policies from western countries to India fail to take into account the realities of the country's river basins - undermining attempts to contain the growing water crisis and reduce vulnerability to drought.

"Water management solutions developed in Europe, North America and Australia cannot be expected to address the more fundamental issues that water sectors in South Asia must contend with. The items that top the water agenda here-such as providing access to water for drinking, growing food and sustainable groundwater management-are either unresolved in the developed world or have become irrelevant due to economic development,"—a new initiative to introduce research knowledge into the policy planning process.

Recent research, which analysed the effectiveness of Integrated River Basin Management (IRBM) models in implementing sustainable water management regimes, found that is many cases these models were not designed to handle the hydrogeology, demography, socio-economics and organisation of the water sector found in South Asia.

This does not mean that India and other South Asian countries cannot learn valuable lessons from these models. Loosely structured, they can serve coordinating mechanisms, facilitating dialogue and negotiation on resource allocation among organised stakeholders and representative bodies. But River Basin Organisations cannot by themselves address the more fundamental issues that water sectors in India must contend with.

"Its an entirely different ball game from IRBM in western countries." "For reform to succeed in developing countries such as India, you have to find ways of influencing huge numbers of small-scale water users who depend on rain-fed agriculture and private or community water storage, without much mediation from public agencies or service providers."

For IRBM to work in India and other countries in South Asia, models have to be properly tailored to local conditions. IWMI-Tata researchers have highlighted four areas policy makers need to consider for the successful application of IRBM.

The Challenge for Developing Countries when Implementing IRBM

- *Regulate the informal water sector:* How do you regulate vast numbers of small-scale users who are not linked to public institutions? One possibility is to find ways of underpinning macro-level institutions with nested organisations of users at the grassroots.

- *Improve the productivity of "Green Water"*: For countries such as India, where the population density is high, both upstream and downstream, increasing the productivity of water diverted from rivers is less important than being able to a capture rainfall and store water effectively in the soil profile ("green water").
- *Manage groundwater:* In South Asia, protecting groundwater from over-exploitation by millions of small unlicensed pumpers is an increasingly pressing issue. Community initiatives for groundwater recharge may offer the most immediate hope for reversing damage in areas, where water tables are dropping as much as a meter each year.
- *Water scarcity:* The heart of the problem in most water-scarce countries is too many people living off a limited natural resource base. Getting more crop, cash and jobs per drop is part of the answer, the other is generating off-farm livelihoods in rural areas.

APPENDIX

THE WATER ACT

Water (Prevention and Control of Pollution) Act, 1974 [No. 6 Of 1974]

An Act to provide for the prevention and control of water pollution and the maintaining or restoring of wholesomeness of water, for the establishment, with a view to carrying out the purposes aforesaid, of Boards for the prevention and control of water pollution, for conferring on and assigning to such Boards powers and functions relating thereto and for matters connected therewith.

Whereas it is expedient to provide for the prevention and control of water pollution and the maintaining or restoring of wholesomeness of water, for the establishment, with a view to carrying out the purposes aforesaid, of Boards for the prevention and control of water pollution and for conferring on and assigning to such Boards powers and functions relating thereto.

And whereas Parliament has no power to make laws for the states with respect to any of the matters aforesaid except as provided in Articles 249 and 250 of the Constitution.

And whereas in pursuance of clause (1) of Article 252 of the Constitution resolutions have been passed by all the Houses of the Legislatures of the states of Assam, Bihar, Gujarat, Haryana, Himachal Pradesh, Jammu and Kashmir, Karnataka, Kerala, Madhya Pradesh, Rajasthan, Tripura and West Bengal to the effect that the matters aforesaid should be regulated in those states by Parliament by law.

Be it enacted by Parliament in the Twenty-fifth Year of the Republic of India as follows:

SECTION 1

Preliminary

1. Short Title, Application and Commencement

(1) This Act may be called the Water (Prevention and Control of Pollution) Act, 1974.

(2) It applies in the first instance to the whole of the states of Assam, Bihar, Gujarat, Haryana, Himachal Pradesh, Jammu and Kashmir, Karnataka Kerala, Madhya Pradesh, Rajasthan, Tripura and West Bengal and the Union territories; and it all shall apply to such other states which adopts this Act by resolution passed in that behalf under clause (1) of Article 252 of the Constitution.

(3) It shall come into force, at once in the states of Assam, Bihar, Gujarat, Haryana, Himachal Pradesh, Jammu and Kashmir, Karnataka, Kerala, Madhya Pradesh, Rajasthan, Tripura and West Bengal and in the Union territories and in any other state which adopts this Act under clause (1) of Article 252 of the Constitution on the date of such adoption and any reference in this Act to the comment cement of this Act shall, in relation to any state or union territory mean the data on which this Act comes into force in such state or union territory.

2. Definitions—In this Act, unless the context otherwise requires—

(a) 'Board' means the Central Board or a State Board;

(b) 'Central Board' means the Central Pollution Control Board constituted under section 3;[1]

(c) 'Member' means a member of a Board and includes the chairman thereof;

(d) 'Occupier', in relation to any factory or premises, means the person who has control over the affairs of the factory or the premises and includes, in relation to any substance, the person in possession of the substance;[2]

(dd) 'Outlet' includes any conduit pipe or channel, open or closed, carrying sewage or trade effluent or any other holding arrangement which causes or is likely to cause, pollution;[3]

(e) 'Pollution' means such contamination of water or such alteration of the physical, chemical or biological properties of water or such discharge of any sewage or trade effluent or of any other liquid, gaseous or solid substance into water (whether directly or indirectly) as may or is likely to, create a nuisance or render such water harmful or injurious to public health or safety, or to domestic, commercial, industrial, agricultural or other legitimate uses or to the life and health of animals or plants or of aquatic organism; (f) 'prescribed' means prescribed by rules made under this Act by the Central Government or, as the case may be, the state government;

(f) 'Prescribed' means prescribed by rules made under this Act by the Central Government or, as the case may be, the state government;

(g) 'Sewage effluent means effluent from any sewerage system or sewage disposal works and includes sullage from open drains;

(gg) 'Sewer' means any conduit pipe or channel, open or closed carrying sewage or trade effluent;[4]

(h) 'State Board' means a State Pollution Control Board constituted under section 4;[5]

(i) 'State government' in relation to a union territory means the administrator thereof appointed under Article 239 of the Constitution;

(j) 'Stream' includes—

(i) river;

(ii) water course (whether flowing or for the time being dry);

(iii) inland water (whether natural or artificial);

(iv) sub-terranean waters;

(v) sea or tidal waters to such extent or, as the case may be, to such point as the state government may, by notification in the Official Gazette, specify in this behalf;

(k) 'Trade effluent' includes any liquid, gaseous or solid substance which is discharged from any premises used for carrying on any [industry, operation, process or treatment and disposal system][6] other than domestic sewage.

SECTION II

The Central and State Boards for Prevention and Control of Water Pollution

3. Constitution of Central Board—(1) The Central Government shall, with effect from such data (being a date not later than six months of the commencement of this Act in the states of Assam, Bihar, Gujarat, Haryana, Himachal Pradesh, Jammu and Kashmir, Karnataka, Kerala, Madhya Pradesh, Rajasthan, Tripura and West Bengal and in the Union territories) as it may, by notification in the Official Gazette, appoint, constitute a Central Board to be called the [Central Pollution Control

Board][7] to exercise the powers conferred on and perform the functions assigned to that Board under this Act.

(2) the Central Board shall consist of the following members, namely:

(a) a full-time chairman, being a person having special knowledge or practical experience in respect of [matters relating to environmental protection][8] or a person having knowledge and experience in administering institutions dealing with the matters aforesaid, to be nominated by the Central Government;

(b) [such number of officials, not exceeding five][9] to be nominated by the Central Government to represent that Government;

(c) such number of persons, not exceeding five, to nominated by the Central Government, from amongst the members of the State Boards, of whom not exceeding two shall be from those referred to in clause (c) of sub-section (2) of section 4;

(d) [such number or non-officials, not exceeding three][10] to be nominated by the Central Government, to represent the interests of agriculture, fishery or industry or trade or any other interest which, in the opinion of the Central Government, ought to be represented;

(e) two persons to represent the companies or corporations owned, controlled or managed by the Central Government, to be nominated by that Government;

(f) a full-time member-secretary, possessing qualifications, knowledge and experience of scientific, engineering or management aspects of pollution control, to be appointed by the Central Government.[11]

(3) The Central Board shall be a body corporate with the name aforesaid having perpetual succession and a common seal with power, subject to the provisions of this Act, to acquire, hold and dispose of property and to contract, and may, by the aforesaid name, sue or be sued.

4. Constitution of State Boards—(1) The state government shall, with effect from such date[***][12] as it may, by notification in the Official Gazettee, appoint, constitute a [State Pollution Control Board][13], under such name as may be specified in the notification, to exercise the powers conferred on and perform the functions assigned to that board under this Act.

(2) A State Board shall consist of the following members namely:

(a) a (***)[14] chairman, being a person having special knowledge or practical experience in respect of [matters relating to environmental protection][15] or a person having knowledge and experience in administering institutions dealing with the matters aforesaid, to be nominated by the State Government:

Provided that the chairman may be either whole-time or part-time as the state government may think fit;[16]

(b) such number of officials, not exceeding five,] to be nominated by the state government to represent that Government;[17]

(c) [such number of persons, not exceeding five,] to be nominated by the state government from amongst the members of the local authorities functioning within the state;[18]

(d) [such number of non-officials not exceeding three,] to be nominated by the state government to represent the interests of agriculture, fishery or industry or trade or any other interest which, in the opinion of the state government, ought to be represented;[19]

(e) two persons to represent the companies or corporations owned, controlled or managed by the state government, to be nominated by that Government;

(f) a full-time member-secretary, possessing qualifications, knowledge and experience of scientific, engineering or management aspects of pollution control, to be appointed by the state government.][20]

(3) Every State Board shall be a body corporate with the name specified by the state government in the notification under sub-section (1), having perpetual succession and a commonweal with power, subject to the provisions of this Act, to acquire, hold and dispose of property and to contract and may, by the said name, sue or be sued.

(4) Notwithstanding anything contained in this section, no State Board shall be constituted for a union territory and in relation to a union territory, the Central Board shall exercise the powers and perform the functions of a State Board for that union territory:

Provided that in relation to any union territory, the Central Board may delegate all or any of its powers and functions under this sub-section to such person or body of persons as the Central Government may specify.

5. **Terms and Conditions of Service of Members.**—(1) Save as otherwise provided by or under this act, a member of a Board, other than a member-secretary, shall hold office for a term of three years from the date of his nomination:

Provided that a member shall, not withstanding the expiration of his term, continue to hold office until his successor enters upon his office.

(2) The term of office of a member of a Board nominated under clause (b) or clause (e) of sub-section (2) of section 3 or clause (b) or clause (e) of sub-section (2) of section 4 shall come to an end as soon as he ceases to hold the office under the Central Government or the state government or, as the case may be, the company or corporation owned, controlled or managed by the Central Government or the state government by virtue of which he was nominated.][21]

(3) The Central Government or, as the case may be, the state government may, if it thinks fit, remove any member of a Board before the expiry of his term of office, after giving him a reasonable opportunity of showing cause against the same.

(4) A member of a Board, other than the member-secretary, may at any time resign his office by writing under his hand addressed—

(a) in the case of the chairman, to the Central Government or as the case may be, the state government; and

(b) in any other case, to the chairman of the board, and the seat of the chairman or such other member shall thereupon become vacant.

(5) A member of a Board, other than the member-secretary, shall be deemed to have vacated his seat if he is absent without reason, sufficient in the opinion of the Board, from three consecutive meetings of the Board,[22] [or where he is nominated under clause (c) or clause (e) of sub-section (2) of section 3 or under clause (c) or clause (e) of sub-section (2) of section 4, if he ceases to be a member of the State Board or of the local authority or, as the case may be of the company or corporation owned, controlled or managed by the Central Government or the state government and such vacation of seat shall, in either case, take effect from such date as the Central Government or, as the case may be, the stage government may, by notification in the Official Gazette, specify].

(6) A casual vacancy in a Board shall be filled by a fresh nomination and the person nominated to fill the vacancy shall hold office only for the remainder of the term for which the member in whose place he was nominated.

(7) A member of a Board shall[23] [be eligible for renomination].

(8) The other terms and conditions of service of a member of a Board, other than the chairman and member-secretary, shall be such as may be prescribed.

(9) The other terms and conditions of service of the chairman shall be such as may be prescribed.

6. Disqualifications—(1) No person shall be a member of a Board, who—

(a) is, or at any time has been adjudged insolvent or has suspended payment of his debts or has compounded with his creditors or

(b) is of unsound mind and stands so declared by a competent court or

(c) is, or has been, convicted of an offence which, in the opinion of the Central Government or, as the case may be, of the state government, involves moral turpitude or

(d) is, or at any time has been, convicted of an offence under this Act or

(e) has directly or indirectly by himself or by any partner, any share or interest in any firm or company carrying on the business of manufacture, sale or hire of machinery, plant, equipment, apparatus or fittings for the treatment of sewage or trade effluents or

(f) is a director or a secretary, manager or other salaried officer or employee of any company or firm having any contract with the Board, or with the Government constituting the Board or with a local authority in the state or with a company or corporation owned, controlled or managed by the Government for the carrying out of sewerage schemes or for the installation of plants for the treatment of sewage or trade effluents or

(g) has so abused, in the opinion of the Central Government or as the case may be, of the state government, his position as a member, as to render his continuance on the Board detrimental to the interest of the general public.

(2) No order of removal shall be made by the Central Government or the state government, as the case may be, under this section unless the member concerned has been given a reasonable opportunity of showing cause against the same.

(3) Notwithstanding anything contained in sub-sections (1) and (7) of section 5, a member who has been removed under this section shall not be eligible for renomination as a member.

7. **Vacation of Seats by Members**—If a member of a Board becomes subject to any of the disqualifications specified in section 6, his seat shall become vacant.

8. **Meetings of Board**— A board shall meet at least once in every three months and shall observe such rules of procedure in regard to the transaction of business at its meetings as may be prescribed:

Provided that if, in the opinion of the chairman, any business of an urgent nature is to be transacted, he may convene a meeting of the Board at such time as the thinks fit for the aforesaid purpose.

9. **Constitution of Committees**—(1) A Board may constitute as many committees

consisting wholly of members or wholly of other persons or partly of members and partly of other persons and for such purpose or purposes as it may think fit.

(2) A committee constituted under this section shall meet at such time and at such place and shall observe such rules of procedure in regard to the transaction of business at its meetings, as may be prescribed.

(3) The members of a committee (other than the members of the Board) shall be paid such fees and allowances, for attending its meetings and for attending to any other work of the Board as may be prescribed.

10. Temporary Association of Persons with Board for Particular Purposes—(1) A Board may associate with itself in such manner, and for such purposes, as may be prescribed any person whose assistance or advice it may desire to obtain in performing may of its functions under this Act.

(2) A person associated with the Board under sub-section (1) for any purpose shall have a right to take part in the discussions of the Board relevant to that purpose, but shall not have a right to vote at a meeting of the Board, and shall not be a member for any other purpose.

(3) A person associated with the Board under sub-section (1) for any purpose shall be paid such fees and allowances, for attending its meetings and for attending to any other work of the Board as may be prescribed.][24]

11. Vacancy in Board not to invalidate acts or proceedings—No act or proceeding of a Board or any committee thereof shall be called in question on the ground merely of the existence of any vacancy in or any defect in the constitution of, the Board or such committee, as the case may be.

11a. Delegation of Powers to Chairman—The chairman of Board shall exercise such powers and perform such duties as may be prescribed or as may, from time to time, be delegated to him by the Board.[25]

12. Member-Secretary and Officers and Other Employees of Board—(1) The terms and conditions of service of the member-secretary shall be such as may be prescribed.

(2) The member-secretary shall exercise such powers and perform such duties as may be prescribed or as may, from time to time, be delegated to him by the Board or its chairman.

(3) Subject to such rules as may be made be the Central Government or, as the case may be, the state government in this behalf, a Board may appoint such officers and employees as it considers necessary for the efficient performance of its functions[26][***].

(3a) The method of recruitment and the terms and conditions of service (including the scales of pay) of the officers (other than the member-secretary) and other employees of the Central Board or a State Board shall be such as may be determined by regulations made by the Central Board or, as the case may be, by the State Board:

Provided that no regulation made under this sub-section shall take effect unless:

(a) in the case of a regulation made by the Central Board, it is approved by the Central Government; and

(b) in the case of a regulation made by a State Board, it is approved by the state government.]

(3b) the Board may, by general or special order and subject to such conditions and limitations, if any, as may be specified in the order, delegate to any officer of the Board such of its powers and functions under this Act as it may deem necessary.][28]

(4) Subject to such conditions as may be prescribed, a Board may from time to time appoint any qualified person to be a consulting engineer to the Board and pay him such salaries and allowances and subject him to such other terms and conditions of service as it thinks fit.

SECTION III

Joint Boards

13. Constitution of Joint Boards—Notwithstanding anything contained in this Act, an agreement may be entered into—

(a) by two or more government of contiguous states, or

(b) by the Central Governments of states contiguous to such union territory or Union territories.

to be in force for such period and to be subject to renewal for such further period, if anyone may be specified in the agreement to provide for the constitution of a Joint Board,—

(i) in a case referred to in clause (a), for all the participating states, and

(ii) in a case referred to in clause (b), for the participating union territory or union territories and the state or states.

(2) An agreement under this section may—

(a) provide, in a case referred to in clause (a) of sub-section (1) for the apportionment between the participating states and in a case referred to in clause (b) of that sub-section, for the apportionments between the Central Government and the participating state government or state governments, of the expenditure in connection with the Joint Board;

(b) determine, in a case referred to in clause (a) of sub-section (1), which of the participating state governments and in a case referred to in clause (b) of that sub-section, whether the Central Government or the participating state government (if there are more than one participating state, also which of the participating state governments) shall exercise and perform the several powers and functions of the state government under this Act and the references in this Act to the state government shall be construed accordingly;

(c) provide for consultation in a case referred to in clause (a) of sub-section (1), between the participating state governments and in a case referred to inclause (b) of that sub-section, between the Central Government and the participating state government or state governments either generally or with reference to particular matters arising under this Act;

(d) make such incidental and ancillary provisions, not in consistent with this Act, as may be deemed necessary or expedient for giving effect to the agreement.

(3) An agreement under this section shall be published, in a case referred to in clause (a) of sub-section (1), in the Official Gazette of the participating states and in a case referred to in clause (b) of that sub-section in the Official Gazette of that participating union territory or Union territories and the participating state or states.

14. Composition of Joint Boards—(1) A Joint Board constituted in pursuance of an agreement entered into under clause (a) of sub-section (1) of section 13 shall consist of the following members, namely:—

(a) a full-time chairman, being a person having special knowledge or practical experience in respect of[29] matters relating to environmental protection] or a person having knowledge and experience in administering institutions dealing with the matters aforesaid, to be nominated by the Central Government;

(b) two officials from each of the participating states to be nominated by the concerned participating state government to represent that Government;

(c) one person to be nominated by each of the participating state governments from amongst the members of the local authorities functioning within the state concerned;

(d) one non-official to be nominated by each of the participating state governments to represent the interests of agriculture, fishery or industry or trade in the state concerned or any other interest which, the opinion of the participating state government, is to be represented;

(e) two persons to be nominated by the Central Government to represent the companies or corporations owned, controlled or managed by the participating state governments;

(f) a full time member-secretary, possessing qualifications, knowledge and experience of scientific, engineering or management aspects of pollution control, to be appointed by the Central Government.[30]

(2) A Joint Board constituted in pursuance of an agreement entered into under clause (b) of sub-section (1) of section 13 shall consist of the following members, namely—

(a) a full-time chairman, being a person having special knowledge or practical experience in respect of[31] [matters relating to environmental protection] or a person having knowledge and experience in administering institutions dealing with the matters aforesaid, to be nominated by the Central Government;

(b) two officials to be nominated by the Central Government from the participating union territory or each of the participating union territories,

as the case may be and two officials to be nominated, from the participating state or each of the participating states, as the case may be, by the concerned participating state government;

(c) one person to be nominated by the Central Government from amongst the members of the local authorities functioning within the participating union territory or each of the participating Union territories, as the case may be, and one person to be nominated, from amongst the members of the local authorities functioning within the participating State or each of the participating states, as the case may be by the concerned participating state government;

(d) one non-officials to be nominated by the Central Government and one person to be nominated by t he participating state government or state governments to represent the interests of agriculture, fishery or industry or trade in the union territory or in each of the union territories or the state or in each of the states, as the case may be or any other interest which in the opinion of the Central Government of, as the case may be, of the state government is to be represented;

(e) two persons to be nominated by the Central Government to represent the companies or corporations owned, controlled or managed by the Central Government and situate in the participating union territory or territories and two persons to be nominated by the Central Government to represent the companies or corporations owned, controlled or managed by the participating state governments;

(f) a full-time member-secretary, possessing qualifi-cations, knowledge and experience of scientific, engineering or management aspects of pollution control, to be appointed by the Central Government.[32]

(3) When a Joint Board is constituted in pursuance of an agreement under clause (b) of sub-section (1) of section 13, the provisions of sub-section (4) of section 4 shall cease to apply in relation to the union territory for which the Joint Board is constituted.

(4) Subject to the provisions of sub-section (3), the provisions of sub-section (3) of section 4 and sections 5 to 12 (inclusive) shall apply in relation to the Joint Board and its member-secretary as they apply in relation to a State Board and its member-secretary.

(5) Any reference in this Act to the State Board shall, unless the context otherwise requires, be construed as including a Joint Board.

15. Special Provision Relating to Giving of Directions— Notwithstanding anything contained in this Act where any Joint Board is constituted under section 13—

(a) the Government of the state for which the Joint Board is constituted shall be competent to give any direction under this Act only in cases where such direction relates to a matter within the exclusive territorial jurisdiction of the state;

(b) the Central Government alone shall be competent to give any direction under this Act where such direction relates to a matter within the territorial jurisdiction of two or more states or pertaining to a union territory.

SECTION IV

Powers and Functions of Boards

16. Functions of Central Board—(1) Subject to the provisions of this Act, the main function of the Central Board shall be to promote cleanliness of streams and wells in different areas of the states.

(2) In particular and without prejudice to the generality of the foregoing function, the Central Board may perform all or any of the following functions, namely;

(a) advice the Central Government on any matter concerning the prevention and control of water pollution;

(b) co-ordinate the activities of the State Boards and resolve disputes among them;

(c) provide technical assistance and guidance to the State Boards, carry out and sponsor investigations and research relating to problems of water pollution and prevention, control or abatement of water pollution;

(d) plan and organise the training of persons engaged or to be engaged in programmes for the prevention, control or abatement of water pollution on such terms ad conditions as the Central Board may specify;

(e) organise through mass media a comprehensive programme regarding the prevention and control of water pollution;

(ee) perform such of the functions of any State Board as may be specified in an order made under sub-section (2) of section 18];[33]

(f) collect, compile and publish technical and statistical data relating to water pollution and the measures devised for its effective prevention and control and prepare manuals, codes or guides relating to treatment and disposal of sewage and trade effluents and disseminate information connected therewith;

(g) lay down, modify or annul, in consultation with the state government concerned, the standards for a stream or well:

Provided that different standards may be laid down for the same stream or well or for different streams or wells, having regard to the quality of water, flow characteristics of the stream or well and the nature of the use of the water in such stream or well or stream or wells;

(h) plan and cause to be executed a nation-wide programme for the prevention, control or abate-ment of water pollution;

(i) perform such other functions as may be prescribed.

(3) The Board may establish or recognise a laboratory or laboratories to enable the Board to perform its functions under this section efficiently, including the analysis of samples of water from any stream or well or of samples of any sewage or trade effluents.

17. Functions of State Board—(1) Subject to the provisions of this Act, the functions of a State Board shall be—

(a) to plan a comprehensive programme for the prevention, control or abatement of pollution of streams and wells in the state and to secure the execution thereof;

(b) to advise the state government on any matter concerning the prevention, control or abatement of water pollution;

(c) to collect and disseminate information relating to water pollution and the prevention, control or abatement thereof;

(d) to encourage, conduct and participate in investigations and research relating to problems of water pollution and prevention, control or abatement of water pollution;

(e) to collaborate with the Central Board in organising the training of persons engaged or to be engaged in programmes relating to prevention control or abatement of water pollution and to organise mass education programmes relating thereto;

(f) to inspect sewage or trade effluents, works and plants for the treatment of sewage and trade effluents and to review plans, specifications or other data relating to plants set up for the treatment of water, works for the purification thereof and the system for the disposal of sewage or trade effluents or in connection with the grant of any consent as required by this Act;

(g) to lay down, modify or annul effluent standards for the sewage and trade effluents and for the quality of receiving waters (not being water in an inter-state stream) resulting from the discharge of effluents and to classify waters of the state;

(h) to evolve economical and reliable methods of treatment of sewage and trade effluents, having regard to the peculiar conditions of soils, climate and water resources of different regions and more especially the prevailing flow characteristics of water in streams and wells which render it impossible to attain even the medium degree of dilution;

(i) to evolve methods of utilisation of sewage and suitable trade effluents in agriculture;

(j) to evolve efficient methods of disposal of sewage and trade effluents on land, as are necessary on account of the predominant conditions of scant stream flows that do not provide for major part of the year the minimum degree of dilution;

(k) to lay down standards of treatment of sewage and trade effluents to be discharged into any particular stream taking into account the minimum fair weather dilution available in that stream and the tolerance limits of pollution permissible in the water of the stream, after the discharge of such effluents;

(l) to make, vary or revoke any order—

(i) for the prevention, control or abatement of discharges of waste into streams or wells;

(ii) requiring any person concerned to construct new systems for the disposal of sewage and trade effluents or to modify, alter or extend any such existing system or to adopt such remedial measures as are necessary to prevent, control or abate water pollution;

(m) to lay down effluent standards to be complied with by persons while causing discharge of sewage or sullage or both and to lay down, modify or annul effluent standards for the sewage and trade effluents;

(n) to advise the stage government with respect to the location of any industry the carrying on of which is likely to pollute a stream or well;

(o) to perform such other functions as may be prescribed or as may, from time to time, be entrusted to it by the Central Board or the state government.

(2) The Board may establish or recognise a laboratory or laboratories to enable the Board to perform its functions under this section efficiently, including the analysis of samples of water from any stream or well or of samples of any sewage or trade effluents.

18. Power to give Directions—[34] (1) In the performance of its functions under this Act—-

(a) the Central Board shall be bound by such directions in writing as the Central Government may give to it; and

(b) every State Board shall be bound by such directions in writing as the Central Board or the state government may give to it;

Provided that where a direction given by the state government is inconsistent with the direction given by the Central Board, the matter shall be referred to the Central Government for its decision.

(2) Where the Central Government is of the opinion that any State Board has defaulted in complying with any directions given by the Central Board under sub-section (1) and as a result of such default a grave emergency has arisen and it is necessary or expedient so to do in the public interest, it may, by order, direct the Central Board to perform any of the functions of the State Board in relation to such area, for such period and for such purposes, as may be specified in the order.

(3) Where the Central Board performs any of the functions of the State Board in pursuance of a direction under sub-section (2), the expenses, if any, incurred by the Central Board with respect to the performance of such functions may, if the State Board is empowered to recover such expenses, be recovered by the Central Board with interest (at such reasonable rate as the Central Government may, by order, fix) from the date when a demand for such expenses is made until it is paid from the person or persons concerned as arrears of land revenue or of public demand.

(4) For the removal of doubts, it is hereby declared that any directions to perform the functions of any State Board given under sub-section (2) in respect of any area would not preclude the State Board from performing such functions in any other are in the state or any of its other functions in that area.

SECTION V

Prevention and Control of Water Pollution

19. Power of State Government to restrict the application of the Act to certain areas—(1) Notwithstanding anything contained in this Act, if the state government, after consultation with or on the recommendation of, the State Board, is of opinion that the provisions of this Act need not apply to the entire state, it may, by notification in the Official Gazette, restrict the application of this Act to such area or areas as may be declared therein as water pollution, prevention and control area or areas and thereupon the provisions of Act shall apply only to such area or areas.

(2) Each water pollution, prevention and control area may be declared either by reference to a map or by reference to the line of any watershed or the boundary of any district or partly by one method and partly by another.

(3) The state government may, by notification in the Official Gazette—

(a) alter any water pollution, prevention and control area whether by way of extension or reduction; or

(b) define a new water pollution, prevention and control area in which may be merged one or more water pollution, prevention and control areas or any part of parts thereof.

20. Power to Obtain Information—(1) For the purpose of enabling a State Board to perform the functions conferred on it by or under this Act, the State Board or any officer empowered by it in that behalf, may make surveys of any area and gauge and keep records of the flow or volume and other characteristics of any stream or well in such area and may take steps for the measurement and recording of the rainfall in such area or any part thereof and for the installation and maintenance for those purposes of gauges or other apparatus and works connected therewith and carry out stream surveys and may take such other steps as may be necessary in order to obtain any information required for the purposes aforesaid.

(2) A State Board may give directions requiring any person who in its opinion is abstracting water from any such stream or well in the area in quantities which are substantial in relation to the flow or volume of that stream or well or is discharging sewage or trade effluent into any such stream or well, to give such information as to the abstraction or the discharge at such times and in such form as may be specified in the directions.

(3) Without prejudice to the provisions of sub-section (2), a State Board may, with a view to preventing or controlling pollution of water, given directions requiring any person in charge of any establishment where any [industry, operation or process or treatment and disposal system][36] is carried on, to furnish to it information regarding the construction, installation or operation of such establishment or of any disposal system or of any extension or addition thereto in such establishment and such other particulars as may be prescribed.

21. Power to take Samples of Effluents and Procedure to be Follow in Connection Therewith—(1) A State Board or any officer empowered by it in this behalf shall have power to take for the purpose of analysis samples of water from any stream or well or samples of any sewage or trade effluent which is passing from any plant or vessel or from or over any place into any such stream or well.

(2) The result of any analysis of a sample of any sewage or trade effluent taken under sub-section (1) shall not be admissible in evidence in any legal proceeding unless the provisions of sub-sections (3), (4) and (5) are complied with.

(3) Subject to the provisions of sub-sections (4) and (5), when a sample (composite or otherwise as may be warranted by the process used) of any sewage or trade effluent is taken for analysis under sub-section (1), the person taking the sample shall—

(a) serve on the person in charge of or having control over, the plant or vessel or in occupation of the place (which person is hereinafter referred to as the occupier) or any agent of such occupier, a notice, then and there in such form as may be prescribed of his intention to have it so analysed;

(b) in the presence of the occupier or his agent, divide the sample into two parts;

(c) cause each part to be placed in a container which shall be marked and sealed and shall also be signed both by the person taking the sample and the occupier or his agent;

(d) send one container forthwith—

(i) in a case where such sample is taken from any area situated in a union territory, to the laboratory established or recognised by the Central Board under section 16; and

(ii) in any other case, to the laboratory established or recognised by the State Board under section 17;

(e) on the request of the occupier or his agent; send the second container—

(i) in a case where such sample is taken from any area situated in a union territory, to the laboratory established or specified under sub-section (1) of section 51; and

(ii) in any other case, to the laboratory established or specified under sub-section (1) of section 51; and

(iii) in any other case, to the laboratory established or specified under sub-section (1) of section 52.

(4) When a sample of any sewage or trade effluent is taken for analysis under sub-section (1) and the person taking the sample serves on the occupier or his agent, a notice under clause (a) of sub-section (3) and the occupier or his agent wilfully absents himself, then—

(a) the sample so taken shall be placed in a container which shall be marked and sealed and shall also be signed by the person taking the sample and the same shall be sent forthwith by such person for analysis to the laboratory referred to in sub-clause (i) or sub-clause (ii), as the case may be, of clause (e) of sub-section (3) and such person shall inform the Government analyst appointed under sub-section (1) or sub-section (2), at the case may be, of section 53, in writing about the wilful absence of the occupier or his agent;

(b) the cost incurred in getting such sample analysed shall be payable by the occupier or his agent and in case of default of such payment, the same shall be recoverable from the occupier or his agent, as the case may be, as an arrear of land revenue or of public demand;

Provided that no such recovery shall be made unless the occupier or, as the case may be, his agent has been given a reasonable opportunity of being heard in the matter.

(5) When a sample of any sewage or trade effluent is taken for analysis under sub-section (1) and the person taking the sample serves on the occupier or his agent a notice under clause (a) of sub-section (3) and the occupier or his agent who is present at the time of taking the sample does not make a request for dividing the sample into two parts as provided in clause (b) of sub-section (3), then the sample so taken shall be placed in a container which shall be marked and sealed and shall also be signed by the person taking the sample and the same shall be sent forthwith by such person for analysis to the laboratory referred to in sub-clause (i) or sub-clause (ii), as the case may be, of clause (d) of sub-section (3).

22. Reports of the Result of Analysis on Samples Taken Under Section 21—

(1) Where a sample of any sewage or trade effluent has been sent for analysis to the laboratory established or recognised by the Central Board or, as the case may be, the State Board, the concerned Board analyst appointed under sub-section (3) of section 53 shall analyse the sample and submit a report in the prescribed form of the result of such analysis in triplicate to the Central Board or the State Board, as the case may be.

(2) On receipt of the report under sub-section (1), one copy of the report shall be sent by the Central Board or the State Board, as the case may be, to the occupier or his agent referred to in section 21, another copy shall be preserved for production before the court in case any legal proceedings are taken against him and the other copy shall be kept by the concerned Board.

(3) Where a sample has been sent for analysis under clause (e) of sub-section (3) or sub-section (4) of section 21 to any laboratory mentioned therein, the Government analyst referred to in that sub-section shall analyse the sample and submit a report in the prescribed form of the result of the analysis in triplicate to the Central Board or, as the case may be, the State Board which shall comply with the provisions of sub-section (2).

(4) If there is any inconsistency or discrepancy between or variation in the results of, the analysis carried out by the laboratory established or recognised by the Central Board or the State Board, as the case may be, and that of the laboratory established or specified under Section 51 or Section 52, as the case may be, the report of the latter shall prevail.

(5) Any cost incurred in getting any sample analysed at the request of the occupier or his agent shall be payable by such occupier or his agent and in case of default the same shall be recoverable from his as arrears of land revenue or of public demand.

23. Power of Entry and Inspection—(1) Subject to the provisions of this section, any person empowered by a State Board in this behalf shall have a right at any time to enter, with such assistance as he considers necessary, any place—

(a) for the purpose of performing any of the functions of the Board entrusted to him;

(b) for the purpose of determining whether and if so in what manner, any such functions are to be performed or whether any provisions of this Act or the rules made thereunder or any notice, order, direction or authorisation served, made, given, or granted under this Act is being or has been complied with;

(c) For the purpose of examining any plant, record, register, document or any other material object or for conducting a search of any place in which he has reason to believe that an offence under this Act or the rules made thereunder has been or is being or is about to be committed and for seizing any such plant, record, register, document or other material object, if he has reason to believe that it may furnish evidence of the commission of an offence punishable under this Act or the rules made thereunder:

Provided that the right to enter under this sub-section for the inspection of a well shall be exercised only at reasonable hours in a case where such well is situated in any premises used for residential purposes and the water thereof is used exclusively for domestic purposess.

(2) The provisions of [the Code of Criminal Procedure, 1973 (2 of 1974),][38] or, in relation to the state of Jammu and Kashmir, the provisions of any corresponding law in force in that state, shall, so far as may be, apply to any search or seizure under [Section 94][39] of the said Code or, as the case may be, under the corresponding provisions of the said law.

Explanation—For the purposes of this section, 'place' includes vessel.

24. Prohibition on use of Stream or Well for Disposal of Polluting Matter etc.—(1) Subject to the provisions of this section.—

(a) no person shall knowingly cause or permit any poisonous, noxious or polluting matter determined in accordance with such standards as may be laid down by the state Board to enter (whether directly or indirectly) into any[40] [stream or well or sewer or on land]; or

(b) no person shall knowingly cause or permit to enter into any stream any other matter which may tend, either directly or in combination with similar matters, to impede the proper flow of the water of the stream in a manner leading or likely to lead to a substantial aggravation of pollution due to other causes or of its consequences.

(2) A person shall not be guilty of an offence under sub-section (1), by reason only of having done or caused to be done any of the following acts, namely:

(a) constructing, improving or maintaining in or across or on the bank or bed of any stream any building, bridge, weir, dam, sluice, dock, pier, drain or sewer or other permanent works which he has a right to construct, improve or maintain;

(b) depositing any materials on the bank or in the bed of any stream for the purpose of reclaiming land or for supporting, repairing or protecting the bank or bed of such stream provided such materials are not capable of polluting such stream;

(c) putting into any stream any sand or gravel or other natural deposit accumulated which has flown from or been deposited by the current of such stream;

(d) causing or permitting, with the consent of the State Board, the deposit accumulated in a well, pond or reservoir to enter into any stream.

(3) The state government may, after consultation with or on the recommendation of, the State Board, exempt, by notification in the Official Gazette, any person from the operation of sub-section (1) subject to such conditions, if any, as may be specified in the notification and any condition so specified may be a like notification be altered, varied or amended.

25. Restrictions on New Outlets and New Discharges—[(1)[41] Subject to the provisions of this section, no person shall, without the previous consent of the State Board—

(a) establish or take any steps to establish any industry, operation or process or any treatment and disposal system or any extension or addition thereto, which is likely to discharge sewage or trade effluent into a stream or well or sewer or on land (such discharge being hereafter in this section referred to as discharge of sewage); or

(b) bring into use any new or altered outlet for the discharge of sewage; or

(c) begin to make any new discharge of sewage;

Provided that a person in the process of taking any steps to establish any industry, operation or process immediately before the commencement of the Water (Prevention and Control of Pollution) Amendment Act, 1988, for which no consent was necessary prior to such commencement, may continue to do so for a period of three months from such commencement or, if he has made an application for such consent, within the said period of three months, till the disposal of such application.

(2) An application for consent of the State Board under sub-section (1) shall be made in such form, contain such particulars and shall be accompanied by such fees as may be prescribed.]

(3) The State Board may make such inquiry as it may deem fit in respect of the application for consent referred to in sub-section (1) and in making any such inquiry shall follow such procedure as may be prescribed.

[4) The State Board may[42]—

(a) grant its consent referred to in sub-section (1), subject to such conditions as it may impose, being—

(i) in cases referred to in clauses (a) and (b) of sub-section (1) of Section 25, conditions as the the point of discharge of sewage or as to the use of that outlet or any other outlet for discharge of sewage;

(ii) in the case of a new discharge, conditions as to the nature and composition, temperature, volume or rate of discharge of the effluent from the land or premises from which the discharge or new discharge is to be made; and

(iii) that the consent will be valid only for such period as may be specified in the order,

and any such conditions imposed shall be binding on any person, establishing or taking any steps to establish any industry, operation or process or treatment and disposal system or extension or addition thereto or using the new or altered outlet or discharging the effluent from the land or premises aforesaid; or

(b) refuse such consent for reasons to be recorded in writing.

(5) Where, without the consent of the State Board, any industry, operation or process or any treatment and disposal system or any extension or addition thereto, is established or any steps for such establishment have been taken or a new or altered outlet is brought into use for the discharge of sewage or a new discharge of sewage is made, the State Board may serve on the person who has established or taken steps to establish any industry, operaction or process or any treatment and disposal system or any extension or addition thereto or using the outlet or making the discharge and the case may be, notice imposing any such conditions as it might have imposed on an application for its consent in respect of such establishment, such outlet or discharge.

(6) Every State Board shall maintain a register containing particulars of the conditions imposed under this section and so much of the register as relates to any

outlet or to any effluent, from any land or premises shall be open to inspection at all reasonable hours by any person interested in, or affected by such outlet, land or premises, as the case may be, or by any person authorised by him in this behalf and the conditions so contained in such register shall be conclusive proof that the consent was granted subject to such conditions.

(7) The consent referred to in sub-section (1) shall, unless given or refused earlier be deemed to have given unconditionally on the expiry of period of four months of the making of an application in this behalf complete in all respects to the State Board.

(8) For the purposes of this section and sections 27 and 30—

(a) the expression new or altered outlet means any outlet which is wholly or partly constructed on or after the commencement of this Act or which whether so constructed or not) is substantially altered after such commencement;

(b) the expression new discharge means a discharge which is not, as respects the nature and composition, temperature, volume and rate of discharge of the effluent substantially continuation of a discharge made within the preceding twelve months (whether by the same or a different outlet), so however that a discharge which is in other respects a continuation of previous discharge made as aforesaid shall not be demand to be a new discharge by reason of any reduction of the temperature or volume or rate of discharge of the effluent as compared with the previous discharge.

26. Provision Regarding Existing Discharge of Sewage or Trade Effluent— Where immediately before the commencement of this Act any person was discharging any sewage or trade effluent into a [stream or well or sewer or on land][43] the provisions of section 25 shall, so far as may apply in relation to such person as they apply in relation to the person referred to in that section subject to the modification that the application for consent to be made under sub-section (2) of that section[44] [shall be made on or before such date as may be specified by the state government by notification in this behalf in the Official Gazette].

27. Refusal or Withdrawal of Consent by State Board—(1)[45] A State Board shall not grant its consent under sub-section (4) of section 25 for the establishment of any industry, operation or process or treatment and disposal system or extension or addition thereto or to the bringing into use of a new or altered outlet unless the industry, operation or process or treatment and disposal system or extension or addition-thereto or the outlet is so established as to comply with any conditions imposed by the Board to enable it to exercise its right to take samples of the effluent.

(2) A State Board may from time to time review—[46]

(a) any condition imposed under section 25 or section 26 and may serve on the person to whom a consent under section 25 or section 26 is granted a notice making any reasonable variation of or revoking any such condition.[47]

(b) the refusal of any consent referred to in sub-section (1) of section 25 or Section 26 or the grant of such consent without any condition and may make such orders as it deems fit.

(3) Any condition imposed under section 25 or section 26 shall be subject to any variation made under sub-section (2) and shall continue in force until revoked under that sub-section.

28. Appeals—(1) Any person aggrieved by an order made by the State Board under section 25, section 26 or section 27 may, within thirty days from the date on which the order is communicated to him, prefer and appeal to such authority (hereinafter referred to as the appellate authority) as the state government may think fit to constitute:

Provided that the appellate authority may entertain the appeal after the expiry of the said period of thirty days if such authority is satisfied that the appellant was prevented by sufficient cause from filing the appeal in time.

(2) An appellate authority shall consist of a single person or three persons, as the state government may think fit, to be appointed by that Government.][48]

(3) The form and manner in which an appeal may be preferred under sub-section (1), the fees payable for such appeal and the procedure to be followed by the appellate authority shall be such as may be prescribed.

(4) On receipt of an appeal preferred under sub-section (1), the appellate authority shall, after giving the appellant and the State Board an opportunity of being head, dispose of the appeal as expeditiously as possible.

(5) If the appellate authority determines that any condition imposed or the variation of any condition, as the case may be, was unreasonable then—

(a) where the appeal is in respect of the unreasonableness of any condition imposed, such authority may direct either that the condition shall be treated as annulled or that there shall be substituted for it such condition as appears to it to be reasonable.

(b) where the appeal is in respect of the unreasonableness of any variation of a condition, such authority may direct either that the condition shall be treated as continuing in force unvaried or that it shall be varied in such manner as appears to it to be reasonable.

29. Revision—(1) The state government may at any time either of its own motion or on an application made to it in this behalf, call for the records of any case where an order has been made by the State Board under section 25, section 26 or section 27 for the purpose of satisfying itself as to the legality or propriety of any such order and may pass such order in relation thereto as it may think fit:

Provided that the state government shall not pass any order under this sub-section without affording the State Board and the person who may be affected by such order a reasonable opportunity of being heard in the matter.

(2) The state government shall not revise any order made under section 25, section 26 or section 27 where an appeal against that order lies to the appellate authority, but has not been preferred or where an appeal has been preferred such appeal is pending before the appellate authority.

30. Power of State Board to Carryout Certain Works[49]— (1) Where under this Act, any conditions have been imposed on any person while granting consent under section 25 or section 26 and such conditions require such person to execute any work in connection therewith and such work has not been executed within such time as may be specified in this behalf, the State Board may serve on the person concerned a notice requiring him within such time (not being less than thirty days) as may be specified in the notice to execute the work specified therein.]

(2) If the person concerned fails to execute the work as required in the notice referred to in sub-section (1), then, after the expiration of the time specified in the said notice, the State Board may itself execute or cause to be executed such work.

(3) All expenses incurred by the State Board for the execution of the aforesaid work, together with interest, at such rate as the state government may, by order, fix, from the date when a demand for the expenses is made until it is paid, may be recovered by that Board from the person concerned, as arrears of land revenue or of public demand.

31. Furnishing of Information to State Board and other Agencies in Certain Cases[50]— (1) If at any place where any industry, operation or process or any treatment and disposal system or any extension or addition thereto is being carried on, due to accident or other unforeseen act or event, any poisonous, noxious or pollution matter is being discharged, or is likely to be discharged into a stream or well or sewer or on land and, as a result of such discharge, the water in any stream or well is being polluted or is likely to be polluted, then the person in charge of such place shall forthwith intimate the occurrence of such accident, act or event to the State Board and such other authorities or agencies as may be prescribed.

(2) Where any local authority operates any sewerage system or sewage works, the provisions of sub-section (1) shall apply to such local authority as they apply in relation to the person in charge of the place where any industry or trade is being carried on.

32. Emergency Measures in Case of Pollution of Stream or Well—(1) Where it appears to the State Board that any poisonous, noxious or polluting matter is present in[51] [any stream or well or on land by reason of the discharge of such matter in such stream or well or on such a land] or has entered into that stream or well due to any accident or other unforeseen act or event, and if the Board is of opinion that it is necessary or expedient to take immediate action, it may for reasons to be recorded in writing, carry out such operations as it may consider necessary for all or any of the, following purposes, that is to say—

(a) removing that matter from the [52][stream or well or land] and disposing it of in such manner as the Board considers appropriate;

(b) remedying or mitigating any pollution caused by its presence in the stream or well;

(c) issuing orders immediately restraining or prohibiting the person concerned from discharging any poisonous, noxious or polluting matter [into the stream or well or on land][53] or from making insanitary use of the stream or well.

(2) The power conferred by sub-section (1) does not include the power to construct any works other than works of a temporary character which are removed on or before the completion of the operations.

33. Power of Board to Make Application to Courts for Restraining Apprehended Pollution of Water in Streams or Wells—[(1) Where it is apprehended by a Board that the water in any stream or well is likely to be polluted by reason of the disposal or likely disposal any matter in such stream or well or in any sewer or on any land, or otherwise, the Board may make an application to a court, not inferior to that of a Metropolitan Magistrate or a Judicial Magistrate of the first class, for restraining the person who is likely to cause such pollution from so causing.][54]

(2) On receipt of an application under sub-section (1) the court may make such order as it deems fit.

(3) Where under sub-section (2) the court makes an order restraining any person from polluting the water in any stream or well, it may in that order—

(i) direct the person who is likely to cause or has caused the pollution of the water in the stream or well, to desist from taking such action as is likely to cause pollution or, as the case may be to remove from such stream or well, such matter, and

(ii) authorise the Board, if the direction under clause (i) (being a direction for the removal of any matter from such stream or well) is not complied with by the person to whom such direction is issued, to undertake the removal and disposal of the matter in such manner as may be specified by the court.

(4) All expenses incurred by the Board in removing any matter in pursuance of the authorisation under clause (ii) of sub-section (3) or in the disposal of any such matter may be defrayed out of any money obtained by the Board from such disposal and any balance outstanding shall be recoverable from the person concerned as arrears of land revenue or of public demand.

33A. Power to Give Directions[55]— Notwithstanding anything contained in any other law, but subject to the provisions of this Act and to any directions that the Central Government may give in this behalf, a Board may, in the exercise of its powers and performance of its functions under this Act, issue any directions in writing to any person, officer or authority, and such person, officer or authority shall be bound to comply with such directions.

Explanation—For the avoidance of doubts, it is hereby declared that the power to issue directions under this section includes the power to direct—

(a) the closure, prohibition or regulation of any industry, operation or process; or

(b) the stoppage or regulation of supply of electricity, water or any other service.

SECTION VI

Funds, Accounts and Audit

34. Contribution by Central Government — The Central Government may, after due appropriation made by Parliament by law in this behalf, make in each financial year such contributions to the Central Board as it may think necessary to enable the Board to perform its functions under this Act.

35. Contribution by State Government—The state government may, after the appropriation made by the Legi-slature of the state by law in this behalf, make in each financial year such contributions to the State Board as it may think necessary to enable that Board to perform its functions under this Act.

36. Fund of Central Board—(1) The Central Board shall have its own fund and all sums which may, from time to time, be paid to it by the Central Government and all other receipts (by way of gifts, grants, donations, benefactions [fees][56] or otherwise) of that Board shall be carried to the fund of the Board and all payments by the Board shall be made therefrom.

(2) The Central Board may expend such sums as it thinks fit for performing its functions under this Act[57] [and, where any law for the time being in force relating to the prevention, control or abatement of air pollution provides for the performance of any function under such law by the Central Board, also for performing its functions under such law] and such sums shall be treated as expenditure payable out of the fund of that Board.

37. Fund of State Board— (1) The State Board shall have its own fund and the sums which may, from time to time, be paid to it by the state government and all other receipts (by way of gifts, grants, donations, benefactions [,fees][58] or otherwise) of that Board shall be carried to the fund of the Board and all payments by the Board shall be made therefrom.

(2) The State Board may expend such sums as it thinks fit for performing its functions under this Act, [59][and, where any law for the time being in force relating to the prevention, control or abatement of air pollution provides for the performance of any function under such law by the State Board, also for performing its functions under such law] and such sums shall be treated as expenditure payable out of the fund of that Board.

37A. Borrowing Powers of Board[60]— A Board may, with the consent of or in accordance with, the terms of any general or special authority given to it by the Central Government or, as the case may be, the state government, borrow money from any source by way of loans or issue of bonds, debentures or such other instruments, as it may deem fit, for the performance of all or any of its functions under this Act.]

38. Budget— The Central Board or, as the case may be, the State Board shall, during each financial year, prepare, in such form and at such time as may be prescribed, a budget in respect of the financial year next ensuing showing the estimated receipt and expenditure and copies thereof shall be forwarded to the Central Government or, as the case may be, the state government.

39. Annual Report[61]— (1) The Central Board shall, during each financial year, prepare, in such form as may be prescribed, an annual report giving full account of its activities under this Act during the previous financial year and copies thereof shall be forwarded to the Central Government within four months from the last date of the previous financial year and that Government shall cause every such report to be laid before both Houses of Parliament within nine months from the last date of the previous financial year.

(2) Every State Board shall, during each financial year, prepare, in such form as may be prescribed, an annual report giving full account of its activities under this Act during the previous financial year and copies thereof shall be forwarded to the state government within four months from the last date of the previous financial year and that Government shall cause every such report to be laid before that State Legislature within a period of nine months from the last date of the previous financial year.

40. Accounts and Audit—(1) Every Board shall maintain proper accounts and other relevant records and prepare an annual statement of accounts in such form as may be prescribed by the Central Government or, as the case may be, the state government.

(2) The accounts of the Board shall be audited by an auditor duly qualified to act as an auditor of companies under section 226 of the Companies Act, 1956 (1 of 1956).

(3) The said auditor shall be appointed by the Central Government or, as the case may be, the state government on the advice of the Comptroller and Auditor General of India.

(4) Every auditor appointed to audit the accounts of the Board under this Act shall have the right to demand the production of books, accounts, connected vouchers and other documents and papers and to inspect any of the offices of the Board.

(5) Every such auditor shall send a copy of his report together with an audited copy of the accounts to the Central Government or, as the case may be, the State Government.

(6) The Central Government shall, as soon as may be after the receipt of the audit report under sub-section (5), cause the same to be laid before both Houses of Parliament.

(7) The state government shall, as soon as may be after the receipt of the audit report under sub-section (5), cause the same to be laid before the State Legislature.

SECTION VII

Penalties and Procedure

41. **Failure to Comply with Directions Under Sub-section (2) or Sub-section (3) of Section 20, or Orders Issued Under Sub-section (2) of Section 33 or Section 33A**—(1) Whoever fails to comply with any direction given under sub-section (2) or sub-section (3) of section 20 within such time as may be specified in the direction shall, on conviction, be punishable with imprisonment for a term which may extend to three months or with fine which may extend to ten thousand rupees or with both and in case the failure continues, with an additional fine which may extend to five thousand rupees for every day during which such failure continues after the conviction for the first such failure.

(2) Whoever fails to comply with any order issued under clause (e) of sub-section (1) of section 32 or any direction issued by a court under sub-section (2) of section 33 or any direction issued under section 33A shall, in respect of each such failure and on conviction, be punishable with imprison-ment for a term which shall not be less than one year and six months but which may extend to six years and with fine, and in case the failure continues, with an additional fine which may extend to five thousand rupees for everyday during which such failure continues after the conviction for the first such failure.

(3) If the failure referred to in sub-section (2) continues beyond a period of one year after the date of conviction, the offender shall, on conviction, be punishable with imprisonment for a term which shall not be less than two years but which may extend to seven years and with fine.]

42. **Penalty for Certain Acts**—(1) Whoever—

(a) destroys, pulls down, removes, injures or defaces any pillar, post or stake fixed in the ground or any notice or other matter put up, inscribed or placed, by or under the authority of the Board, or

(b) obstructs any person acting under the orders or directions of the Board from exercising this powers and performing his functions under this Act or

(c) damages any works or property, belonging to the Board, or

(d) Fails to furnish to any officer or other employee of the Board any information required by him for the purpose of this Act, or

(e) fails to intimate the occurrence of any accident or other unforcessen act or event under Section 31 to the Board and other authorities or agencies as required by that section, or

(f) in giving any information which he is required to give under this Act, knowingly or wilfully makes a statement which is false in any material particular or

(g) for the purpose of obtaining any consent under section 25 or section 26, knowingly or will fully makes a statement which is false in any material particular,

shall be punishable with imprisonment for a term which may extend to three months or with fine which may extend to [ten][63] thousand rupees or with both.

(2) Where for the grant of a consent in pursuance of the provisions of section 25 or section 26, the use of a meter or gauge or other measure or monitoring device is required and such device is used for the purposes of those provisions, any person who knowingly or wilfully alters or interferes with that device so as to prevent it from monitoring or measuring correctly shall be punishable with imprisonment for a term which may extend to three months or with fine which may extend to one thousand rupees or with both.

43. Penalty for Contravention of Provisions of Section 24— Whoever contravenes the Provisions of Section 24 shall be punishable with imprisonment for a term which shall not be less than [one year and six months][64] but which may extend to six years and with fine.

44. Penalty for Controvention of Section 25 or Section 26— Whoever contravenes the provisions of Section 25 or Section 26 shall be punishable with imprisonment for a term which shall not be less than [one year and six month][65] but which may extend to six years and with fine.

45. Enhanced penalty after previous conviction—If any person who has been convicted of an offence under Section 24 or section 25 or Section 26 is again found guilty of an offence involving a contravention of the same proviso, he shall, on the second and on every subsequent conviction be punishable with imprisonment for a term which shall not be less than [two years][66] but which may extend to seven years and with fine:

Provided that for the purpose of this section no cognisance shall be taken of any conviction made more than two years before the commission of the offence which is being punished.

45A. Penalty for Contravention of Certain Provisions of the Act[67]— Whoever contravenes any of the provisions of this Act or fails to comply with any order or direction given under this Act, for which no penalty has been elsewhere provided in this Act, shall be punishable with imprisonment which may extend to three months or with fine which may extend to ten thousand rupees or with both and in the case of a continuing contravention or failure, with an additional fine which may extend to five thousand rupees for every-day during which such contravention or failure continues after conviction for the first such contravention or failure.

46. Publication of Names of Offenders— If any person convicted of an offence under this Act commits a like offence afterwards it shall be lawful for the court before which the second or subsequent conviction takes place to cause the offender's name and place of residence, the offence and the penalty imposed to be published at the offender's expense in such newspapers or in such other manner as the court may direct and the expenses of such publication shall be deemed to be part of the cost attending the conviction and shall be recoverable in the same manner as a fine.

47. Offences by Companies—(1) Where an offence under this Act has been committed by company, every person who at the time the offence was committed was in charge of, and was responsible to the company for the conduct of, the business of the company, as well as the company, shall be deemed to be guilty of the offence and shall be liable to be proceeded against and punished accordingly:

Provided that nothing contained in this sub-section shall render any such person liable to any punishment provided in this Act if he proves that the offence was committed without his knowledge or that he exercised all due diligence to prevent the commission of such offence.

(2) Notwithstanding anything contained in sub-section (1), where an offence under this Act has been committed by a company and it is proved that the offence has been committed with the consent or connivance of or is attributable to any neglect on the part of, any director, manager, secretory or other officer of the company, such director, manager, secretary or other officer shall also be deemed to be guilty of that offence and shall be liable to be proceeded against and punished accordingly.

Explanation—For the purposes of this section—

(a) 'company' means any body corporate and includes a firm or other association of individuals; and

(b) 'director' in relation to a firm means a partner in the firm.

48. Offences by Government Departments—Where an offence under this Act has been committed by any Department of Government, the Head of the department shall be deemed to be guilty of the offence and shall be liable to be proceeded against and punished accordingly:

Provided that nothing contained in this section shall render such Head of the Department liable to any punishment if he proves that the offence was committed without his knowledge or that he exercised all due diligence to prevent the commission of such offence.

49. Cognisance of Offences— (1) No court shall take cognizance of any offence under this Act except on a complaint made by-[68]

(a) a Board or any officer authorised in this behalf by it; or

(b) any person who has given notice of not less than sixty days, in the manner prescribed, of the alleged offence and of his intention to make a complaint, to the Board or officer authorised as aforesaid,

and no court inferior to that of a Metropolitan Magistrate or a Judicial Magistrate of the first class shall try any offence punishable under this Act.

(2) Where a complaint has been made under clause (b) of sub-section[69] (1), the Board shall, on demand by such person, make available the relevant reports in its possession to that person:

Provided that the Board may refuse to make any such report available to such person if the same is, in its opinion, against the public interest.]

(3) Notwithstanding anything contained in[70] [Section 29 of the Code of Criminal Procedure, 1973 (2 of 1974),][71] it shall be lawful for any [Judicial Magistrate of the first class or for any Metropolitan Magistrate] to pass a sentence of imprisonment of a term exceeding two years or of fine exceeding two thousand rupees on any person convicted of an offence punishable under this Act.[72]

50. Members, Officers and Servants of Boards to be Public Servants—All members, officers and servants of a Board when acting or purporting to act in pursuance of any of the provisions of this Act and the rules made thereunder shall be deemed to be public servants within the meaning of Section 21 of the Indian Penal Code (45 of 1860).

SECTION VIII

Miscellaneous

51. Central Water Laboratory—(1) The Central Government may, by notification in the Official Gazette.—

(a) establish a Central Water Laboratory; or

(b) specify any laboratory or institute as a Central Water Laboratory, to carry out the functions entrusted to the Central Water Laboratory under this Act.

(2) The Central Government may, after consultation with the Central Board, make rules prescribing—

(a) the functions of the Central Water Laboratory;

(b) the procedure for the submission to the said laboratory of samples of water or of sewage or trade effluent for analysis or tests, the form of the laboratory's report thereon and the fees payable in respect of such report;

(c) such other matters as may be necessary or expedient to enable that laboratory to carry out its functioning.

52. State Water Laboratory—(1) The state government may, by notification in the Official Gazette—

(a) establish a State Water Laboratory; or

(b) specify any laboratory or institute as a State Water Laboratory, to carry out the functions entrusted to the State Water Laboratory under this Act.

(2) The state government may, after consultation with the State Board, make rules prescribing—

(a) the functions of the State Water Laboratory;

(b) the procedure for the submission to the said labora-tory of samples of water or of sewage or trade effluent for analysis or test, the form of the laboratory's report thereon and the fees payable in respect of such report;

(c) such other matters as may be necessary or expedient to enable that laboratory to carry out its functions.

53. Analysts—(1) The Central Government may, by notification in the Official Gazette, appoint such persons as it thinks fit and having the prescribed qualifications to be Government analysts for the purpose of analysis of samples of water or of sewage or trade effluent sent for analysis to any laboratory established or specified under sub-section (1) of section 51.

(2) The state government may, by notification in the Official Gazette, appoint such persons as it thinks fit and having the prescribed qualifications to be Government analysts for the purpose of analysis of samples of water or of sewage or trade effluent sent for analysis to any laboratory established of specified under sub-section (1) of section 52.

(3) Without prejudice to the provisions of sub-section (3) of section 12, the Central Board or, as the case may be, the State Board may, by notification in the Official Gazette and with the approval of the Central Government or the state government, as the case may be, appoint such persons as it thinks fit and having the prescribed qualifications to be Board analysts for the purpose of analysis of samples of water or of sewage or trade effluent sent for analysis to any laboratory

established or recognised under Section 16, or as the case may be, under Section 17.

54. Reports of Analysts—Any document purporting to be a report signed by a Government analyst or, as the case may be, a Board analyst may be used as evidence of the exacts stated therein in any proceeding under this Act.

55. Local Authorities to Assist—All local authorities shall render such help and assistance and furnish such information to the Board as it may require for the discharge of its functions and shall make available to the Board for inspection and examination such records, maps, plans and other documents as may be necessary for the discharge of its functions.

56. Compulsory Acquisition of Land for the State Board—Any land required by a State Board for the efficient performance of its functions under this Act shall be deemed to be needed for a public purpose and such land shall be acquired for the State Board under the provisions of the Land Acquisition Act, 1894 (1 of 1894), or under any other corresponding law for the time being in force.

57. Returns and Reports—The Central Board shall furnish to the Central Government, and a State Board shall furnish to the state government and to the Central Board such reports, returns, statistics, accounts and other information with respect to its fund or activities as that Government or as the case may be, the Central Board may, from time to time, require.

58. Bar of Jurisdiction—No civil court shall have jurisdiction to entertain any suit or proceeding in respect of any matter which an appellate authority consistuted under this Act is empowered by or under this Act to determine and no injunction shall be granted by any court or other authority in respect of any action taken or to be taken in pursuance of any power conferred by or under this Act.

59. Protection of Action taken in Good Faith—No suit or other legal proceedings shall lie against the Government or any officer of Government or any member or officer of a Board in respect of anything which is in good faith done or intended to be done in pursuance of this Act or the rules made thereunder.

60. Overriding Effect—The provisions of this Act shall have effect notwithstanding anything inconsistent therewith contained in any enactment other than this Act.

61. Power of Central Government not Supersede the Central Board and Joint Boards—(1) If at any time the Central Government is of opinion—

(a) that the Central Board or any Joint Board has persistently made default in the performance of the functions imposed on it by or under this Act; or

(b) that circumstances exist which render it necessary in the public interest so to do,

The Central Government may, by notification in the Official Gazette, supersede the Central Board or such Joint Board, as the case may be, for such period, not exceeding one year, as may be specified in the notification:

Provided that before issuing a notification under this sub-sectionfor the reasons mentioned in clause (a), the Central Government shall give a reasonable opportunity to the Central Board or such Joint Board, as the case may be, to show cause why it should not be superseded and shall consider the explanations and objections, if any, of the Central Board or such Joint Board, as the case may be.

(2) Upon the publication of a notification under sub-section (1) superseding the Central Board or any Joint Board—

(a) all the members shall, as from the date of supersession vacate their offices as such;

(b) all the powers, functions and duties which may, by or under this Act, be exercised performed or discharged by the Central Board or such Joint Board shall, until the Central Board or the Joint Board, as the case may be, is reconstituted under subsection (3) be exercised, performed or discharged by such person or persons as the Centrals Government may direct;

(c) all property owned or controlled by the Central Board or such Joint Board shall, until the Central Board or the Joint Board, as the case may be, is reconstituted under sub-section (3) vest in the Central Government.

(3) On the expiration of the period of supersession specified in the notification issued under sub-section (1), the Central Government may—

(a) extend the period of supersession for such further term, not exceeding six months, as it may consider necessary; or

(b) reconstitute the Central Board or the Joint Board, as the case may be, by fresh nomination or appointment, as the case may be and in such case any person who vacated his office under clause (a) of sub-section (2) shall not be deemed disqualified for nomination or appointment:

Provided that the Central Government may at any time before the expiration of the period of supersession, whether originally specified under sub-section (1) or as extended under this sub-section, take action under clause (b) of this sub-section.

62. Power of State Government to Supersede State Board—(1) If at any time the state government is of opinion—

(a) that the State Board has persistently made default in the performance of the functions imposed on it by or under this Act; or

(b) that circumstances exist which render it necessary in the public interest so to do,

The state government may, by notification in the Official Gazette, supersede the State Board for such period, not exceeding one year, as may be specified in the notification:

Provided that before issuing a notification under this sub-section for the reasons mentioned in clause (a), the state government shall give a reasonable opportunity to the State Board to shown cause why it should not be superseded and shall consider the explanations and objections,if any, of the State Board.

(2) Upon the publication of a notification under sub-section (1) superseding the State Board, the provisions of sub-sections (2) and (3) of Section 61 shall apply in relation to the supersession of the State Board as they apply in relation to the supersession of the Central Board or a Joint Board by the Central Government.

63. Power of Central Government to make Rules—(1) The Central Government may, simultaneously with the constitution of the Central Board, make rules in respect of the matter specified in sub-section (2):

Provided that when the Central Board has been constituted, no such rule shall be made, varied, amended or repealed without consulting the Board.

(2) In particular and without prejudice to the generality of the foregoing power, such rules may provide for all or any of the following matters, namely;

(a) the terms and conditions of service of the members (other than the chairman and member-secretary) of the Central Board under sub-section (8) of section 5;

(b) the intervals and the time and place at which meetings of the Central Board or of any committee thereof constituted under this Act, shall be held and the procedure to be followed at such meetings, including the quorum necessary for the transaction of business under Section 8 and under sub section (2) of Section 9;

(c) the fees and allowances to be paid to such members of a committee of the Central Board as are not members of the Board under sub-section (3) of Section 9;

(d) the manner in which and the purposes for which persons may be associated with the Central Board under sub-section (1) of Section 10 and the fees and allowances payable to such persons;[73]

(e) the terms and conditions of service of the chairman and the member-secretary of the Central Board under sub-section (9) of Section 5 and under sub-section (1) of Section 12;

(f) conditions subject to which a person may be appointed as a consulting engineer to the Central Board under sub-section (4) of Section 12;

(g) the powers and duties to be exercised and performed by the chairman and the member-secretary of the Central Board;[74]

(j) the form of the report of the Central Board analyst under sub-section (1) of Section 22;

(k) the form of the report of the Government analyst under sub-section (3) of Section 22;

(l) the form in which and the time within which the budget of the Central Board may be prepared and forwarded to the Central Government under section 38;[75]

(la) the form in which the annual report of the Central Board may be prepared under Section 39;

(m) the form in which the accounts of the Central Board may be maintained under Section 40;

[(m(a)) the manner in which notice of intention to make a complaint shall be given to the Central Board or office authorised by it under Section 49;[76]]

(n) any other matter relating to the Central Board, including the powers, and functions of that Board in relation to Union territories;

(o) any other matter which has to be or may be prescribed.

(3) Every rule made by the Central Government under this Act shall be laid, as soon as may be after it is made, before each House of Parliament while it is in sessions for a total period of thirty days which may be comprised in one session or in two or more successive session and if, [before the expiry of the session immediately following the session or the successive sessions aforesaid], both Houses agree in making any modification in the rule or both Houses agree that the rule should not be made, the rule shall thereafter have effect only in such modified form or be of no effect, as the case may be; so, however, that any such modification or annulment shall be without prejudice to the validity of anything previously done under that rule.

64. Power of State Government to Make Rules—(1) The state government may, simultaneously with the constitution of the State Board, make rules to carry out the purposes of this Act in respect of matters not falling within the purview of Section 63:

Provided that when the State Board has been constituted, no such rule shall be made, amended or repealed without consulting that Board.

(2) In particular and without prejudice to the generality of the foregoing power, such rules may provide for all or any of the following matters, namely:

(a) the terms and conditions of service of the members (other than the chairman and the member-secretary) of the State Board under sub-section (8) of Section 5;

(b) the time and place of meetings of the State Board or of any committee of that Board constituted under this Act and the procedure to be followed at such meeting, including in the quorum necessary for the transaction of business under section 8 and under sub-section (2) of Section 9;

(c) the fees and allowances to be paid to such members of a committee of the State Board as are not members of the Board under sub-section (3) of Section 9;

(d) the manner in which and the purposes for which persons may be associated with the State Board under sub-section (1) of Section 10 [and the fees and allowances payable to such persons;][78]

(e) the terms and conditions of service of the chairman and the member secretary of the State Board under sub-section (9) of Section 5 and under sub-section (1) of section 12;

(f) the conditions subject to which a person may be appointed as a consulting engineer to the State Board under sub-section (4) of Section 12;

(g) the powers and duties to be exercised and discharged by the chairman and the member-secretary of the State Board.

(h) the form of the notice referred to in Section 21;

(i) the form of the report of the State Board analyst under sub-section (1) of Section 22;

(j) the form of the report of the Government analyst under sub-section (3) of section 22;

(k) the form of application for the consent of the State Board under sub-section (2) of section 25 and the particulars it may contain;

(l) the manner in which inquiry under sub-section (3) of section 25 may be made in respect of an application for obtaining consent of the State Board and the matters to be taken into account in granting or refusing such consent;

(m) the form and manner in which appeals may be filed, the fees payable in respect of such appeals and the procedure to be followed by the appellate authority in disposing of the appeals under sub-section (3) of Section 28;

(n) the form in which and the time within which the budget of the State Board may be prepared and forwarded to the State Government under section 38;[79]

(a) the form in which the annual report of the State Board may be prepared under section 39;

(o) the form in which the accounts of the State Board may be maintained under sub-section (1) of section 40;

(a) the manner in which notice of intention to make a complaint shall be given to the State Board or officer authorised by it under section 49;[80]

(p) any other matter which has to be or may be prescribed.

REFERENCES

1. *Subs.* by Act 53 of 1988.
2. *Subs.* by *ibid.*
3. *Ins.* by Act 44 of 1978.
4. *Ins.* by *ibid.*
5. *Subs.* by Act 53 of 1988.
6. *Subs.* by *ibid.*
7. *Subs.* by *ibid.*
8. *Subs.* by Act 44 of 1978.
9. *Subs.* by *ibid.*
10. *Subs.* by *ibid.*
11. *Subs.* by Act 53 of 1988.
12. *Omitted* by Act 44 of 1978.
13. *Subs.* by Act 53 of 1988.
14. *Omitted* by Act 44 of 1978.
15. *Subs.* by *ibid.*
16. *Ins.* by *ibid.*
17. *Subs.* by *ibid.*
18. *Subs.* by *ibid.*

19. *Subs.* by *ibid.*
20. *Subs.* by *Act 53 of 1988.*
21. *Subs.* by *Act 44 of 1978.*
22. *Subs.* by *ibid.*
23. *Subs.* by *Act 53 of 1988.*
24. *Ins.* by *Act 44 of 1978.*
25. *Subs.* by *ibid.*
26. *Omitted* by *ibid.*
27. *Ins.* by *ibid.*
28. *Ins.* by *Act 53 of 1988.*
29. *Subs.* by Act 44 of 1978.
30. *Subs.* by Act 53 of 1988.
31. *Subs.* by Act 44 of 1978.
32. *Subs.* by Act 53 of 1988.
33. *Ins.* by *ibid.*
34. *Renumbered* by Act 53 of 1988 and after sub-section (1) as so *renumbered* sub-sections (2) and (3) *Ins. by ibid.*
35. *Subs.* by *ibid.*
36. *Subs.* by Act 53 of 1988.
37. *Subs.* by Act 44 of 1978.
38. *Subs.* by *ibid.*
39. *Subs.* by *ibid.*
40. *Subs.* by Act 53 of 1988.
41. *Subs.* by *ibid.*
42. *Subs.* by *ibid.*
43. *Subs.* by Act 44 of 1978.
44. *Subs.* by *ibid.*
45. *Subs.* by Act 44 of 1988.
46. *Subs.* by Act 44 of 1978.
47. *Subs.* by Act 53 of 1988.
48. *Subs.* by Act 44 of 1978.
49. *Subs.* by Act 53 of 1988.
50. *Subs.* by *ibid.*
51. *Subs.* by *ibid.*

52. *Subs.* by *ibid.*

53. *Subs.* by *ibid.*

54. *Subs.* by *ibid.*

55. *Ins.* by Act 53 of 1988.

56. *Ins.* by Act 44 of 1978.

57. *Ins.* by *ibid.*

58. *Ins.* by *ibid.*

59. *Ins.* by *ibid.*

60. *Ins.* by Act 53 of 1988.

61. *Subs.* by *ibid.*

62. *Subs.* by Act 53 of 1988.

63. *Subs.* by *ibid.*

64. *Subs.* by *ibid.*

65. *Subs.* by *ibid.*

66. *Subs.* by *ibid.*

67. *Ins.* by *ibid.*

68. *Subs.* by Act 53 of 1988.

69. *Ins.* by *ibid.*

70. *Renumbered* by *ibid.*

71. *Subs.* by Act 44 of 1978.

72. *Subs.* by *ibid.*

73. *Subs.* by Act 44 of 1978.

74. *Omitted by ibid.*

75. *Subs.* by Act 53 of 1988.

76. *Ins.* by *ibid.*

77. *Subs.* by Act 44 of 1978.

78. *Ins.* by *ibid.*

79. *Subs.* by Act 53 of 1988.

80. *Ins.* by *ibid.*

APPENDIX

CLEAN WATER ACT

The **Clean Water Act** is the primary *federal law in the United States* governing *water pollution.*[1] Commonly abbreviated as the **CWA**, the act established the symbolic goals of eliminating releases to water of high amounts of *toxic substances*, eliminating additional water pollution by 1985, and ensuring that surface waters would meet standards necessary for human sports and recreation by 1983.

The principal body of law currently in effect is based on the *Federal Water Pollution Control Amendments of 1972*, which significantly expanded and strengthened earlier legislation.[2] Major amendments were enacted in the Clean Water Act of 1977 enacted by the *95th United States Congress*[3] and the Water Quality Act of 1987 enacted by the 100th United States Congress.[4]

Pollution Control Strategy in the CWA

Point Sources

The 1972 act introduced a permit system for regulating *point sources* of pollution. Point sources include:

- industrial facilities (including manufacturing, mining, oil and gas extraction, and service industries)
- municipal governments and other government facilities (such as military bases), and
- some agricultural facilities, such as animal *feedlots.*

Point sources may not discharge pollutants to surface waters without a permit from the National Pollutant Discharge Elimination System (NPDES). This system is managed by the *United States Environmental Protection Agency* (EPA) in partnership with state environmental agencies. EPA has authorized 45 states to issue permits directly to the discharging facilities. In the remaining states and territories, the permits are issued by an EPA regional office.[5]

In previous legislation, *Congress* had authorized states to develop water quality standards, which would limit discharges from facilities based on the characteristics of individual water bodies. However, these standards were only to be developed for interstate waters, and the science to support this process (i.e. data, methodology) was in the early stages of development. This system was not effective and there was no permit system in place to enforce the requirements. In the 1972 CWA Congress added the permit system and a requirement for technology-based effluent limitations.[6]

Technology-Based Standards

The 1972 CWA created a new requirement for technology-based standards for point source discharges. EPA develops these standards for categories of dischargers, based on the performance of pollution control technologies without regard to the conditions of a particular receiving water body. The standard becomes the minimum regulatory requirement in a permit.[7]

Water Quality Standards

The 1972 act authorized continued use of the water quality-based approach, but in coordination with the technology-based standards. After application of technology-based standards to a permit, if water quality is still impaired for the particular water body, then the permit agency (state or EPA) may add water quality-based limitations to that permit. The additional limitations are to be more stringent than the technology-based limitations and would require the permittee to install additional controls.

Nonpoint Sources

Congress exempted some water pollution sources from the point source definition in the 1972 CWA, and was unclear on the status of some other sources. These sources were therefore considered to be **nonpoint sources** that were not subject to the permit program.

Agricultural stormwater discharges and irrigation return flows were specifically exempted from permit requirements.[8] Congress, however, provided support for research programs at the U.S. *Department of Agriculture* to improve runoff management practices on farms.

Stormwater runoff from industrial sources, municipal storm drains, and other sources were not specifically addressed in the 1972 law. EPA declined to include urban and industrial stormwater discharges in the NPDES program and consequently was sued by an environmental group. The courts ruled that stormwater discharges must be covered by the permit program.[9]

A growing body of research during the late 1970's and 1980's indicated that stormwater runoff was a significant cause of water quality impairment in many parts of the U.S. In the early 1980's EPA conducted the *Nationwide Urban Runoff Program* (NURP) to document the extent of the urban stormwater problem. The agency began to develop regulations for stormwater permit coverage, but encountered resistance from industry and municipalities, and there were additional rounds of litigation.

In the *Water Quality Act of 1987* (1987 WQA) Congress responded to the stormwater problem by requiring that industrial stormwater dischargers and municipal separate *storm sewer* systems (often called "MS4") obtain NPDES permits, by specific deadlines. The permit exemption for agricultural discharges continued, but Congress created a nonpoint source pollution demonstration grant program at EPA to expand the research and development of nonpoint controls and management practices.

Financing of Pollution Controls

Congress created a major public works financing program for municipal sewage treatment in the 1972 CWA. A system of grants for construction of municipal *wastewater treatment plants* was authorized and funded in. In the initial program the federal portion of each grant was up to 75 percent of a facility's capital cost, with the remainder financed by the state. In subsequent amendments Congress reduced the federal proportion of the grants and in the 1987 WQA transitioned to a revolving loan program. Industrial and other private facilities are required to finance their own treatment improvements on the "polluter pays" principle.

Major Statutory Provisions

The Act is comprised of six titles.

Research and Related Programs

Title I includes a *Declaration of Goals and Policy*[10] and various grant authorizations for research programs and pollution control programs. Some of the programs authorized by the 1972 law are ongoing (e.g. section 104 research programs, section 106 pollution control programs, section 117 *Chesapeake Bay Program)* while other programs are no longer operational.

Grants for Construction of Treatment Works

To assist municipalities in creating or expanding wastewater treatment plants Title II established a system of construction grants. This was replaced by the Clean Water State Revolving Fund in the 1987 WQA.

Standards and Enforcement

Technology-Based Standards Program

Under the 1972 act EPA began to issue technology-based standards for municipal and industrial sources.

- Municipal sewage treatment plants, also called *publicly-owned treatment works (POTW)* are required to meet *secondary treatment standards.*[11]

- *Effluent guidelines* (for existing sources) and *New Source Performance Standards* are issued for categories of industrial facilities discharging directly to surface waters.[12]

- Categorical Pretreatment Standards are issued to industrial users (also called "indirect dischargers") contributing wastes to POTW.[13] These standards are developed in conjunction with the effluent guidelines program.

To date, the effluent guidelines and categorical pretreatment standards regulations have been published for 56 categories and apply to between 35,000 and 45,000 facilities that discharge directly to the nation's waters. These regulations are responsible for preventing the discharge of almost 700 billion pounds of pollutants each year.[14] EPA has updated some categories since their initial promulgation and has added new categories.

The secondary treatment standards for POTWs and the effluent guidelines are implemented through NPDES permits. The categorical pretreatment standards are typically implemented by POTWs through permits that they issue to their industrial users.[15]

Water Quality Standards Program

Water quality standards (WQS) are risk-based (also called hazard-based) requirements which set site-specific allowable pollutant levels for individual water bodies, such as rivers, lakes, streams and *wetlands.* States set WQS by designating uses for the water body (e.g., recreation, water supply, aquatic life, agriculture) and applying *water quality criteria* (numeric pollutant concentrations and narrative requirements) to protect the designated uses. An *antidegradation policy* is also issued by each state to maintain and protect existing uses and high quality waters.[16]

A *Total Maximum Daily Load* (TMDL), is a calculation of the maximum amount of a pollutant that a water body can receive and still meet WQS. Over 60,000 TMDLs are proposed or in development for U.S. waters in the next decade and a half.

Following the issuance of a water quality standard or TMDL for a water body, implementation of the requirements involves modification to NPDES permits for facilities discharging to the water body.

While the effluent guidelines have been largely successful, because they apply to specific sources and are enforceable, the WQS have been much less so. As of 2007, approximately half of the rivers, lakes, and bays under EPA oversight were not safe enough for fishing and swimming. [17]

National Water Quality Inventory

Section 305(b) requires EPA and the states to compile a biennial *Report to Congress on the nation's water quality.*[18]

Enforcement

Under section 309, EPA can issue administrative orders against violators, and seek civil or criminal penalties when necessary.[19]

- For a first offense of criminal negligence, the minimum fine is $2,500, with a maximum of $25,000 fine per day of violation. A violator may also receive up to a year in jail. On a second offense, a maximum fine of $50,000 per day may be issued.

- For a knowing endangerment violation, i.e. placing another person in imminent danger of death or serious bodily injury, a fine may be issued up to $250,000 and/or imprisonment up to 15 years for an individual, or up to $1,000,000 for an organization.

States that are authorized by EPA to administer the NPDES program must have authority to enforce permit requirements under their respective state laws.

Federal Facilities

Military bases, national parks and other federal facilities must comply with CWA provisions.[20]

Thermal Pollution

Section 316 requires standards for *thermal pollution* discharges, as well as standards for *cooling water* intake structures.[21] These standards are applicable to *power plants* and other industrial facilities.

Nonpoint Source Management Program

The 1987 amendments created the *Nonpoint Source* Management Program under CWA section 319.[22]

Permits and Licenses

NPDES Permits for Point Sources

The NPDES permit program is authorized by CWA section 402.[23] The 1987 WQA expanded the program to cover *stormwater* discharges from municipal separate storm sewer systems (MS4) and industrial sources.[24]

NPDES permits must be reissued every five years. Permit agencies (EPA and states) must provide notice to the public of pending permits and provide an opportunity for public comment.

Dredge and Fill Permits (Wetlands)

The discharge of dredged and fill material into "Waters of the United States," including wetlands, is subject to a separate permit program administered by the *Army Corps of Engineers* under Section 404.[25] Essentially, all discharges of fill or dredged material affecting the bottom elevation of a jurisdictional water of the U.S. require a permit from the Army Corps. These permits are an essential part of protecting *wetlands,* which are often filled by *land developers.* Wetlands are vital to the ecosystem in filtering streams and rivers and providing habitat for wildlife.

There are two main types of permits—general permits, and individual permits. General permits change periodically and cover broad categories of activities, and require the user to comply with all stated conditions. General permits (such as the Nationwide Permits) are issued for fill activities that will result in minimal adverse effects to the environment. Individual permits are utilized for actions that are not addressed by a general permit, or that do not meet the conditions of a General Permit. In addition, Individual Permits (generally) require more analysis than do the general permits, and typically require much more time to prepare the application and to process the permit.

When the Corps processes an application for an Individual Permit, the Corps must publish/issue a public notice (typically in the Federal Register) describing the proposed action described in the permit application. The public notice must be issued no later than fifteen days after the Corps determines the application to be complete. Although the District Engineer makes the decision to grant a permit, this authority is usually delegated to is granted or not the Administrator is able to take-away permits if they feel that the permit is not reasonable; before making this decision though the Administrator must consult with the secretary. A permit expires after five years of being granted.

When a state wants a permit, they make sure that all other states being affected are aware they will be sent a copy of the request and the state is able to write a recommendation. A state permit also expires after five years of being granted.

POTW Biosolids Management Program

The 1987 WQA created a program for management of biosolids (sludge) generated by POTWs.[26]

Title V - General Provisions

Citizen Suits

U.S. citizens may file suit against a CWA violator if EPA or a state fails to take enforcement action.[27]

Employee protection

The 1972 act added an employee *("whistleblower")* protection provision. Employees in the U.S. who believe they were fired or suffered adverse action related to enforcement of the CWA may file a written complaint with the *Occupational Safety and Health Administration.*[28]

State Water Pollution Control Revolving Funds

The *Clean Water State Revolving Fund* (CWSRF) program was authorized by the 1987 WQA.[29] This replaced the municipal construction grants program, which was authorized in the 1972 law under Title II. In the CWSRF, federal funds are provided to the states and Puerto Rico to capitalize their respective revolving funds, which are used to provide financial assistance (loans or grants) to local governments for wastewater treatment, nonpoint source pollution control and estuary protection.

The fund provides loans to municipalities at lower-than-market rates. As of 2007 the average rate was 2.1 percent nationwide, compared to an average market rate of 4.3 percent.[30] In 2006, CWSRF assistance totaling $5 billion was provided to 1,858 local projects across the country.[31]

Earlier legislation

Congress first addressed water pollution issues in the *Rivers and Harbors Act of 1899*.[32] Portions of this law remain in effect, including the *Refuse Act*, while others have been superseded by various amendments, including the 1972 CWA.

Other notable predecessor legislation includes the following.

- **Public Health Service Act of 1912.** Expanded the mission of the *United States Public Health Service* to study problems of sanitation, sewage and pollution.[33]

- **Oil Pollution Act of 1924.** Prohibited the intentional discharge or fuel oil into coastal waters.[34] Repealed by 1972 CWA.

- **Federal Water Pollution Control Act of 1948.** Created a comprehensive set of water quality programs that also provided some financing for state and local governments. Enforcement was limited to interstate waters. The Public Health Service provided financial and technical assistance.[35]

- **Water Quality Act of 1965.** Required states to issue water quality standards for interstate waters, and authorized the newly-created Federal Water Pollution Control Administration to set standards where states failed to do so.[36]

Recent developments

On *July 25, 2007*, Senator Russell Feingold, Democrat from Wisconsin, introduced legislation to reiterate the Congress' objective in passing the *Federal Water Pollution Control Amendments of 1972*. The bill states that it was Congress' intention to protect all waters of the United States. Known as the Clean Water Restoration Act and co-sponsored by 19 Senators, the bill being reviewed by the House Transportation and Infrastructure Committee. This is considered by many environmental groups to be a necessary step towards reversing recent *Supreme Court of the United States* rulings that have repealed protection for as much as 60 percent of the nation's waters.

Case law

- *United States v. Riverside Bayview Homes, Inc.*, 474 U.S. 121 (1985), upholding the Act's hold in regulating wetlands that intermingle with *navigable waters*.

- *Solid Waste Agency of North Cook County (SWANCC) v. United States Army Corps of Engineers,* 531 U.S. 159 (2001), possibly denying the CWA's hold in isolated intra-state waters and certainly denying the validity of the 1986 *"Migratory Bird Rule."*

- *S. D. Warren Co. v. Maine Bd. of Env. Protection,* 547 U.S. 370 (2006), involving section 401 state certification requirements for federally licensed activities that cause a discharge into navigable waters.

- *Rapanos v. United States,* 547 U.S. 715 (2006), in separate controlling opinions questioned the Act's use of the terms "navigable waters" and "waters of the United States" and questioned the reach of the Act to regulate wetlands that possess a "significant nexus" with such waters.

- *National Association of Home Builders v. Defenders of Wildlife,* 551 U.S., 127 S.Ct. 2518 (June 25, 2007). Slip Opinion No. 06-340. Upheld EPA's approval of NPDES program for State of *Arizona.* EPA was not required to consult with the *Fish and Wildlife Service,* under the *Endangered Species Act,* during the approval process.

REFERENCES

1. 33 U.S.C., 1251 et seq.
2. Pub.L. 92-500, October 18, 1972.
3. Pub.L. 95-217, December 27, 1977.
4. Pub.L. 100-4, February 4, 1987.
5. U.S. Environmental Protection Agency. Washington, D.C. NPDES State Program Status
6. Water Pollution Control Foundation (WPCF): "The Clean Water Act of 1987." Joan M. Kovalic et al. Alexandria, VA, 1987. .
7. U.S. Environmental Protection Agency. Washington, D.C. "NPDES Permit Writers' Manual." Chapter 1. December 1996. Document No. EPA-833-B-96-003.
8. CWA 502(14), 33 U.S.C. 1362.
9. *Natural Resources Defense Council v. Train,* 396 F.Supp. 1393 (D.D.C. 1975), aff'd. by *NRDC v. Costle,* 568 F.2d 1369 (D.C. Cir. 1977).
10. CWA 101, 33 U.S.C. § 1251.
11. CWA 304(d)(1), 33 U.S.C. 1314(d)(1) and *Secondary Treatment Regulation Code of Federal Regulations,* 40 CFR Part 133

12. CWA 301, 33 U.S.C. 1311; CWA 304(b), 33 U.S.C. § 1314(b); and CWA 306, 33 U.S.C. 1316.

13. CWA 307(b), 33 U.S.C. - 1317(b); and CWA 307(c), 33 U.S.C. -1317(c).

14. U.S. Environmental Protection Agency. Washington, D.C. *EPA Evaluation Report: Effectiveness of Effluent Guidelines Program for Reducing Pollutant Discharges Uncertain.* Report No. 2004-P-00025. August 24, 2004.

15. U.S. Environmental Protection Agency. Washington, D.C."Introduction to the National Pretreatment Program." February 1999. Document No. EPA-833-B-98-002.

16. U.S. Environmental Protection Agency. Washington, D.C. "NPDES Permit Writers' Manual." Chapter 6. December 1996. Document No. EPA-833-B-96-003.

17. National Public Radio. Cities Battle Over River's Pollution Level. Susan Sharon. May 17, 2007.

18. CWA 305(b), 33 U.S.C. 1315(b).

19. CWA 309, 33 U.S.C. 1319.

20. CWA 313, 33 U.S.C. 1323.

21. 33 U.S.C. 1326.

22. 33 U.S.C. 1329.

23. 33 U.S.C. 1342.

24. CWA 402(p), 33 U.S.C. 1342(p).

25. 33 U.S.C. 1344.

26. CWA 405, 33 U.S.C. 1345.

27. CWA 505, 33 U.S.C. 1365.

28. CWA 507, 33 U.S.C. 1367.

29. CWA 601, 33 U.S.C. 1381 et seq.

30. U.S. Environmental Protection Agency. Washington, D.C."*Clean Water State Revolving Fund.*" Accessed 2008-01-12.

31. U.S. Environmental Protection Agency. Washington, D.C. "*Clean Water State Revolving Fund Programs: 2006 Annual Report,*" p. 24. March 2007. Document No. EPA-832-R-07-001.

32. Ch. 425, Sec. 9, 30 Stat. 1151. 33 U.S.C. § 401. March 3, 1899.

33. 7 Stat. 309. August 14, 1912.

34. 43 Stat. 604.

35. Pub.L. 80-845, June 30, 1948.

36. Pub.L. 89-234, October 2, 1965

BIBLIOGRAPHY

Arizona Municipal Water Users Association (AMWUA). *Converting to Xeriscape: Renovate Your Landscape with Style*. Phoenix, AZ: AMWUA, 1997.

AMWUA, *Xeriscape Gardens: Plants for the Desert Southwest*. Phoenix AZ: AMWUA, 1998.

AMWUA, *Xeriscape: A New Look for Arizona Gardens*. Phoenix, AZ: AMWUA. 1997.

AMWUA, *Visions of Xeriscape,* Phoenix, AZ: AMWUA, 1997..

Brookbank, George, *Desert Landscaping*. Tucson, AZ: University of Arizona Press, 1992, 253 pp.

Duffield, M. and Warren D. Jones. *Plants for Dry Climates*. 2nd Edition. Tucson, AZ: H.P. Books, 1992.

Johnson, Eric A. *Pruning, Planting and Care*. Tucson, AZ: Ironwood Press, 1997.

Johnson, Eric A. and Scott Millard. *The Low-Water Flower Gardener*. Tucson, AZ: Ironwood Press. 1993.

McPherson, E. Gregory and Charles Sacamano. *Southwestern Landscaping that Saves Energy and Water*. Tucson. AZ: College of Agriculture, University of Arizona. 1989.

McPherson, E. Gregory and Gary C. Woodard. "Cooling the Urban Heat Island with Water-and-Energy Efficient Landscapes" in *Arizona Review*. Tucson, AZ: College of Business and Public Administration, University of Arizona. Spring 1990.

Mielke, Judy, *Native Plants for Southwestern Landscapes*. Austin, TX: University of Texas Press, 1993.

Miller, George O. *Landscaping with Native Plants of Texas and the Southwest*. Still Water, MN: Voyageur Press, 1991.

Perty, Robert. *Landscape Plants for Western Regions*. Claremont, CA: Land Design Publishing Co. 1992..

Phillips, Judith, *Southwestern Landscaping with Native Plants,* Santa Fe, NM: Museum of New Mexico Press. 1987.

Postel, S.L. and A.T. Wolf, "Dehydrating Conflict," Foreign Policy, 126, (2001).

Rasler, Karen A. and W.r. Thompson, "contested Territory, Strategic rivalries, and Conflict Esclation." International Studies quarterly, 50. 1. 2006.

Shuler, Carol. *Low Water Use Plants for California and the Southwest*. Tucson, AZ: Fisher Books, 1993..

Sunset Magazine and Books. *Waterwise Gardening*. Menlo Park, CA: Lane Publishing, 1995.

Sunset Magazine and Books. *Sunset Western Garden Book*. 6th Edition. Menlo Park, CA: Lane Publishing Co. 1995.

Sunset Magazine and Books. *Sunset Western Landscaping*. Menlo Park, CA: Sunset Books, Inc. 1997.

Wolf, Aaron T. "Water and Human Secrity," *Journal of contemporary Water Research and Education*. 118 2001.

INDEX

***